PRAISE FOR
A MIND FOR BUSINESS

'This book demonstrates the value of taking care of your mind and mental wellbeing on a day-to-day basis, offering practical tips and advice to help you think smarter and live better.'
Patrick Watt, Corporate Director, Bupa

'If enough managers read this highly readable and very useful book we might just increase national productivity and make our work a whole lot more enjoyable and fulfilling too.'
Matthew Taylor, Chief Executive, The RSA

'Insightful, entertaining and accessible. Something I can see myself coming back to many times over my career to help me, my colleagues and my team get the best out of themselves.'
Roger Edmonds, Senior Marketing Manager, PepsiCo

'A well-written, useful guide to mental good health at work with loads of sensible, practical advice for all and essential for anyone who runs an organisation and cares about their staff.'
Tony Cohen, Chair of Trustees, Barnardo's, and former CEO, FremantleMedia

'An MOT and tune-up for your mind, in and out of business, that will help you stay on track.'
Paul Birch, angel investor and Founder @ Makeshift

'A thought-provoking journey into mental wellbeing in the workplace and essential reading for companies who want staff to flourish.'
John Attley BA

A MIND FOR BUSINESS

GET INSIDE YOUR HEAD TO
TRANSFORM HOW YOU WORK

ANDY GIBSON

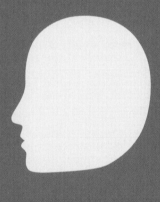

PEARSON

Harlow, England • London • New York • Boston • San Francisco • Toronto • Sydney
Auckland • Singapore • Hong Kong • Tokyo • Seoul • Taipei • New Delhi
Cape Town • São Paulo • Mexico City • Madrid • Amsterdam • Munich • Paris • Milan

Pearson Education Limited
Edinburgh Gate
Harlow CM20 2JE
United Kingdom
Tel: +44 (0)1279 623623
Web: www.pearson.com/uk

First edition published 2015 (print and electronic)

ISBN: 978-1-292-01467-8 (print)
       978-1-292-01470-8 (PDF)
       978-1-292-01469-2 (ePub)
       978-1-292-01468-5 (eText)

British Library Cataloguing-in-Publication Data
A catalogue record for the print edition is available from the British Library

Library of Congress Cataloging-in-Publication Data
A catalog record for the print edition is available from the Library of Congress

Cover design by redeyoffdesign.com
Cover concept by Owen Tozer
Text design by Design Deluxe
Images by Owen Tozer

Print edition typeset in 10.5pt Stone Sans by 3
Print edition printed by Ashford Colour Press Ltd, Gosport

NOTE THAT ANY PAGE CROSS REFERENCES REFER TO THE PRINT EDITION

For all the growers of mindapples,
especially Jo for inspiring me to start this journey,
my parents for supporting me on it,
and Esther and Ruta for coming with me.

CONTENTS

1 FEED YOUR MIND   1

Your mind is your greatest asset, so how can you take care of it and keep it performing at its best? Learn how to nourish your mind and stay mentally healthy and productive at work.

2 MASTER YOUR MOODS   33

Our thoughts, judgements and decisions are shaped by our moods. Learn to manage your moods and emotions to remain calm, focussed and energetic throughout the working day.

3 GET MOTIVATED   55

The best businesses engage their staff and get maximum effort from their people. Find out what really drives us to succeed and spot better ways to motivate yourself and others.

4 HANDLE PRESSURE 77

Pressure is a reality of modern business, but stress can harm our health and productivity. Understand the psychology of pressure and learn practical tools to reduce stress at work.

5 KNOW YOURSELF 101

We're all different. By understanding the characteristics that make each of us unique, we can play to our strengths, manage our weaknesses and work better together.

6 TRAIN YOUR MIND 129

Is it possible to increase your intelligence or change your habits? Explore how our minds acquire knowledge and learn new skills and find out what it really means to train your mind.

7 MAKE SMARTER DECISIONS 159

Businesses depend on people making the right decisions at the right times. Understand our decision-making processes and how to support informed, rational decisions at work.

8 INFLUENCE PEOPLE 181

We influence each other all the time, positively and negatively, often without realising it. Learn to manage your influence, build better relationships, and inspire others.

9 WORK COLLABORATIVELY   205

When we work together we can work smarter and get more done. Learn how to share ideas clearly with others and explore better ways to communicate and collaborate.

10 THINK CREATIVELY   231

Organisations that fail to innovate are increasingly being left behind. Explore how to nurture creativity, find ingenious solutions and become more innovative at work.

THE 10 HABITS OF A MIND FOR BUSINESS   253
CONCLUSION: A BUSINESS FOR MINDS   255

ABOUT THE AUTHOR

Andy Gibson is an award-winning entrepreneur, speaker and consultant with a decade of experience advising organisations on innovation and performance.

He founded Mindapples in 2008, which has now reached thousands of people all around the world with positive messages about understanding our minds. This book is the culmination of three years of development of the Mindapples training programme *Your Mind: A User's Guide*, which is now used by a number of major multinational corporations and small businesses to increase the performance of their staff.

Andy has worked with some of the biggest names in global business to help them get the best from their staff, including several of the world's leading financial institutions, Bupa, News UK, L'Oréal, PricewaterhouseCoopers and the Wellcome Trust. He has advised the UK Government on public health promotion, supported many entrepreneurs to launch and grow their ventures, and speaks internationally about business innovation and social change. He is also a Trustee of the Royal Society for the Encouragement of Arts, Manufactures and Commerce, and *Wired* magazine once named him the 78th most influential person in UK technology – although they changed their minds again the following year. He lives in London.

www.mindapples.org/business
www.twitter.com/gandy

ACKNOWLEDGEMENTS

This book and the Mindapples training programme that inspired it only exist thanks to the many people who have helped Mindapples grow over the years, and particularly my colleagues Ruta Marcinkus and Esther King.

Ruta's research, insights and uncompromising drive for the truth have made this book far better than I could ever have managed alone, whilst Esther and I have built Mindapples together from the ground up and still managed to look after each other's minds in the process.

I'm also indebted to John Attley, Dr Natalie Banner, Dwayne Baraka, Roger Edmonds, Dr Alex Fradera, Jon Lloyd, Dr Sam Spedding and Colin Tate for their insightful feedback on this text and its content, and to Nathalie Nahai and Tessy Britton for their contributions in the early stages of our training programme. Indirect thanks are also due to Dr Daniel Freeman, Malcolm Gladwell, Prof Jonathan Haidt, Prof Daniel Kahneman, Daniel Pink and all the staff and speakers of the RSA, who have inspired me more than they know.

Finally, I would like to thank Gloria Else, Sophie Boswell, Colin Tate, Marya Goga and Seeta Patel for looking after my mind whilst I wrote this book, and my dear friend Jo Worsley who first said to me *'our minds are what separate us from animals, so why are we taught so little about how they work?'* I hope this book sets in motion the changes we both hope to see in the world.

A Mind for Business is based on the Mindapples training programme *Your Mind: A User's Guide*, developed by Andy Gibson, Ruta Marcinkus, Esther King, Dr Alex Fradera, Dr Sam Spedding and Owen Tozer.

PUBLISHER'S ACKNOWLEDGEMENTS

We are grateful to the following for permission to use copyright material:

Figure on page 37 is adapted from Plutchik, Robert, *Emotion: A Psychoevolutionary Synthesis*, 1st edn., © 1979. Reprinted and electronically reproduced by permission of Pearson Education, Inc., Upper Saddle River, New Jersey; figure on page 39 is adapted from Thayer, R. E., *The Origin of Everyday Moods* (OUP USA, 1986); figure on page 44 is adapted from Larsen, R. J., Toward a science of mood regulation, *Psychological Inquiry*, vol 11, no 3, 129–41 (Taylor & Francis, 2000), reprinted by permission of the publisher (Taylor & Francis Ltd, http://www.tandfonline.com); figure on page 92 is adapted from Dodge, R., Daly, A., Huyton, J. and Sanders, L., The challenge of defining wellbeing, *International Journal of Wellbeing*, 2(3), 222–35 (2012). Reproduced by permission of the authors; figure on page 113 is adapted from DeYoung, C. G., Personality neuroscience and the biology of traits, *Social and Personality Psychology Compass* vol 4, no. 12, 1165–1180 (John Wiley & Sons Ltd, 2010); figure on page 146 is adapted from the original by Anton Ioukhnovets that appeared in Duhigg, C., *The Power of Habit: Why We Do What We Do, And How To Change* (Random House, 2013); figure on page 216 modified and reproduced by special permission of the Publisher, CPP, Inc., Mountain View, CA 94043 from the Thomas-Kilmann Conflict Mode Instrument by Kenneth W. Thomas and Ralph H. Kilmann. Copyright 1974, 2002 by CPP, Inc. All rights reserved. Further reproduction is prohibited without the Publisher's consent.

The publisher would also like to thank Owen Tozer for providing the illustrations in this book.

In some instances we have been unable to trace the owners of copyright material, and we would appreciate any information that would enable us to do so.

INTRODUCTION

The fundamental unit of modern business is not the dollar, or the yen, the pound or the euro: it is the human being.

People buy your products, deliver your services, manage your projects and account for your money; they are your partners, your colleagues, your friends and collaborators. Most businesses spend more money on people than on anything else. People are your business.

Or, more specifically, people's minds are your business. In the knowledge economy, the performance of any business depends on the performance of the minds of its staff. Our work is becoming less mechanistic and more analytic, using more brainpower and relying increasingly on human ingenuity to generate a competitive edge. The human mind is our greatest asset, and the key unit of production.

Yet most businesses seem to know surprisingly little about minds. We learn very little about them in school and college, and we rarely talk about them at work either, so we are left to rely on personal experience and folk psychology to guide us – which is bad for us, and bad for our businesses.

The good news is that advances in neuroscience and psychology mean that, perhaps for the first time in our history, we are reaching some level of consensus about the basic workings of our minds and what they need to perform well. Although this is still a comparatively young area of scientific research and continues to provoke intense debate and disagreement, some conclusions can now be drawn about how we work, and how we can work better.

This is a book about how people work.

Like the Mindapples training programmes upon which it

is based, it shares practical insights from neuroscience and psychology to help you work successfully and sustainably. It is structured around the key capabilities that are needed in modern business, so whether you want to engage your staff, support your colleagues, reduce your stress levels or come up with new ideas, there should be something here for you.

It is not intended as a rulebook to follow, or a replacement for your own observations and judgement. Our minds are far too complex to lend themselves to one-size-fits-all solutions, and no two minds are the same. Everything presented here is, by necessity, a generalisation. Our purpose here is rather to set in motion a more informed type of enquiry, applying experimentally validated insights to business practice and making more accurate, insightful observations about how we work.

This is not about changing our minds to fit our work; it is about changing how we work to fit us better. The more aware we become of how our minds work and what they need to thrive, the more informed we can be in our choices, and the better we will perform at work.

And if we go further, and use this knowledge to improve our working practices and redesign our businesses, then everything will start to change. We have an opportunity to create workplaces that get the best from our minds, by harnessing and developing the mental resources of their people and giving each of us a chance to thrive.

The knowledge is here; the case is clear. Now it is up to us to put these findings into practice, to work smarter, build better businesses, and perhaps even enjoy ourselves a little more in the process.

IN A NUTSHELL

Mind too full? Here's what's coming up...

THE TWITTER VERSION

To be successful in business, you need to make time for your mind, maintain your mental resources and create environments for minds to thrive.

THE SUMMARY VERSION

In the knowledge economy, businesses rely almost entirely on the minds of their staff to succeed. Yet most businesses spend more maintaining their photocopiers than the minds of their staff.

Modern neuroscience and psychology have given us a better model for managing our minds, and our businesses, better. The principles are simple: maintain mental energy levels, avoid unnecessary tasks and interruptions, manage relationships and emotional dynamics, tap into people's skills and passions, and promote a diverse, flexible and open-minded working culture.

Progressive businesses will take this one stage further and use this model to manage every aspect of their work, from dealing with clients to developing talent. Looking after our minds is a keystone habit of successful businesses, and one which brings both quality of life, and commercial success.

CHAPTER 1
FEED YOUR MIND

Your mind is the most sophisticated tool you will ever own, and like any other tool it works best when you take care of it.

Our minds aren't quite as simple as other tools though. Looking after this particular asset takes a little more effort.

When you leave the office and head home of an evening, you can leave behind most of the tools of your trade – your files, your meetings, your colleagues, your contact lists. The one thing you can't leave behind is your mind. Instead, you leave it running all the time, checking messages, pondering problems, thinking not only of the work of today, but the work of tomorrow, and the next day, and the next day.

Without proper care and attention, fatigue sets in, and your work and your life falters. It may be in little ways, or it may be dramatic – either way, you're not performing at your best.

So, to be successful in business, you need to know how your mind works and how to take care of it – both inside and outside work.

CHANGING MINDS

The case for looking after our minds is obvious.

Whatever your goals in your life and work, you will need your mind. No wonder, then, that in a survey by Mindapples and the charity Mind, 84 per cent of people judged their mental health to be as important as their physical health.[1]

Yet we do surprisingly little to look after our minds. Despite saying their mental health is important, 56 per cent of respondents said they had never thought about it before. We know our minds matter, but turning that into positive actions seems to be more of a struggle.

One of the biggest obstacles is that the term 'mental health' has become hugely associated with illness. Ask people what word first comes into their heads when they hear the term 'mental health', and they say 'depression', 'illness', 'crazy' or 'breakdown'; ask them the same question about 'physical health' and they talk about 'the gym', 'fitness', 'healthy eating' and 'five-a-day'.[2]

Whilst physical health is something to be proud of, mental health has become something to be avoided, only relevant for sick people and certainly too sensitive a topic for the workplace. People even talk about 'having mental health' as meaning having an illness.

The impact of this is bigger than we might think. We have no positive image to move towards, so we struggle to take action. Perhaps this is why 72 per cent of our respondents felt mental health and wellbeing issues were not discussed openly enough in society.

Another part of the problem is our collective ignorance about our minds. As children, most of us were bombarded with information about plaque on our teeth, germs on our hands and salt in our food, yet we were taught almost nothing about our minds. We don't learn the concepts, and we don't know what's normal.

The result is that our minds can feel shadowy and mysterious, something over which we have little control. So we tune out the messages, ignore our minds and focus on easier things like watching our waistlines or cutting down on sugar, and hope the experts will fix us if something goes wrong.

We are increasingly very interested in our minds though. There is a growing public interest in neuroscience and psychology, from media stories about brain scanning, to books about the 'hidden secrets' of psychology. In fact, 52 per cent of our survey respondents said they would like to know more about looking after their mental health and wellbeing. When it comes to engaging people in thinking more about the health of their minds, we are pushing at an open door.

It's time for a change. We all have mental health, and looking after our minds is a normal part of having a successful life. So, if we can look after our bodies by brushing our teeth, or eating an apple, what about our minds?

MEET YOUR MIND

Let's start by looking at this thing we call a 'mind', what it is, and how to keep it in good working order.[3]

When we think about our minds, we usually think about brains. Modern neuroscience has revealed the hive of activity that takes place inside our heads. Whilst we still know relatively little about what really goes on up there, we do know a fair amount about how our brains are constructed and why they work the way they do.

The evolution of the human race is very much the story of brain development. We didn't reach the top of the food chain by being bigger or stronger than the other creatures: we grew bigger brains than them. In fact our brains grow so much larger than those of comparable creatures,[4] that, technically, our young have to be born premature, so that their brains can continue to grow outside the womb.[5]

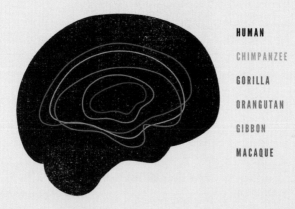

HUMAN

CHIMPANZEE

GORILLA

ORANGUTAN

GIBBON

MACAQUE

In the 1960s, Paul D. McLean mapped the sections of our brains to three distinct stages of our evolutionary development.[6] All these parts are deeply interlinked, but they offer us a useful way to explore the functional structure of our brains.

The first and most primitive part handles basic functioning, the **primal systems** that keep us alive. Even lizards have similar systems, so it is sometimes called the 'lizard brain'.

The second section is the limbic system or 'mammalian brain', which is of course found in all mammals. This handles **emotional responses**, and also body temperature.

And finally, wrapped around all this is the neocortex, which is uniquely large in humans and gives us our distinctive capacity for **abstract thought and planning**.

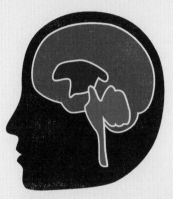

PRIMAL

Vital functions (blood pressure, heart rate, breathing, hunger and digestion)

Sleep and waking

Arousal and alertness

EMOTIONAL

Emotional responses (joy, sadness, disgust)

Behavioural responses (risks, aggression)

Body temperature

Pleasure, reward, motivation

INTELLECTUAL

Abstract thought

Willpower and inhibition

Planning and organising

Ideas and imagination

Language and learning

Problem-solving and analysis

Although these sections reflect different evolutionary purposes, they are not actually separate, but deeply interconnected. Each part is involved in how we think and feel, and impulses pass smoothly between them.

We are more than just our brains too: our 'primal' systems extend all through our bodies. There are over five hundred million neurons in our digestive system,[7] neurons in our hearts,[8] and in fact our whole body is wired into one complex, integrated nervous system.

For example, if you feel hungry – a primal instinct – you might then experience an emotional impulse to eat cake, because you associate cake with feeling full. Then your intellectual side might step in to remind you that cake is fattening and you should stick to your diet. This in turn reminds you that you are worried about your weight, another emotional response. Your primal system still craves sugar though, and your emotional side feels uncomfortable. So you decide you deserve a treat – but rationalise it by planning to go to the gym later.

So that original impulse to eat cake might not even have come from your brain, but from deeper in your nervous system. This complex nervous system underpins our minds, and much of the power of how our minds work lies not in our cognitive processes, but in the complex set of instincts and automatic systems that underpin them.

This is why it is so complicated being us. Our nervous systems blend together a range of different structures and processes, which we experience as one single mind.

PROCESSING POWER

The mind, then, is much more than just our conscious thoughts, and it relies on more to function than just our brain too. Our minds are complex, interconnected systems, and each part relies on the rest to function. So if you thought feeding your mind was just a matter of doing crosswords and maths problems, think again.

The true power of your mind lies in the mental processes of which you are not consciously aware – your unconscious mind.[9] The key to the unconscious lies in its ability to do more than one thing at once. Whilst your conscious attention is preoccupied with a particular task, your unconscious mind is keeping everything else running.

Autonomic processes like heart rate, breathing patterns and body clock, memories, associations, reminders of things to do later – your unconscious handles it all for you, leaving you free to think about more important things. Most of what is going on in your mind happens beneath your conscious awareness.

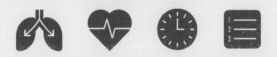

So if you want to be successful at work, you need to take care of your unconscious mind.

THE ELEPHANT AND THE RIDER

The psychologist Jonathan Haidt has a delightful metaphor for our reliance on our unconscious minds. Inspired by the Buddha, who likened the mind to a wild elephant, he describes the mind as *'the elephant and the rider'* – our animal and human sides combined.[10]

We like to see ourselves as the conscious rider, planning ahead, choosing where to go, but we are also the elephant – the large body of unconscious processes on which our minds rely.

The elephant is larger and more powerful than the rider. Unlike a car or a computer, we cannot program it or force it to do our bidding. It has its own needs and instincts. If the elephant wants cake, the elephant usually gets cake.

Maintaining a good relationship with your 'elephant' is essential for having a healthy and productive mind.

WHAT AFFECTS OUR MINDS?

To take better care of our minds – not just the rational, human side, but our primal and emotional 'elephants' too – we need to know what affects them. So what factors affect how we feel, and how our minds perform?

Our minds are more sensitive than we might think. Whilst we go about our lives unaware of most of the things around us, our unconscious 'elephants' are taking in all these sights, sounds and sensations and feeding selective insights to our conscious mind.

This means our minds are influenced by our environment all the time, but we might only be aware of a handful of these influences. These influences affect our judgement, our moods, our relationships, even our life expectancy.

By becoming more aware of how our minds are influenced, we can start to identify the positive and negative factors that affect our wellbeing and performance and manage them accordingly.

NOISES AND DISTRACTIONS

All kinds of distractions can be bad for our minds. One thing in particular that affects our minds is noise. Loud noises, especially **intermittent noise**, can interfere with our concentration and harm our mental wellbeing.[11]

Noise isn't always bad for us though, and everyone has **different sensitivities**.[12] Some people work best with some background noise or music, whilst others need total silence to concentrate. Different ambient noise levels are also more suited to different tasks. The optimum level for creative tasks, for instance, seems to be that of a coffee shop.[13]

Being able to **control** noise levels is the key: noise that is out of your control is generally much more disruptive.[14]

LIGHT

Sunlight isn't just pleasant – it's good for us too. Natural light during the day helps us sleep better at night and promotes vitamin D production, which is good for mental alertness and general wellbeing.[15]

Some **electronic devices** though, such as mobile phones, emit a light similar to natural daylight. This can stimulate our mood and mental performance, but can also affect our sleep – so if you're struggling to sleep, it's probably best not to check your phone at bedtime.[16]

Watch out for **fluorescent lights** too: they can make us feel stressed.[17] If your office has a lot of fluorescent lights, make sure you get regular time outside to refresh your mind.

SLEEP

Going without sleep is extremely bad for our minds.

Sleep deprivation makes us less alert and impairs mental performance. It actually has similar effects on the mind to being **drunk**. Small amounts of sleep deprivation seem to have similar or worse effects to being over the legal alcohol limit for driving.[18]

That doesn't mean we all need our 'eight hours' though: we each need **different amounts** of sleep to function, and we typically need less as we get older.[19] There is also research suggesting that how we think about sleep makes a difference to our mental performance.[20] Listen to your mind: if you feel like you've had enough sleep, don't worry – and if you haven't, well, try not to lose sleep over it.

PHYSICAL HEALTH AND FITNESS

Our general physical health affects our minds too. **Illness, pain and exhaustion** can all affect how we think and feel, from that foggy-headed feeling during a bout of 'flu to being distracted when you're in pain.[21] Taking care of your body is an excellent way to take care of your mind.

Exercise is particularly beneficial: even gentle physical activity is good for our minds. Vigorous physical exercise can help reduce stress and anxiety, and regular physical activity can help boost mood and improve wellbeing. [22]

Whether you prefer gardening or kickboxing, walking or rock climbing, exercise can be a great mind-booster.

NUTRITION

What we eat and drink affects our minds much more than most of us realise. Managing your diet is a simple and effective way to improve your mental wellbeing.

Food gives our minds energy and when we eat slow energy-release foods like porridge and pulses, we have more concentration and mental energy through the day.

There are also many **vitamins and minerals** that our brains need to function, such as iron, selenium and vitamin D. A handful of brazil nuts, fortified cereals and some seeds and pulses can all have beneficial effects on the mind as well as the body – in moderation of course. The brain is 70 per cent fat too, so **fatty acids** like Omega-3 are important – although the exact effects of these on mental health and cognitive performance are still being studied.[23]

Some food and drink can have particularly strong effects on our minds. **Highly sugary foods** do give our brains more energy in the short term, but they can cause us to 'crash' later and affect our moods and mental energy. **Caffeine** similarly gives us a short-term sense of alertness but has been linked to anxiety and can increase tension.[24]

There's no need to be puritanical about your diet, but it is good to remember that what you eat has an impact on how you think and feel. Consider what you put into your body and how it affects your mind. If you feel unusually anxious, low or tired, think about what you've eaten and drunk that day: the key to how you feel may lie there.[25]

WATER

Water deserves special mention. One of the best ways you can look after your mind is to drink more water.

Research has shown that dehydration not only affects our physical wellbeing, but also our mood and our ability to think clearly. Lack of water has been linked to **reduced working memory capacity**, poor mental performance, and even depression.

Studies have shown that even mild dehydration – as little as one-and-a-half per cent below normal water levels – caused participants to experience **fatigue, tension and anxiety**, and difficulty working on mental tasks. [26]

The impact of dehydration on mood seems to be particularly prominent in women. One study also found that staying hydrated is as important for those who work sitting down in an office as it is for those who are physically active.[27]

Dieticians recommend **two litres of water a day** – roughly eight glasses – to stay hydrated and mentally alert. We get a lot of water from our food of course, so it's not all about buying bottled water. However, mild dehydration can be as little as five hundred millilitres – the equivalent of one small bottle of water.

So if your mind is feeling sluggish or lacking in energy, drink more water. It's free! Well, most of the time.

OTHER PEOPLE

Positive contact with other people is very important for our mental wellbeing. Isolation is very bad for our minds.

Social contact has been linked to all sorts of health and wellbeing factors, including reduced stress, better physical health and lower mortality.[28] One substantial review concluded that lack of friendships has a similar impact on our life expectancy to smoking, alcohol and obesity.[29]

This applies to professional relationships too: despite all the stresses and strains of work, **feeling useful** to other people and being part of a team are generally good for us. This may explain why retirement and unemployment can be so bad for our mental health.[30]

Not all social contact is good for us though. **Bullying and unfair treatment** are very bad for our mental health,[31] particularly if it makes us feel unsafe,[32] so aggressive or contemptuous people tend to be destructive to our ability to think and work and should be avoided. And remember not to treat people badly yourself either.

We also have a tendency to tune into each other emotionally, so **other people's emotional states** have an influence on our own. Happy people can make us feel happier. Anxious people can make us feel more anxious.[33] Sometimes the source of our good or bad feelings is not even in our own minds, but those of the people around us.

Other people can be a great asset for our mental wellbeing and ability to work productively though. Investing in positive relationships and spending time with people you like can benefit your health, and also your work performance.

MENTAL RESOURCES

Many different internal and external factors affect our minds. By being more conscious of these factors, we can work to our potential in most common situations.

One important concept is 'mental resources' – essentially the amount of energy your mind has at any given time.[34]

Using your conscious mind takes mental effort, so how it performs is affected by how much mental energy you have. If your mind is tired and sluggish, you may struggle with basic mental tasks; if you feel alert and engaged, with lots of mental resources to call on, you can think more clearly, remember things better and have more control over your decisions. Your mental resources affect how well your mind performs, and hence how well you perform.[35]

Anything that depletes your mental resources can reduce your ability to work. This can include physical lack of energy or nutrients, and also distractions, rumination and other emotional factors. Stress and anxiety can also impair your ability to think clearly.[36] The more tired, worried, stressed or distracted you are, the harder you will find it to use your mind.[37]

Mental resources are vital to achieving high professional performance. There are surprisingly few ways to make yourself smarter, but there are many ways to make yourself stupider. If you stop doing these things, you should notice how smart you really are.[38]

So if you want to make the most of your mind, maintaining your mental resources is a great habit to learn. Get plenty of sleep, drink water, eat well, take exercise – because all these things give your mind a better chance of thinking and working better.[39]

RESILIENCE

Resilience is our capacity to maintain our wellbeing in the face of life events and environment.[40] It is not an end in itself, but a useful ability when we are faced with difficult situations and challenges.

Much of the research on resilience focusses on dealing with setbacks and coping with stress (more on that later), but on some level we are all required to be resilient in our day-to-day lives. Noisy neighbours, a missed lunch or a bad night's sleep can all affect the mind, and we each need to find our own ways of coping with our challenges.

Part of this is about mental attitude: some people will shrug off a bad day and come back stronger for it, whilst others of us may still be feeling unbalanced a couple of days later.[41] Part of it is also about compensating for bad events with positive actions, such as drinking more water when you know you haven't had enough sleep, or going outside to get some perspective and recharge your mind.

Sometimes, though, resilience is also about changing your environment, seeking out positive situations and avoiding things that you know are bad for your mind. By noticing the effects that things around you have on your mind, you can seek out the situations in which you work best, and avoid things that distract you or sap your mental energy.

No one can tell you what to put up with in your life and what not to, but the two aren't mutually exclusive. Learning how to manage your mind in difficult situations can make it easier to change things for the better. Where possible, try to change your situation to suit what your mind needs. Where that isn't possible though, you may need to learn how to cope with things you can't change.

LOOKING AFTER YOUR MIND

So what can we do to maintain our mental wellbeing and conserve mental resources amidst all these influences?

Research from the field of positive psychology suggests that a considerable proportion of our mental wellbeing may be down to our outlook and activities – the choices we make, and the actions we take.[42]

Put in basic terms, the formula for wellbeing is fairly simple:[43]

Genetics + Conditions of Life + Your Actions = Wellbeing

Your genetic make-up and innate personality traits certainly affect your wellbeing.[44] When it comes to our minds, we are not all created equal. Conditions of life – your upbringing, childhood experiences and current circumstances – do make a difference too. We can't blame people for how they feel, and we certainly shouldn't underestimate the impact trauma can have, or the value of a safe, nurturing environment.[45]

Nevertheless, more and more research is showing us that a significant contribution to how our minds feel comes from the things we do – our choices, attitudes and behaviour. As individuals, and as a society, we have a huge opportunity to influence our minds for the better. What we do affects how we feel.

So, how are you using this opportunity? Are you using your daily routine to improve your mind, or making it less healthy and efficient? What do *you* do that is good for your mind?

WHAT ARE YOUR MINDAPPLES?

The Mindapples campaign encourages everyone to care for their minds just like we care for our bodies.[46]

A 'mindapple' is anything you do to look after your mind. Drawing inspiration from the '5-a-day' campaign to encourage people to eat more fruit and vegetables, Mindapples asks people to share a '5-a-day' for their mind, building awareness of what we can all do to improve our mental health and getting everyone talking and learning about their minds.

Thousands of people have shared their mindapples all around the world. Responses range from gentle activities like reading and walking in nature, to more active pursuits like *'dancing my socks off'*. Sometimes they are quite psychological, such as practising mindfulness or being grateful; others are more primal, like *'scream my head off'* or *'eat cake and don't care'*. Many are good for our bodies, others not so much – a glass of wine to unwind, a bacon butty for breakfast or a big cup of coffee.

Actions can be solitary or social too, from getting a bit of 'me time' to talking to old ladies at bus stops. We like our pets too – one response was *'take my dog dancing'* – although another was *'pet something furry (dog or boyfriend)'*. It's not all about indulging ourselves either: constructive and altruistic activities like *'take care of my kids'* and *'do something I'm good at'* are popular too.

So what are your mindapples? Think about what you do every day, or regularly, to look after your mind. They can be anything you like. After all, it's your mind.[47]

We do seem to agree on a few things that are good for our minds. In a poll of two thousand people around the UK, using a similar question, these were the key themes:[48]

- 61 per cent mentioned **physical activity** of some kind.
- 53 per cent mentioned spending time with **other people**.
- 35 per cent mentioned **learning and creativity**.
- 35 per cent mentioned **food or drink** (although only 22 per cent were talking about doing it healthily).
- 31 per cent mentioned some form of 'me time' or **relaxation**.

Keeping physically and mentally active, spending time with people, learning new things and enjoying our food – there are lots of things we feel are good for our minds. Sadly though, only four per cent mentioned going to work.

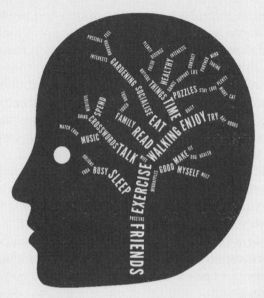

WHAT WORKS FOR YOU

There are various official lists of things that we can do to look after our minds. One often used by UK policymakers and health practitioners is the Five Ways to Wellbeing, developed by the New Economics Foundation:[49]

1 **Connect**
   Spend quality time with other people.
2 **Be active**
   Take some exercise, however gentle.
3 **Take notice**
   Appreciate the world around you.
4 **Keep learning**
   Mental challenge is good for you.
5 **Give**
   Helping others makes you feel good too.

The Five Ways can be a useful framework for thinking about how to maintain your mental wellbeing. Think of them as categories of activity to consider when you want to add a new 'mindapple' to your daily routine.

What is most important though is to find healthy activities that you enjoy and fit your lifestyle. We all know that taking time out to have fun makes us feel good, but engaging in activities that you find enjoyable or fulfilling really does seem to lead to increased mental wellbeing.

Research has shown that when we choose to engage in pleasurable activities free from the demands of work and responsibilities, this has surprisingly measurable positive effects on our mental wellbeing.[50]

People who spend more time engaging in enjoyable activities tend to have more positive emotions and life satisfaction, lower depression scores, reduced stress levels, lower blood pressure and better physical health.

Taking time out to relax can serve as a 'breather', a chance to take a break and distract oneself from demands and concerns that occupy the mind. Leisure activities can also act as 'restorers', helping us cope with stress and adversity by replenishing our resources.

So, whilst it might not feel quite as virtuous as quitting smoking or getting an early night, it seems you really can take care of your health by spending more time doing things you enjoy. Having fun really is good for you.

As a result of this, the list of activities that are good for our mental wellbeing is endless and reductive. There are research papers showing the health benefits of music, art and nature. Science says that hugging is good for our wellbeing.[51] Retail therapy – buying small treats to cheer ourselves up or to celebrate success – can lead to short-term mood boosts.[52] There is even a study that says watching *Lord of the Rings* is good for your mind.[53]

Don't worry too much about one-size-fits-all solutions for maintaining your mind. When it comes to our day-to-day wellbeing, what works for one person doesn't necessarily work for everybody else.

Anything you do to maintain your mind will be more successful if you have chosen it yourself, and if you enjoy it. Scientists can tell you what has worked for other people, but they can't tell you what you enjoy, or choose for you.

So make time for your mind. Keep noticing what it needs, and make time for whatever 'breathers' and 'restorers' you enjoy to keep your mind in good condition. Your health, and your professional performance, may depend on it.

MINDFULNESS

One increasingly popular tool for improving mental wellbeing and performance is the meditative practice of 'mindfulness', which is now one of the best-researched topics in this area and is worthy of particular consideration.

Mindfulness has some of its roots in spiritual practices,[54] but it has secular applications too, as a technique for training your attention to become more aware of what is happening in your mind and body. One study defined it as *'the non-judgmental awareness of experiences in the present moment'.*[55] It is not about clearing your mind, but about noticing more, in yourself and your surroundings.

If you devote time to it, the benefits of regular mindfulness meditation seem to be extensive. One review concluded that mindfulness-based therapy is *'an effective treatment for a variety of psychological problems, and is especially effective for reducing anxiety, depression, and stress'.*[56] A University of Utah study found mindfulness training can help us control our emotions and sleep better at night.[57] There are physical health benefits too:[58] another study even showed it can improve our immune systems.[59]

Although there has been slightly less research on mindfulness in business contexts, the initial findings also seem to be positive, and one review found correlations between mindfulness and job performance.[60]

Whether you practise meditation regularly or just make a conscious effort to be more calm and present, mindfulness seems to be very good for our minds.

As mindfulness pioneer Jon Kabat-Zinn puts it: *'We call ourselves human beings, but we behave more like human doings.'*[61] Perhaps it's time to change that.

REMEMBER THE BASICS

Listen to your mind and learn what works for you to keep yourself calm, healthy, present and energetic. The more you can tune into how you are feeling and respond appropriately, the more you can start to manage how you think and feel.

It's not always possible to make time for your mind, and there will be days when you have to send your 'elephant' out into the jungle without everything it needs. During those times though, little things can still make a big difference.

If you feel sluggish, down or distracted, ask yourself:

1 **Have I had enough sleep?**
2 **Have I drunk enough water?**
3 **What did I eat and drink today?**
4 **Have I had enough natural light?**
5 **Have I been physically active lately?**

Take care of the basics, and the more advanced aspects of looking after your mind will start to feel easier. Build good habits, and make time for your own 'mindapples' when you can, and you should notice the benefits to your mental health and your professional performance.

Most of all, remember that caring for your mind is not a

luxury but an essential ingredient of success in life and work. To paraphrase a popular saying about our bodies:[62]

> ## Take care of your mind.
> ## It's the only place you
> ## have to live.

HABIT 1
LOOK AFTER YOUR HEALTH AND FIND BREATHERS AND RESTORERS TO GET THE 5-A-DAY FOR YOUR MIND

FEED YOUR MIND
IN A NUTSHELL

THE TWITTER VERSION

Your mind works best when you give it regular breaks, get your #mindapples and manage your energy levels and mental resources.

THE SUMMARY VERSION

Looking after your mind isn't a luxury to be tackled once the work is finished: it is a key tool in getting work done.

Your mind is complex and many of the factors that affect your physical and emotional state, like lack of food, dehydration, distractions and other people around you, also affect your intellectual abilities. These external factors need to be managed, and you can manage them better if your mind has energy. Maintaining your mental resources is the best way to stay resilient and improve your performance at work.

You can maintain your mental performance proactively, by watching your diet and taking exercise, sleeping well, drinking water, getting natural light, and most importantly, by doing things that you enjoy. In fact, the more time you make for doing things you enjoy, the better your mind will perform. Having fun really is good for you.

Your mind is your greatest asset, and if you want to succeed you need to take care of it, both inside and outside work. So ask yourself, have you had *your* mindapples?

NOTES

1 **in a survey by Mindapples...** This survey was conducted by Populus for Mind and Mindapples between 7 and 9 June 2013. In the survey, 2053 people were polled from a representative range of backgrounds and occupations around the UK.

2 **Ask people what word first comes into their heads...** We have been asking these questions at Mindapples events and training sessions for four years now and the responses here are typical of what people tend to say in a wide range of settings – although of course attitudes do vary.

3 **first we need to understand what we mean by 'mind'...** We will use the term 'mind' throughout this book, but there is not necessarily wide agreement on its definition. Here we take it to mean both the physical aspects of the brain and nervous system, and also the subjective experience of being in them. The mind is essentially an abstraction of course: what we are really talking about here is people, and how they experience their lives.

4 **our brains grow so much larger...** Brain size is measured in many ways, primarily volume, mass, and the ratio of these to the body. Human brains are not at the top of any of these charts, but our brains are still considerably larger relative to those of similar creatures.

5 **our young have to be born premature...** See for example Cameron, N. (2001). *Human Growth and Development*. Academic Press, 311.

6 **In a classic model, Paul D MacLean...** MacLean, P.D. (1990). *The Triune Brain in Evolution: Role in Paleocerebral Functions*. Plenum.

7 **over five hundred million neurons in the human digestive system...** See for example Sherwood, L. (2008). *Human Physiology: From Cells to Systems*. Brooks/Cole 595.

8 **neurons in our hearts...** Sperelakis, N., Kurachi, Y., Terzic, A., Cohen, M.V. (2000). *Heart Physiology and Pathophysiology*. Academic Press, 48.

9 **The true power of your mind...** There are many different definitions of the unconscious. Here we use it not in the Freudian sense, but in the modern psychological sense, to mean mental activity that is not mediated by conscious awareness. We will be using 'unconscious' rather than 'subconscious' throughout for consistency too, although the words are increasingly used interchangeably.

10 **Haidt describes the mind as 'the elephant and the rider'...** Haidt, J. (2007). *The Happiness Hypothesis*. Arrow Books.

11 **Loud noises, especially intermittent noise...** One commonly-cited review of this well-researched area is Broadbent, D.E. (1958). *The Effects of Noise on Behaviour*. Elmsford, New York: Pergamon Press.

12 **Noise isn't always bad for us though...** See for example studies investigating the beneficial effects of background noise for children with attention problems, such as, Söderlund, G.B.W., Sikström, S., Loftesnes, J.M. & Sonuga-Barke, E.J. (2010). 'The effects of background white noise on memory performance in inattentive school children'. *Behavioral and Brain Functions*,

6: 55. And also Söderlund G.B.W., Sikström S, Smart A. (2007). 'Listen to the noise: Noise is beneficial for cognitive performance in ADHD'. *Journal of Child Psychology and Psychiatry* 48(8): 840–7.

13 **The optimum level for creative tasks...** Mehta, R., Zhu, R., Cheema, A. (2012). 'Is noise always bad? Exploring the effects of ambient noise on creative cognition'. *Journal of Consumer Research*, 39: 784–99.

14 **Being able to control noise levels is the key...** Glass, D.C. & Singer, J.E. (1972). *Urban Stress: Experiments on Noise and Social Stressors*. New York: Academic Press.

15 **Sunlight isn't just pleasant...** Wirz-Justice, A., Bucheli, C., Graw, P., Kielholz, P., Fisch, H.-U. & Waggon, B. (1986). 'Light treatment of seasonal affective disorder in Switzerland'. *Acta Psychiatrica Scandinavica*, 74(2): 193–204. And see also Hubalek, S., Brink, M. & Schierz, C. (2010). 'Office workers' daily exposure to light and its influence on sleep quality and mood'. *Lighting Research and Technology* 42(1): 33–50.

16 **Some electronic devices though...** King, D., Delfabbro, P.H., Zwaans, T. & Kaptsis, D. (2014). 'Sleep interference effects of pathological electronic media use during adolescence'. *International Journal of Mental Health and Addiction*. ISSN: 1557–1874 (Print) 1557–1882.

17 **Watch out for fluorescent lights too...** See Hollwich, F. and Dieckhues, B. (1980). 'The effect of natural and artificial light via the eye on the hormonal and metabolic balance of animal and man'. *Opthalmologica*, 180(4): 188–197. And also see Küller, R. & Wetterberg, L. (1993). 'Melatonin, cortisol, EEG, ECG and subjective comfort in healthy humans: impact of two fluorescent lamp types at two light intensities'. *Lighting Research and Technology.* 25(2): 71–80.

18 **Sleep deprivation has similar effects to being drunk...** Dawson, D. & Reid, K. (1997). 'Fatigue, alcohol and performance impairment'. *Nature*, 388: 235.

19 **That doesn't mean we all need our eight hours...** See for example Ferrara M., De Gennaro L. (2001). 'How much sleep do we need?' *Sleep Medicine Reviews* 5(2): 155–179. For more on sleep patterns see Daniel and Jason Freeman's excellent introduction in their 2011 book *Use Your Head*. John Murray, Chapter 7.

20 **how we think about sleep makes a difference...** Draganich C. & Erdal K. (2014). 'Placebo sleep affects cognitive functioning'. *Journal of Experimental Psychology, Learning Memory and Cognition.* 40(3): 857–64.

21 **being distracted when you're in pain...** An interesting take on the impact of chronic pain on wellbeing can be found in Smith, J.A. & Osborn, M. (2007). 'Pain as an assault on the self: An interpretative phenomenological analysis of the psychological impact of chronic benign low back pain'. *Psychology & Health*, 22(5): 517–34.

22 **Exercise is particularly beneficial...** Fox, K.R. (1999). 'The influence of physical activity on mental well-being'. *Public Health Nutrition*, 2(3A),

411–418. And see also Biddle, S.J.H., Fox, K.R., Boutcher, H.S. (2000) *Physical Activity and Psychological Well-being,* Routledge Chapman & Hall.

23 **fatty acids like Omega-3...** Desai, A., Rush, J., Naveen, L. & Thaipisuttikul, P. (2011). 'Nutrition and nutritional supplements to promote brain health', Enhancing Cognitive Fitness in Adults. Springer. 249–69.

24 **Caffeine similarly gives us...** Childs, E., Hohoff, C., Deckert, J., Xu, K., Badner, J. & de Witt, H. (2008), 'Association between ADORA2A and DRD2 polymorphisms and caffeine-induced Anxiety'. *Neuropsychopharmacology,* 33(12): 2791–800.

25 **Consider what you put into your body...** I am greatly indebted in this section to Alison Clark of AC Health & Nutrition (www.achn.co.uk) for her advice on diet, wellbeing and 'good mood food'.

26 **Lack of water has been linked to poor mental performance...** Ganio M.S., Armstrong, L.E., Casa, D.J., McDermott, B.P., Lee, E.C., Yamamoto, L.M., Marzano, S., Lopez, R.M., Jimenez, L., Le Bellego, L., Chevillotte, E. & Lieberman, H.R. (2011). 'Mild dehydration impairs cognitive performance and mood of men'. *British Journal of Nutrition* 106: 1535–1543.

27 **The impact of dehydration on mood...** Armstrong, L.E., Ganio, M.S., Casa, D.J., Lee, E.C., McDermott, B.P., Klau, J.F., Jimenez, L., Le Bellego, L., Chevillotte, E. &. Lieberman, H.R. (2012). 'Mild dehydration affects mood in healthy young women'. *Journal of Nutrition* 142(2): 382–388.

28 **Social contact has been linked to all sorts of health and wellbeing factors...** See for example Thoits, P.A. (1995). 'Stress, coping and social support processes: where are we? What next?' *Journal of Health and Social Behaviour* (extra issue), 35: 53–79. And also Uchino, B.N., Cacioppo, J.T. & Kiecolt-Glaser J.K (1996). 'The relationship between social support and physiological processes: A review with emphasis on underlying mechanisms and implications for health'. *Psychological Bulletin,* 119: 488–531.

29 **lack of friendships has a similar impact on our life expectancy...** Holt-Lunstad, J., Smith, T.B., Layton, J.B. (2010). 'Social relationships and mortality risk: a meta-analytic review'. *PLoS Med.* 7(7).

30 **This may explain why retirement and unemployment can be so bad for our mental health...** There is a wealth of evidence on the effects of work on our minds. See for example Waddell, G. & Burton, A.K. (2006). *Is Work Good for Your Health and Well-being?* Department of Work and Pensions, UK. And also Sahlgren, G.H. (2013). 'Work longer, live healthier. The relationship between economic activity, health and government policy'. IEA Discussion Paper No. 46.

31 **Bullying and unfair treatment are very bad for our mental health...** Dr Lynne Friedli's work is the best place to start on the negative health impact of bullying and inequality, such as Friedli, L. (2009). *Mental Health, Resilience and Inequalities – A Report for WHO Europe and the Mental Health Foundation.* London/Copenhagen: Mental Health Foundation and WHO Europe.

32 **particularly if it makes us feel unsafe...** There are many social

determinants of mental health and wellbeing, but an interesting local study is Shipton, D. & Whyte, B. (2011). *Mental Health in Focus: A Profile of Mental Health and Wellbeing in Greater Glasgow & Clyde.* Glasgow: Glasgow Centre for Population Health.

33 **Happy people can make us happier...** See Chapter 8 for more on how we unconsciously influence each other.

34 **One important concept is that of 'mental resources'...** Mental resources can mean a few different things, but here and elsewhere in this book we are using it in the sense of the mental energy we have for making decisions, exercising willpower and using our conscious minds to control our thoughts and actions. This is related to the concept of 'ego depletion' described in Baumeister, R.F., Bratslavsky, E., Muraven, M. & Tice, D.M. (1998). 'Ego depletion: Is the active self a limited resource?' *Journal of Personality and Social Psychology* 74 (5): 1252–1265.

35 **Using your conscious mind takes mental effort...** For an excellent introduction to how self-control and cognitive effort are a form of mental work, see Kahneman, D. (2012). *Thinking, Fast and Slow.* Penguin. Chapter 3.

36 **Stress and anxiety can also impair your ability to think clearly...** See Chapter 4 for a more detailed look at the impact of stress on mind and body.

37 **the harder you will find it to use your mind...** See for instance Pocheptsova, A., Amir, O., Dhar, R. & Baumeister, R. (2009). 'Deciding without resources: Resource depletion and choice in context'. *Journal of Marketing Research*, 46(3): 344–355. Read more on how mental resources can affect decision-making in Chapter 7.

38 **There are surprisingly few ways to make yourself smarter...** Read more about the merits, or otherwise, of brain training and other activities that claim to increase intelligence in Chapter 6.

39 **So if you want to make the most of your mind...** See for example this 2006 study linking healthy lifestyle to memory performance. Small, G.W.; Silverman, D.H.; Siddarth, P.; et al. (2006). 'Effects of a 14-day healthy longevity lifestyle program on cognition and brain function'. *American Journal of Geriatric Psychiatry* 14(6): 538–45.

40 **Resilience is our capacity to maintain our mental wellbeing...** This term has become widely overused and means different things to different people. It was popularised by Norman Garmezy in the 1970s and the literature on it is now quite extensive. For a couple of perspectives on it, see Luthar, S.S., Cicchetti, D. & Becker, B. (2000). 'The construct of resilience: A critical evaluation and guidelines for future work'. *Child Development* 71(3): 543–562. Also see Rutter, M. (2012). 'Resilience as a dynamic concept'. *Development and Psychopathology* 24: 335–344.

41 **Part of this is about psychological attitude...** For more on differing mindsets and managing emotions, see the material on self-regulation in Chapter 2 and neuroticism in Chapter 5.

42 **the choices we make, and the actions we take...** For a round-up

of research into how our wellbeing can be influenced by our actions, see Lyubomirsky, S., Sheldon, K.M. & Schkade, D. (2005). 'Pursuing happiness: The architecture of sustainable change'. *Review of General Psychology*, 9: 111–131. Far too much has been made of this research by some commentators though and generalisations should be avoided, particularly around the relative contributions of each factor to our wellbeing.

43 **Put in crude terms...** The research here is complex and contentious so we are broadly following Jonathan Haidt's summary in his book, *The Happiness Hypothesis* (2007), Chapter 5. The formula is more usually applied to 'happiness' or 'eudemonic wellbeing', but the terminology can be a bit confusing so we've stuck with 'wellbeing' for consistency.

44 **Your genetic make-up...** Around 50 per cent in fact, according to Lykken, D. & Tellegen, A. (1996). 'Happiness is a Stochastic Phenomenon'. *Psychological Science*, 7(3): 186–9. Steven Pinker also argues strongly for the role of genes in our future character and life chances in Pinker, S. (2003). *The Blank Slate: The Modern Denial of Human Nature*. Penguin Press Science.

45 **Conditions of life...** For a therapeutic perspective on how early experiences affect our minds, see Sue Gerhardt's book (2004) *Why Love Matters: How Affection Shapes a Baby's Brain*. Routledge.

46 **The Mindapples campaign...** Disclosure: I founded this organisation in 2008, so I would recommend it wouldn't I? Mindapples is an independent non-profit organisation, and you can read more about its campaign work at www.mindapples.org/about/projects.

47 **So what are your mindapples?** You can share the '5-a-day for your mind', and find out what other people say works for them, at www.mindapples.org.

48 **In a poll of two thousand people...** This poll of 2000 broadly representative members of the UK public was conducted by Populus for Mind and Mindapples in June 2013. The question asked was: 'What five things, if any, do you currently do in the knowledge that they will contribute to your mental health and wellbeing?'

49 **the Five Ways to Wellbeing...** For the evidence behind NEF's Five Ways to Wellbeing see Huppert, F. (2008). 'Psychological Well-being: Evidence Regarding its Causes and its Consequences'. *Appl. Physiol: Health and Well-Being*, 1(2): 137–64.

50 **pleasurable activities free from the demands of work...** Pressman, S.D., Matthews, K.A., Cohen, S., Martire, L.M., Scheier, M., Baum, A. & Schulz, R. (2009). 'Association of enjoyable leisure activities with psychological and physical well-being. *Psychosomatic Medicine*, 71: 725–732.

51 **Hugging is good for our health...** Field, T. (2010). 'Touch for socioemotional and physical well-being: A review'. *Developmental Review*, 30: 367–383. (Beware of anyone who needs scientific evidence to justify hugging you though: these people tend to be a little peculiar.)

52 **Retail therapy...** Atalay, A. & Meloy, M. (2011). 'Retail therapy: A strategic effort to improve mood'. *Psychology and Marketing*, 28(6): 638–659.

53 **watching *Lord of the Rings* is good for your mind...** Powell, M.L. & Newgent, R.A. (2010). 'Improving the empirical credibility of cinematherapy: A single-subject interrupted time-series design'. *Counseling Outcome Research and Evaluation* 1: 40–49.

54 **Mindfulness has some of its roots in spiritual practices...** Most popular modern mindfulness tools and techniques are inspired by Buddhist meditative practices, but the idea of being present and mindful is found in a range of spiritual and secular practices throughout the ages.

55 **'the non-judgmental awareness of experiences in the present moment'** Hölzel, B.K., Lazar, S.W, Gard, T., Schuman-Olivier, Z., Vago, D.R. & Ott, U.. (2011). 'How does mindfulness meditation work? Proposing mechanisms of action from a conceptual and neural perspective'. *Perspectives on Psychological Science*, 6(6): 537–559.

56 **'especially effective for reducing anxiety, depression, and stress'...** Khoury, B., Lecomte, T., Fortin, G., Masse, M., Therien, P., Bouchard, V., Chapleau M-A., Paquin, K. & Hofmann, S.G. (2013). 'Mindfulness-based therapy: A comprehensive meta-analysis'. *Clinical Psychology Review*, 33(6): 763–771.

57 **and sleep better at night...** Howell, A.J., Digdon, N.L., Buro, K. & Sheptycki, A.R. (2008). 'Relations among mindfulness, well-being, and sleep'. *Personality and Individual Differences*, 45(8): 773–777.

58 **There are physical health benefits too...** Brown, K.W. & Ryan, R.M. (2003) 'The benefits of being present: mindfulness and its role in psychological well-being'. *Journal of Personal and Social Psychology*. 84(4): 822–48.

59 **it can improve our immune systems...** Davidson R.J., Kabat-Zinn J., Schumacher J., Rosenkranz M., Muller D., Santorelli S.F., Urbanowski F., Harrington A., Bonus K., Sheridan J.F. (2003). 'Alterations in brain and immune function produced by mindfulness meditation'. *Psychosomatic Medicine*, 65(4): 564–70.

60 **correlations between mindfulness and job performance...** Dane, E. & Brummel, B. J. (2014). 'Examining workplace mindfulness and its relations to job performance and turnover intention'. *Human Relations*, 67(1): 105–128.

61 **'We call ourselves human beings, but we behave more like human doings.'** Jon Kabat-Zinn, quoted by the author from a lecture at Friends House, London, 28 March 2013, and also elsewhere.

62 **a popular saying about our bodies...** The lovely line 'Take care of your body. It's the only place you have to live' is often attributed to Jim Rohn but may have originated elsewhere. Try this for starters Rohn, J. (2002), *The Keys to Success*. Brolga Publishing.

CHAPTER 2
MASTER YOUR MOODS

We aren't always comfortable talking about our feelings.

Discussing our emotions can feel too personal, even self-indulgent, particularly in a business context. Calling someone 'emotional' can even sound like an insult, implying that their judgement is unsound or their behaviour unpredictable. For some people, emotions just aren't very 'business like'.

However, managing our emotions at work is essential to working well. We all experience moods and emotions all the time, both positive and negative, and our emotional state contributes directly to our professional performance.

Moods and emotions affect our work. Positive moods have been linked to learning, creativity and mental performance, whilst negative moods can narrow our focus, blind us to possibilities and change how we see risks and opportunities.

Managing the emotional side of work can give businesses the edge. Whether we like it or not, talking about our feelings is good for business.

AN EMOTIONAL BUSINESS

Our emotional states have a lot of effects on our thoughts and behaviour, and consequently on our work.

Positive emotions like joy and excitement seem to increase our capacity for making decisions,[1] improve our memories[2] and encourage people to be helpful and collaborative.[3] Staff in positive emotional states also make more time for interesting tasks whilst still doing boring, necessary tasks just as accurately.[4]

Positive emotions allow us to be more creative and open to new opportunities. We tend to have more flexible thought patterns, be more responsive to new information, and process ideas in novel ways.[5] They allow us to broaden our attention and our thinking, whereas negative emotions – anger, anxiety, depression, or feelings of threat – narrow our attention and blind us to possibilities.

The 'broaden and build' theory developed by Barbara Fredrickson suggests why this might be the case.[6]

Negative emotions such as fear or anger are signals for us to escape or attack. They limit our options in order to enable quick, decisive action and maximise our chances of survival. They are useful because they help us focus on threats and learn from bad experiences, but not so useful when they dominate our thinking and stop us from thinking clearly or spotting opportunities.[7]

Positive emotions, on the other hand, signal safety and opportunities for exploration and creation, broadening our minds and allowing us to think in more flexible ways. They make it easier for us to approach new experiences, increasing our attention for new ideas and relationships – which is more useful for most situations at work.

When we are in positive states of mind, we literally see more of the world around us.[8] Conversely, negative emotions can cause us to miss opportunities and pay more attention to negative events and bad memories.[9] We filter the world according to our moods and emotional states. They shape how we see the world, affecting our decisions.

A University of Warwick study also showed positive emotions increase productivity by helping us engage more in our work. *'Happier workers,'* said the study authors, *'were 12 per cent more productive. Unhappier workers were 10 per cent less productive'*. According to their findings, *'the effect operates through a rise in sheer output...Effort increases. Precision remains unaltered'*.[10]

When we are in a positive state of mind, we tend to race through our task lists and work more efficiently and accurately. When we feel good emotionally, it helps us reach a state of flow.

So managing our moods and emotions affects more than just our health and wellbeing. It can aid our professional development, help us develop new skills and capabilities, promote creativity and collaboration, and help us get more done.

If you want to be successful at work, you need to manage your emotions, not just your intellectual abilities.

As Barbara Fredrickson put it:

'Positive emotions are worth cultivating, not just as end states in themselves but also as a means to achieving psychological growth and improved well-being.'[11]

SEEING THE WOOD FOR THE TREES

The first obstacle to managing our emotional states is that most of us struggle to answer even simple questions about how we feel. We can't easily put our feelings into words, or talk about them comfortably with other people.

We need to find a better language for describing this sensitive, personal topic – particularly at work.

There are many models of emotion but Robert Plutchik's classic 'wheel of emotions' offers a detailed starting point, mapping the twenty-four most common emotions by their type and intensity.[12] Less intense varieties are on the outside of the wheel, more intense closer to the centre.

Plutchik's model reveals the variety and complexity of our emotional reactions. It is instructive, too, to see how many different words we have to describe how we feel. For all our awkwardness, we certainly like talking about our feelings.

This model is pretty complicated though. It can be tricky to identify our feelings to this level of precision, and very few people sit in the office discussing their pensiveness or rage.

The wheel is actually constructed around four basic emotions – fear, anger, sadness and joy – which simplifies things a little. If you know how you feel in relation to each of these, that's a good start.

The other problem though is that we are not always aware of what we're feeling. We can feel several emotions at the same time, and experience emotions on different levels:[13]

1 Conscious
Aware of how we feel and can explain it
2 Partially conscious
Fleeting awareness of the feeling
3 Unconscious
No awareness of the feeling or its effects

So there is usually at least some aspect of how you feel that is beneath your conscious awareness, making it impossible to regulate every aspect of your emotional state. Knowing how your emotions are affecting you can be challenging.

No wonder, then, that psychologists are increasingly seeking less subjective ways to map how we feel. Influential psychologist James Russell even said of our popular language of emotions that *'these guideposts might not have pointed in the best direction'.*[14] If we want to make managing our feelings a day-to-day habit, we may need to look a little further.

WHAT ABOUT MOODS?

We use the word 'mood' frequently in everyday conversation – 'he's in a mood', 'I'm in such a good mood today' and so on – but we rarely stop to consider what it means.

Psychologists distinguish carefully between 'moods' and 'emotions'. Emotional reactions relate to specific events, and may come and go relatively quickly. Moods, meanwhile, are persistent states that can last for hours or even days. They aren't linked to a single event: they are background feelings, sometimes called 'core affect'.

Moods are natural, and present in everyone, a bit like an emotional body temperature. We notice them when they are particularly intense, but they are always there.

Our moods affect our emotional reactions, and vice versa. Both provide useful insights into how the events in our lives affect us. Here is a useful distinction developed by the influential mood researcher William N. Morris and summed up by Randy J. Larsen:[15]

> *'Emotions provide information about the environment and the demands being placed on us.*
> *Moods...provide information about our internal state of affairs.'*

Moods, then, show us what we have taken on emotionally from the events in our lives. Managing our moods can help us manage the impact that our emotions and the world around us have on our thoughts and behaviour, both at work and in our lives more generally.

TRACKING YOUR MOODS

Although we typically talk about being in a 'good' mood or a 'bad' mood, psychologists generally measure mood in two dimensions, most commonly mapping our emotional state against levels of energy or 'arousal'.[16]

One of the more accessible models, proposed in the 1990s by psychologist Robert Thayer, describes mood as a product of tension and energy. We can be tired and also feel tense, or energetic but also relaxed. In his book *The Origin of Everyday Moods*, Thayer argued that people feel, and perform, best when they are in a relaxed, energised state.[17]

Here is a model of how Thayer's two dimensions of mood can be mapped to some of our familiar mood states.[18]

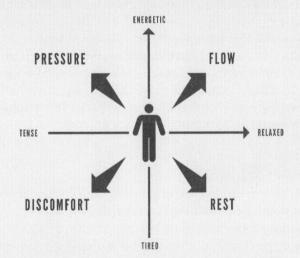

You can use this model to help you recognise when you are in a particular mood. By tracking your levels of energy and tension and becoming more aware of how and why they change, you can begin to manage them.[19]

Knowing how we feel is important: if our underlying moods change our perception and behaviour, then the more conscious we are of our moods, the more we can correct for these effects. Most of us have had the experience of noticing that we are reacting angrily or struggling to concentrate.

Being aware of your underlying levels of tension and energy can help you notice when you are in a productive state of mind, and also when to come back to things later.

Thayer's model doesn't tell you everything about how you are feeling. We feel many different things and there are many models for mapping these sensations.

However, this model is both a good start for managing your own state, and a useful way to talk about moods at work. We may not feel comfortable telling our colleagues when we feel sad or fearful, but we are much more comfortable talking about how much energy we have, and whether we are feeling tense.

Thayer said that *'our moods are infallible indicators, or barometers, of our most basic functions'.*[20] Knowing your moods is a powerful tool for self-management. If you at least know, on a day-to-day basis, how energised you are feeling, and how tense you are feeling, that will take you a long way towards improving your performance at work.

MANAGING YOUR MOODS

So maintaining our tension and energy levels offers a good starting point for managing our everyday moods.

Managing these moods isn't straightforward though. Compared to emotions, they are longer lasting, less related to external events, and harder to express directly, which can make it tricky to know how to process them. Many different factors affect your moods:[21]

- **Your personality**
  Your natural personality traits affect your average mood levels, volatility and sensitivity to life events.

- **Hormones**
  Body chemicals and other internal physiological systems
  affect and interact with moods (in men and women).
- **Nutrition**
  What you eat and drink alters your mood, especially
  substances like caffeine, sugar and alcohol.
- **Environment**
  Events, context, other people and your day-to-day
  emotional reactions affect your mood over the long term.

Some of these things are outside our control, but a great
many are down to our own outlook, choices and actions. So
although external factors affect our moods, there is usually
also something we can do to manage them.

Thayer's research suggests that we all unconsciously seek
to manage our moods through our daily actions, instinctively
raising energy and reducing tension through our actions.

Think about the regular actions you take – consciously or
unconsciously – to raise your energy and reduce your tension.
Consider your daily routine: what you do when you wake up
in the morning, and get home at night. Even the little things
can make a big difference.

If you are unaware of your unconscious need to regulate
our moods, then you may find yourself unthinkingly doing
whatever you can to shift your moods quickly, particularly
when you are in a state of discomfort. This can lead to
harmful and addictive behaviour patterns that provide
short-term relief, but which may cause long-term problems.

Just as with maintaining our general mental wellbeing,
there is no universal technique for regulating energy and
tension. The things we do to manage our moods tend to be
very personal and vary according to culture, lifestyle, interests,
age, health and personality.

For example, some people find gentle activities like music
and gardening can relax them, whilst others prefer more

energetic pursuits like socialising and sports. What one person finds energising might feel exhausting for someone else, and many things people say are relaxing may be stressful to somebody else. We're all different.

Some people find it easier to identify energising actions, others relaxing actions, and often the things we do to recharge and stay calm can be the same. There's no set rule about how we manage energy and tension.

The most important thing is to find what works for you. We generally do whatever feels easiest and most comfortable, so your self-management behaviours need to fit in with your lifestyle. Find your own relaxing 'breathers' and energising 'restorers' and build them into your daily routine, to maintain your emotional wellbeing and keep yourself focussed and productive.[22]

MANAGING DISCOMFORT

If we are unaware of the importance of managing our moods, we can end up being managed by them.

Thayer's research suggests that although we take many healthy actions to manage our moods, our behaviour becomes more compulsive when we reach the 'discomfort zone' of low energy and high tension. We find this state unbearable and will do almost anything to escape from it, including reaching for quick-fix solutions that are not beneficial for us in the long term.

These quick fixes might include cigarettes, alcohol, drugs and stimulants, comfort eating, and even shopping. They shift our moods rapidly, but come with other negative consequences.

Coffee to wake us up, cigarettes to calm us down, shopping to lift our spirits – all these actions are attempts at mood management. By recognising this, we can start to identify whether these actions are really working for us, and begin to manage our moods proactively.

The most important thing is to broaden your choices about what you can do. The more actions you have to choose from to raise your energy and reduce your tension, the easier you will find it to keep yourself comfortable and well.

So keep thinking about your lists of actions, try to find more ways to manage energy and tension, and build yourself a toolbox of activities to change how you feel in healthy, sustainable ways. Try to keep yourself out of that state of discomfort too, because the more time you spend in that tense, tired state, the more compulsive your actions are likely to become.[23]

SELF-REGULATION

The deliberate and habitual ways in which we manage and change how we feel through our actions is often known in psychology as 'self-regulation'.[24]

Self-regulation is not a tool for emergencies, but a good habit to develop in your life and work.[25] Sometimes you may need to dampen the intensity of emotions to enable you to focus more on your situation; other times you may want to maintain a positive or productive mood. Whatever you're using these techniques for, the most valuable thing is to feel that you have some influence over how you feel, rather than being a slave to your emotions.

There are three levels to emotional self-regulation:

---

1 **Awareness**
Knowing your emotional state and understanding your impact on others.
2 **Surface acting**
Managing your impact on others despite how you feel at the time.
3 **Deep acting**
Managing your underlying emotional state to be appropriate to the context.

Surface acting is tiring and uses up your mental resources, and this kind of 'emotional labour' can affect wellbeing and work performance. Genuinely managing your emotions is far more efficient and effective. If you can adjust your underlying state to 'tune in' to the people around you, you can relate to them better.[26]

Learning to do this, then, is a very useful skill. We are all different, in how often we self-regulate, the strategies we prefer to use, and how successful we are. The more tools we have, and the more insights we have into why we feel the way we do, the more likely we are to be able to manage our reactions and cope with difficult situations.

Using research data from a number of studies, Randy J. Larsen collected some of the most common strategies that people employ to regulate their moods and emotions.[27]

	ACTIONS	THOUGHTS
PROBLEM FOCUS	Fix the problem	Reframe the situation
	Plan for the future	Think of what's going well
	Talk it through	Think of others worse off
	Try harder	Have faith
	Hide or run away!	Just accept it
MOOD ITSELF	Keep busy	Relax or meditate
	Help others	Draw strength from it
	Seek pleasure	Daydream to forget
	Socialise	Focus on the future
	Vent	Refuse to think about it
	Suppress it	Intellectualise
	Exercise	
	Ingest substances	

The list he gathered is not designed to be advice, but simply a reflection back of what people actually do, both good and bad, to manage their moods. He distinguished particularly between strategies that focus on the problem itself, and those that focus on the feelings it provokes.

There is no consistent one-size-fits-all solution to managing your moods and emotions: different strategies work for different feelings. Whether you choose to change how you feel, or change your situation, is up to you. Every situation is different and no-one can tell you what to put up with in your life and what not to.

Take responsibility for how you react to your moods and emotions. Be aware of your options, and choose the most appropriate response for you and others at the time.

SELF-REGULATION AT WORK

Given the impact our emotional state has on our ability to concentrate, think clearly, learn new skills and relate to others, mood regulation is very important if we want to perform at our best at work.

If we are unaware of the importance of mood regulation though, we may regard these instinctive self-regulation behaviours as 'time-wasting', when in fact we are simply trying to shift our mental state in order to tackle our workload more effectively. Going for a walk, checking Facebook, chatting to colleagues – these things can all help keep people positive and enable them to work better.

Mood management represents something of a challenge for businesses then. Seemingly unproductive activities might actually make us more efficient at work because they improve our mood and help us concentrate and make better decisions. Managers need to know their people well enough to be able to tell the difference between positive self-regulation activities, and plain old time-wasting.

Everyone is different, so it is difficult to put organisation-wide policies in place to support mood management. What is really needed is good, supportive management to give people the space and autonomy to make their own choices and manage their energy levels and emotional state in their own ways.

This means we all need to do our bit to promote a positive culture in the workplace, to avoid spreading our anxieties onto others and be aware of our emotional impact. We influence each other's moods a lot through our reactions and behaviour too, so the more conscious we can be of our own moods and emotions, the better we can manage them, and make a positive contribution at work.

EMOTIONAL INTELLIGENCE

Mood regulation is part of a wider area of research called 'emotional intelligence'. Emotional intelligence is a popular term for our ability to recognise and manage emotions effectively, in ourselves and others. It is important for managing our minds, maintaining wellbeing and relating to others, and is widely recognised as a key predictor of personal and professional success.[28]

People high in emotional intelligence are more likely to forego short-term pleasures for greater and more sustained long-term pleasures, strive towards emotions that are both good for them and good for those around them, and appreciate that emotions are context-dependent and different emotions are helpful in different situations.

Emotional intelligence is particularly useful in social settings: if we can recognise and manage our own emotions, we can have a positive impact on others. Being aware of other people's emotional states, and understanding your own moods and how they affect other people, enables you to respond appropriately.

This is not just about being perpetually cheerful. If you are very happy whilst others around you are sad or angry, you will struggle to relate to them. Sometimes the most appropriate response is to be sombre, sad or angry.

Learning when, and when not, to express your emotions, both good and bad, is an important aspect of emotional intelligence.

GETTING THE MESSAGE

Emotions are important signals though, and not something to be suppressed or 'fixed'. Our emotions are telling us how we feel about the events in our lives, and our moods are telling us about our inner state and mental condition. We may need to put these messages aside to get things done, but we ignore them at our peril.[29]

Moods also have a natural rhythm, and it is not always healthy, or possible, to control your emotional states. Any emotion can be healthy and useful in the right context, and sometimes the most appropriate response is to feel angry or unhappy. Too much emotional self-regulation can even make us over-vigilant, always looking for deeper levels of feeling in case there is something we have missed.

Listen to your mind and notice what it needs to be calm, energetic and productive, but don't worry too much about trying to stay in one particular mood all the time. The key is to understand and process your moods effectively, to manage your activities and routine accordingly, and not to get stuck for too long in unhelpful feelings.

Use your moods to monitor your mental state, and then let them go when they are no longer useful to you.

As Randy J. Larsen summed it up, self-regulation is:[30]

> **the ability to hang up the phone after getting the message.**

HABIT 2
TRACK THE ACTIONS YOU TAKE TO RAISE ENERGY AND REDUCE TENSION AND BUILD THEM INTO YOUR DAY

MASTER YOUR MOODS
IN A NUTSHELL

THE TWITTER VERSION

Your moods affect your mind and need to be managed, so maintain your energy and reduce your tension through your daily actions.

THE SUMMARY VERSION

Moods and emotions affect our relationships, our productivity and even how we see the world, but we tend to be afraid of talking about them, particularly at work. Part of this is about language: we need a better way to talk about our feelings.

Emotions give you information about the events in your life, whilst moods are background feelings and tell you about your inner state. Everyone has moods, and they naturally vary with life events, nutrition, hormones and other factors.

Moods are more than just good or bad: they also involve energy. One good model involves managing your levels of energy and tension. We all instinctively raise our energy and reduce our tension through our actions. Think about what works best for you to stay energised and free from tension. If you don't, you may find yourself relying on unhealthy quick fixes to escape discomfort.

All this is part of emotional intelligence: the ability to process your emotions and deal sensitively with others. Don't obsess about changing your moods though: just learn how to get what they are telling you, and then move on with your day.

NOTES

1 **increase our capacity for making decisions...**Isen, A.M. (2000). 'Positive affect and decision making'. In Lewis, M. & Haviland, J.M. (Eds.), *Handbook of Emotions*. 2nd ed. New York: The Guilford Press.
2 **improve our memories...** Isen, A.M., Shalker, T.E., Clark, M. & Karp, L. (1978). 'Affect, accessibility of material in memory, and behaviour: A cognitive loop?' *Journal of Personality and Social Psychology*, 36, 1–12; and see also Teasdale, J.D. & Fogarty, S.J. (1979). 'Differential effects of induced mood on retrieval of pleasant and unpleasant events from episodic memory'. *Journal of Abnormal Psychology*, 88: 248–257.
3 **encourage people to be helpful and collaborative...** Isen, A.M. & Simmonds, S. (1978). 'The effect of feeling good on a helping task that is incompatible with good mood'. *Social Psychology Quarterly*, 41: 346–349.
4 **make more time for interesting tasks..** Isen, A. M. & Reeve, J. (2005). 'The influence of positive affect on intrinsic and extrinsic motivation: Facilitating enjoyment of play, responsible work behavior, and selfcontrol'. *Motivation and Emotion, 29:* 297–325.
5 **We tend to have more flexible thought patterns...** Isen, A.M. (2000). 'Positive affect and decision making'. In Lewis, M. & Haviland, M.J. (Eds.), *Handbook of Emotions*. 2nd edn. Guilford Press, pp. 417–435.
6 **The 'broaden and build' theory...** Fredrickson, B.L. (1998). 'What good are positive emotions?' *Review of General Psychology*, 2: 300–319.
7 **Negative emotions such as fear or anger...** Tooby, J. & Cosmides, L. (1990). 'The past explains the present: Emotional adaptations and the structure of ancestral environments'. *Ethology and Sociobiology*, 11: 375–424.
8 **we literally see more...**Schmitz, T.W., De Rosa, E. & Anderson, A.K. (2009). 'Opposing influences of affective state valence on visual cortical encoding'. *The Journal of Neuroscience* 22: 7199–7207.
9 **negative emotions can cause us to miss opportunities...** Harris, J.C. (1995). *Developmental Neuropsychiatry: Fundamentals*. Oxford University Press.
10 **positive emotions increase productivity...** Oswald, A.J., Proto, E. & Sgroi, D. (2009). 'Happiness and productivity'. *IZA Discussion Papers*, 4645.
11 **'Positive emotions are worth cultivating...'** Fredrickson, B.L. (2001). 'The role of positive emotions in positive psychology: The broaden-and-build theory of positive emotions'. *American Psychologist,* 56: 218–226.
12 **Robert Plutchik's classic 'wheel of emotions'...** adapted from Plutchik, R., *Emotion: A Psychoevolutionary Synthesis*, 1st edn., © 1979. Reprinted and electronically reproduced by permission of Pearson Education, Inc., Upper Saddle River, New Jersey.
13 **experience emotions on different levels...** Mayer, J.D. & Salovey, P. (1995). 'Emotional intelligence and the construction and regulation of feelings'. *Applied and Preventive Psychology*, 4: 197–208.
14 **'these guideposts might not have pointed in the best direction'**

Russell, J.A. (2003) 'Core affect and the psychological construction of emotion'. *Psychological Review*, 110: 145–172.

15 **'Emotions provide information...'** Larsen, R.J. (2000). Toward a science of mood regulation'. *Psychological Inquiry*, 11(3): 129–141, referencing Morris, W.N. (1992) 'A functional analysis of the role of mood in affective systems' in Clark, M.S. (Ed) (1992). *Emotion. Review of Personality and Social Psychology*. Sage, No.13, pp. 256–93.

16 **psychologists generally measure mood in two dimensions...** For an excellent review of the main models of mood tracking, including those of Robert Thayer, see Russell, J.A. & Feldman Barrett, L. (1999). 'Core affect, prototypical emotional episodes, and other things called emotion. Dissecting the elephant'. *Journal of Personality and Social Psychology*, 76(5): 805–819.

17 **mood as a product of tension and energy...** Thayer, R. (1996). *The Origin of Everyday Moods: Managing Energy, Tension, and Stress*. Oxford University Press USA.

18 **how Thayer's two dimensions of mood can be mapped...** This illustration is based on Robert Thayer's two dimensions of mood, tension and energy, but the labels and representation are our interpretation. For Thayer's version, see Thayer, R.E., (1996) *The Origin of Everyday Moods*. Oxford University Press USA.

19 **By tracking your levels of energy and tension...** You can also track and share your moods on a variant of this two-axis model using the *Moodbug* phone app developed by us at Mindapples, available at www.moodbug.me.

20 **'our moods are infallible indicators...'** Thayer, R. (1996). *The Origin of Everyday Moods: Managing Energy, Tension, and Stress*. Oxford University Press USA: 21.

21 **Many different factors affect our moods...** For a more complex breakdown of the sources of our moods, see Russell, J.A. (2003). 'Core affect and the psychological construction of emotion'. *Psychological Review*, 110(1): 145–172.

22 **The most important thing is to find what works for you...** Read more about the individual variations in what we find comfortable and energising in Chapter 5.

23 **the more compulsive your actions are likely to become...** Read more about the limits of willpower and our ability to delay gratification in Chapter 3.

24 **self-regulation...** Gross, J.J. (1998). 'The emerging field of emotion regulation: An integrative review'. *Review of General Psychology*, 2: 271–299.

25 **Self-regulation is not a tool for emergencies...** See for example the discussion of the distinction between self-regulation and 'coping' in Larsen, R.J. (2000) 'Toward a science of mood regulation'. *Psychological Inquiry: An International Journal for the Advancement of Psychological Theory*, 11(3): 129–141.

26 **Surface acting is tiring...** Grandey, A.A. (2003). 'When ''the show must go

on'': Surface acting and deep acting as determinants of emotional exhaustion and peer-rated service delivery'. *Academy of Management Journal*, 46: 86–96. And also Zapf, D. (2002). 'Emotion work and psychological well-being: A review of the literature and some conceptual considerations'. *Human Resource Management Review* 12: 237–268.

27 **Randy J Larsen collected some of the most common strategies...** Larsen, R.J. (2000). 'Toward a science of mood regulation'. *Psychological Inquiry: An International Journal for the Advancement of Psychological Theory*, 11(3): 129–141. Reprinted by permission of the publisher (Taylor & Francis Ltd, http://www.tandfonline.com).

For a more detailed exploration of the various strategies for managing moods, see Eid, M. & Larsen R.J. (Eds) (2008). *The Science of Subjective Well-Being*. The Guildford Press.

And see also the comprehensive review by Augustine, A.A. & Hemenover, S.H. (2009). 'On the relative effectiveness of affect regulation strategies: A meta-analysis'. *Cognition and Emotion*, 23(6), 1181–220.

28 **a wider area of research called 'emotional intelligence'...** The idea of emotional intelligence has been popularised by Daniel Goleman, particularly in Goleman, D. (1996) *Emotional Intelligence. Why it Can Matter More than IQ*. Bloomsbury. The classification of these emotional skills as a form of 'intelligence' though, is a little contentious and 'educated understanding' may be more appropriate. See Mayer, J.D., & Salovey, P. (1995). 'Emotional intelligence and the construction and regulation of feelings'. *Applied and Preventive Psychology*, 4: 197–208.

29 **Our emotions are telling us how we feel...** For more on the very useful idea that feelings provide information to inform our judgements, see for example Schwarz, N. (2010). 'Feelings-as-information theory'. In Van Lange, P., Kruglanski, A. & Higgins E.T. (eds.), *Handbook of Theories of Social Psychology*. Sage Publications.

30 **'the ability to hang up the phone after getting the message'** Larsen, R.J. (2000) 'Toward a Science of Mood Regulation', *Psychological Inquiry: An International Journal for the Advancement of Psychological Theory*, 11(3): 129–41.

CHAPTER 3
GET MOTIVATED

Most of us have to work hard to stay motivated in some aspects of our lives. Whether it's sticking to a diet, doing boring tasks, or even finding the time to do things we love, doing what we said we would do is a very human struggle.

Motivation means an eagerness to act, not just deciding to do something. There is often a gap between what we intend to do, and what we are motivated to do. We can commit to a course of action, but it is our motivation to do it that makes one thing feel easy and another feel hard.

Motivation is one of the most popular and widely researched topics in psychology and neuroscience. It is the study of what drives human behaviour: the underlying factors that make us do the things we do.

It is big business too. Highly engaged employees have a significant influence on sales performance,[1] whilst a 20 per cent increase in employee commitment can lead to an increase in sales of 9 per cent each month.[2] Motivation is one of the most fundamental ingredients of a successful business. Whether our goal is to motivate ourselves or others, most of us can learn a lot from the study of motivation.

THE LIMITS OF WILLPOWER

So why do we find some tasks easier than others? Why is it sometimes so hard to make time for things we enjoy? And what can we do to make the things we have to do, feel easy to do?

If we decide to do something we don't want to do, we usually rely on willpower. Willpower is a deliberate process by which we override our natural inclinations and force ourselves to act in line with our decisions.

We can boost our short-term motivation by consciously reminding ourselves why we are doing something:

- **'I need the money'**
- **'I believe in this'**
- **'I need to practise'**

The trouble is, willpower seems to be a finite resource.[3] Continually reminding ourselves why we need to do something takes energy and can lead to mental fatigue.

We seem to have less willpower when we are mentally tired, either from previous acts of self-control or lack of physical energy such as low glucose levels,[4] so we find it harder to control ourselves when we are tired or busy.

We can give ourselves more willpower if we keep ourselves fit, healthy, well-fed and rested, but it is still an uphill struggle that uses up mental resources we could be using for other things. We can practise it, but we can't do it indefinitely.[5]

So if willpower takes valuable energy that would be better spent on the task at hand, how can we boost our motivation without using willpower?

A MODEL OF MOTIVATION

Based on the motivation research of Gagné, Deci and Kehr,[6] here is an integrated model of three connected factors that, together, seem to get us motivated.

In order to feel motivated by a task, we need a clear external incentive for taking action, an inner drive for what we are doing, and a sense that we have the ability to succeed.

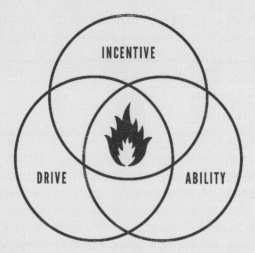

Combining these factors is the key to getting ourselves, and others, genuinely motivated.

EXTERNAL INCENTIVE

First, we need an external **incentive**.

External or 'extrinsic' motivators come from outside us, pulling us into action. They might be positive or negative, such as to gain a reward, avoid a threat or protect something important to us. They are the elements of motivation that relate to the situation we are in, and change with our circumstances.

Anything external that inspires us to take action can be classed as an extrinsic motivator. Some examples include:

- **Money, qualifications or awards**
- **Praise, status or prizes**
- **Deadlines, threats or evaluation**
- **Penalties, fines or disciplinary action**

Sometimes we act in pursuit of rewards, but extrinsic motivators also include negative factors too. When we act out of pressure, fear of punishment or criticism, or to avoid disappointing people, we are motivated by external incentives. This is classic 'carrot and stick' management.[7]

The impact of external incentives varies according to the type of task. For more dull, repetitive or mechanical tasks with no intrinsic interest, people usually want **increasing rewards** because they find them increasingly boring.[8] For more complex or creative tasks though, too much focus on external incentives can make us do less, not more.

In classic experiments in the 1970s by Edward Deci,[9] some participants were paid for completing interesting puzzles, whilst others were given nothing. Surprisingly, the unpaid participants spent more time solving the puzzles, even though they had no external incentive to do so. Paying people made them reduce their discretionary effort and 'work to rule'.

Money is still very important though. Being worried about money can make us distracted and demoralised. We also need to feel **fairly compensated** for our contributions or we may feel resentful or undervalued.[10] But beyond that, money doesn't seem to translate easily into effort.

This applies to negative incentives too. Some participants in the same study were also criticised or threatened with punishment if they failed, and they too stopped solving the puzzles sooner, just like their paid counterparts.

Negative motivators can be problematic in other ways too. We do have a strong motivation to **avoid loss** and protect what we have,[11] but our minds are not very good at processing negative instructions. When we try not to do something, it makes us think about it even more – a phenomenon known as 'ironic process theory'.[12] We also tend to **underestimate threats** and bad outcomes,[13] so threats can be surprisingly ineffective. Positive goals tend to be more motivating than threats of negative consequences.[14]

Whether we employ the carrot or the stick though, it seems external incentives alone are not enough to motivate us.

INNER DRIVE

Incentives aren't everything: we also need **drive**.

Internal or 'intrinsic' motivators come from within, and describe the values, beliefs and desires that consistently motivate us, regardless of context. They push us into action, whether there is an external benefit or not.

If a task is in line with our inner drivers, we are more likely to do it, and to concentrate more whilst we are doing it. Intrinsic drivers are also particularly important for highly creative or cognitive tasks, including problem-solving and innovation.

We can have all the incentives for being clever and creative we like, but unless we have that inner drive, we will struggle to focus our minds on the task at hand.

We all have inner drivers, even if we might struggle to identify them. Many things drive us, including:

- **Enjoyment or interest**
- **Beliefs, values or purpose**
- **Self-esteem and esteem of others**
- **Sense of autonomy and control**
- **Sense of accomplishment or satisfaction**
- **Helping people you care about**
- **Improving or protecting relationships**

Two of our most powerful inner drivers are our sense of autonomy and our social relationships.

Autonomy is our desire to be independent and free to choose. In a study of students, participants who were allowed to choose from similar activities persisted longer at problem-solving tasks than those given no choice between activities.[15] Whilst it is not always easy to choose what we do, whatever small choices we can make about what we do or how we do it will enhance our motivation – something micro-managers would do well to remember.

Alongside a desire for choice and autonomy, we have a strong desire for **'relatedness'** – good social relationships with others. Our need to belong is a powerful motivator.[16] We will usually be very motivated to do things that enhance our social standing and relationships, and to protect important relationships with people we care about.

One study showed we are more motivated by rewards and incentives when they are accompanied by positive feedback.[17] Another study found a small improvement in a person's relationship with their boss can improve their job satisfaction by as much as a thirty per cent increase in salary.[18] The human side of management really does matter.

These two inner drivers – to be independent and to be interconnected – underpin much of our behaviour. They are not opposing forces: some researchers are developing the concept of 'relational autonomy'. Rather than being competitive, autonomy is all about good relationships, because other people can help us achieve our goals.[19]

Intrinsic motivation is a very personal thing. It is particularly important that a task fits with a person's inner **beliefs and values**, a sense of higher purpose. If we can find a way to connect our actions to something we agree with or believe in, we will find it easier to do them.

As Dan Pink, author of the excellent *Drive*, puts it:[20]

'We have oversold carrot and stick motivators and undersold motivators like autonomy, mastery and purpose.'

ABILITY TO SUCCEED

Along with external incentives and inner drive, we also need to feel we have the **ability** to accomplish the task.

This obvious point can easily be forgotten amidst all this talk of incentives and values. The more we feel we have the **skills and resources** to accomplish a task, the more likely we are to want to do it. If we don't feel we have the ability to do it successfully, we are much more likely to give up.

Our perception of our ability to complete a task depends on the resources we can bring to it, including:[21]

- **Knowledge, skills and abilities**
- **Self-belief and confidence**
- **Resourcefulness or adaptability**
- **Social status and supporting relationships**
- **Money and physical assets**

The more of these skills and resources we have to bring to a task, the more motivated we will feel about doing it. In fact, the actual experience of **competence** and self-efficacy, of doing something we are good at, can itself be motivating, even when we derive no benefit from the task itself.[22]

There are links between perceived ability at tasks like sports, music and academia and motivation to pursue them. As a general rule, we like using our abilities.

Improving our abilities can itself be motivating. Studies by Carol Dweck and others have shown that people who attribute their successes to hard work rather than innate talent are more likely to persevere. The more **self-belief** you have in your capacity to improve your skills and work towards the things you care about, the more motivated you will feel about taking on new challenges.[23]

Mental **challenge** can be motivating too though. If a task is too easy we are unlikely to give it our full attention, and we may even put it off in favour of more challenging tasks. New challenges tap into our desire for mastery, to improve our skills and become more competent. Rising to challenges and stretching our abilities make us feel good, and make future tasks feel more manageable too.[24]

There is a balancing act to be struck with challenge though. Too little challenge and we get bored; too much and we may get overwhelmed and disengage. This is often to protect ourselves from **potential stress**.

When we care deeply about a task, we are more likely to get stressed if it goes wrong. Stress occurs when things we are motivated to do feel beyond our control. If we can't make the task feel more manageable, then the easiest way to avoid stress is to stop caring about it and disengage.

The optimum level of challenge is when we feel that a task requires us to use the full extent of our abilities. The more we push ourselves, and the more motivated we become, the more vigilant we need to be of stress.[25]

We never quite know what we're capable of doing until we try of course: some of the greatest achievements come from people overestimating their chances of success. However, stress is not in itself a motivator: if you believe in what you're doing, and you have the promise of a reward if you succeed, and you also have the skills to do it, you can find the energy you need for the task without having to stress out about it.

GETTING MOTIVATED

If you don't feel motivated, the first step is to work out why. When one or more of the three factors in this motivation model goes missing, we struggle to take action.

If you are struggling to find the energy for an important task, or if someone you work with is feeling demoralised, this three factor model can be a useful tool for identifying the problem.

Sometimes the problem is a lack of inner drive. When we need to do something we don't enjoy or find fulfilling, we disengage. The result is low effort, **working to rule**, and is a common result of focussing too much on goals and not enough on enjoyment and fulfilment.

We may also experience the opposite problem, of having inner drive but no incentive. We can find a task fulfilling and enjoyable, and have the resources to do it – and yet still not make time for it. Without a clear sense of how we will benefit from taking action now, we may **procrastinate**, putting off things we really want to do in favour of more immediate concerns. No incentive, no priority.

Sometimes we find ourselves with an incentive to do something that we really enjoy or believe in, and yet if we feel it is beyond our ability, we may still **give up**. This is often a defence mechanism to protect ourselves from potential stress: if something important to us feels out of our control, we may stop caring to protect ourselves.

Each of these problems requires a different approach to solve it. Find the source of the problem, and then finding your motivation becomes much easier.

MOTIVATING YOURSELF
Here are a few things you can try to increase your motivation for a task, without resorting to willpower.[26]

---

* **Set yourself goals**
  Setting your own (realistic) incentives can keep you motivated, particularly for things you've been putting off. The process of goal-setting can help you reflect on how your actions relate to your values, whilst completing a goal can boost your autonomy and perceived abilities. Bargaining with yourself and setting your own rewards can also help you get routine or boring tasks done. Set realistic

goals too: lots of smaller goals can help you get to a big goal.

- **Find your passion**
  It is much easier to motivate yourself to do something you believe in. This doesn't have to be about great moral crusades: it is about connecting your work to something that matters to you, such as feeding your family, achieving an ambition or improving your surroundings. Increasing your sense of having chosen to do it also helps. Even minor choices can make you feel more attached to a task, so if you can't change the task, change how you'll do it and make it your own.

- **Increase your abilities**
  Practising an activity can make you feel more competent and motivate you to carry on doing it. Seeing improvements in your ability and rising to challenges also gives you an intrinsic sense of mastery and accomplishment, increasing your motivation. Confidence matters too: sometimes you have all the resources you need to succeed, but you don't believe you can.

The exact strategy you adopt will depend on which part of the motivation model is missing. As always, there isn't one single answer, but you do have a wide range of options.

MOTIVATING OTHERS

This model can also be helpful for line management and appraisals. When team members are feeling demotivated, discussing the three factors of motivation can help people understand where they are stuck, and find ways to get themselves motivated.

If your goal is to motivate your team or organisation, there are also a few ways you can apply these principles to inspire motivation in other people, including:

- Set **clear, achievable goals** and give people the autonomy and resources to accomplish them.
- Connect the work of your organisation to something you **care deeply about**, and share it.
- Build **positive, trusting relationships** between colleagues and between staff and management.
- Treat people according to their **abilities, interests and personality**, particularly in setting incentives.

Clarity of objectives is particularly important. If staff don't know what they have to do, individually and for the company as a whole, this can affect every factor in the model. You can pay people to turn up to work, but if they don't know what success looks like or why it matters, they will only bring their bodies to work. If you want their minds, you need to give them clarity.

It isn't always possible to give people tasks that fit with their talents and passions of course, and sometimes people need to get on with tasks that don't really inspire them. In these situations, explaining why the task matters, for the company or for colleagues, can help. If we know the rationale for a task, it can help us make time for it.

INTERNALISING GOALS

Our ability to find meaning in external incentives is called internalisation, and it is one of the best ways to boost your motivation when you lack inner drive for a task.[27]

Internalisation is the process by which we take on the values, attitudes or structures of our situation and integrate them into our world view. Psychologists describe three levels by which we take on goals from our environment:[28]

1 Introjection
The task matters to us because of external feedback or conditions ('I do this because it's what people expect')

2 Identification
The task matters because we can connect it to a larger goal we believe in ('I do this because it's important').

3 Integration
The task matters to us because doing it is part of our identity, how we see ourselves or aspire to be ('I do this because I am a caring person').

The more you can connect the goal to something you find fulfilling or meaningful, the easier you will find it. This is not about lip service, but a genuine process of exploring what matters to you about the task at hand.

If you want to increase your motivation for something that you need to do but don't really want to, there is one exercise in particular that seems to help. First, you need to identify a task that you feel unenthusiastic about doing (this should be the easy bit). It should be something you have a clear reason to do, and that you know is achievable, but does not feel interesting, fulfilling or meaningful to you at the moment.

Next, take a couple of minutes to write down how the task connects to your life, your beliefs and the things you care about. This could be anything from how the task will help you achieve your goals or benefit someone you love, to what you find ethical or meaningful about it, or even why you might enjoy it.

When a group of high school students was asked to do this simple exercise in an experiment, it did indeed increase their motivation. One group was asked to write about how science related to their lives, whilst another group simply summarised what they had learned in class. Those who had thought about the importance of science in their lives became more interested and motivated than the other group, and improved their grades more.[29]

Reflecting on how the task fits with your beliefs and goals can help to turn external incentives into internal drivers, and make an unfulfilling task feel easier to do. Assigning value to an activity can also boost your sense of autonomy and make you more invested in a goal.

This won't make you love everything on your to-do list though, but writing down why you are doing something can reduce the need for conscious willpower and make it feel that little bit easier. Connect your external goals to what you really believe in, and you will find it easier to stay motivated.

And if you still feel demotivated, ask yourself:

What if I just didn't do it?

If you really can't think of a reason, you've just saved yourself a lot of time.

REACHING FLOW

The goal of motivation is to reach a state of 'flow' – our optimum state of untroubled concentration in which action feels easy. Flow is our most engaged and productive state. It comes from feeling challenged but not overwhelmed. Successful people, and successful businesses, maximise the time they spend in a state of flow.[30]

Give yourself clear, achievable goals and reward yourself when you reach each one. Think consciously about your beliefs and values and connect your tasks to what matters to you. Learn what you're good at and build your abilities, particularly during quiet periods. All these things will help you to stay motivated, even with very challenging tasks.

As with most aspects of our minds, motivation isn't an exact science. What motivates us depends on our personal values, the things we enjoy, the causes we believe in, the talents we have. It can be hard for organisations to harness these drivers through one-size-fits-all solutions. Most incentive structures will only take you halfway to a motivated, engaged workforce.

In the knowledge economy, businesses need to connect to what their employees care about, and help them believe in the intrinsic value of the work of the organisation. Businesses that know what they are for, beyond the money, will have an edge in motivating their employees. To really motivate people, businesses need a purpose.

As Daisy Yuhas once put it in *Scientific American*:[31]

> # Motivation blossoms when you stay true to your beliefs and values.

HABIT 3
CONNECT YOUR WORK TO YOUR SKILLS AND VALUES TO MOTIVATE YOURSELF AND OTHERS

GET MOTIVATED
IN A NUTSHELL

THE TWITTER VERSION

Using willpower drains your mental energy so get motivated instead by combining external incentives, inner drive and the ability to succeed.

THE SUMMARY VERSION

Motivation is not the same as willpower. Some actions feel harder than others, and this is because of motivation. Motivation makes action easy. We can have all the intentions we like, but without motivation, work is a struggle.

Motivation comes from more than just external incentives. Money and threats can make people work to rule, which is no good for complex and creative work. To really get motivated, you also need inner drive and the ability to succeed. If you enjoy or believe in what you are doing, and you feel you have the ability to do it, you will feel more motivated.

When you aren't motivated, it's usually because one of these three factors is missing. If you lack ability, you may give up, so build your skills and resources to make tasks feel achievable. If you lack an incentive you may procrastinate, so set yourself goals and rewards to keep you going. If you lack inner drive, relate what you're doing to your life and values.

The goal of motivation is flow, when action feels easy. The more time you spend in this state, the more creative and productive you become, and the more successful you will be.

NOTES

1   **a significant influence on sales performance...** Barber L., Hayday S. & Bevan S. (1999). *From People to Profits: The HR Link in the Service-Profit Chain*, Report 355, Institute for Employment Studies.

2   **an increase in sales of 9 per cent each month...** See Barber et al (1999) above, and also Bates, K., Bates, H. & Johnston, R. (2003). 'Linking service to profit: the business case for service excellence'. *International Journal of Service Industry Management*, 14(2): 173–183.

3   **Willpower seems to be a finite resource...** Baumeister, R.F.; Bratslavsky, E.; Muraven, M.; Tice, D.M. (1998). 'Ego depletion: Is the active self a limited resource?' *Journal of Personality and Social Psychology* 74: 1252–1265.

4   **lack of physical energy such as low glucose levels...** Gailliot, M.T., Baumeister, R.F., DeWall, C.N., Maner, J.K., Plant, E.A., Tice, D.M.; Brewer, L.E. & Schmeichel, B.J. (2007). 'Self-control relies on glucose as a limited energy source: Willpower is more than a metaphor'. *Journal of Personality and Social Psychology* 92 (2): 325–336. However, some experiments have suggested the psychological reward of sugar matters more than the energy itself, so who knows. See for example Hagger, M.S. &, Chatzisarantis, N.L. (2013). 'The sweet taste of success: The presence of glucose in the oral cavity moderates the depletion of self-control resources'. *Personality and Social Psychology Bulletin*, 39: 28–42.

5   **We can practise it...** Muraven, M. & Baumeister, R.F. (2000). 'Self-regulation and depletion of limited resources: does self-control resemble a muscle?' *Psychological Bulletin*, 126(2): 247–259. Well, possibly anyway. As we'll see in Chapter 5, willpower is linked to the personality trait of conscientiousness, which may suggest some people naturally have more than others.

6   **Based on the motivation research...** What follows is a synthesis of two related models of motivation. Gagné, M. & Deci, E.L. (2005). 'Self-determination theory and work motivation'. *Journal of Organizational Behavior*, 26: 331–362. Kehr, H.M. (2004). 'Integrating implicit motives, explicit motives, and perceived abilities: The compensatory model of work motivation and volition'. *Academy of Management Review*, 29: 479–499.

7   **This is classic 'carrot and stick' management...** For one perspective on the use of threats and opportunities in workplace motivation see Steinmetz, L. (1983) *Nice Guys Finish Last: Management Myths and Reality.* Horizon Publications.

8   **For dull, repetitive or mechanical tasks...** Deci, L., Koestner, R. & Ryan, R.M. (2001). 'Extrinsic rewards and intrinsic motivation in education: Reconsidered once again'. *Review of Educational Research*, 71(1): 1–27. See also Pink, D.H. (2011). *Drive: The Surprising Truth About What Motivates Us.* Canongate Books.

9   **In classic experiments in the 1970s by Edward Deci...** Deci, E.L. (1972). 'The effects of contingent and noncontingent rewards on intrinsic motivation

and controls'. *Organizational Behavior and Human Performance*, 8: 217–229. The study has been repeated many times in different contexts and cultures.

10 **We also need to feel fairly compensated...** Fairness may be innate and instinctive, as argued from Brosnan, S.F. & de Waal, F.B.M. (2003). 'Monkeys reject unequal pay'. *Nature* 425: 297–299. Fairness is not an exact science though, since it is about perception rather than reality. For one detailed study in the workplace see Wu. X., Sturman, M.C. & Wang, C. (2013). 'The motivational effect of pay fairness: A longitudinal study in Chinese star-level hotels'. *Cornell Hospitality Quarterly*, 54(2): 185–198.

11 **We do have a strong motivation to avoid loss...** Kahneman, D. & Tversky, A. (1984). 'Choices, values, and frames'. *American Psychologist* 39(4): 341–350.

12 **a phenomenon known as 'ironic process theory'...** Wegner, D.M. (1994). 'Ironic processes of mental control'. *Psychological Review*, 101(1): 34–52.

13 **We also tend to underestimate threats...** This phenomenon is known as 'optimism bias' and is explored in more detail in Chapter 7.

14 **positive goals tend to be more motivating...** See for example Janis, I.L. & Feshbach, S. (1953). 'Effects of fear-arousing communications'. *The Journal of Abnormal and Social Psychology*, 48(1): 78–92.

15 **In a study of students...** Moller, A.C., Deci, E.L & Ryan, R.M. (2006). 'Choice and ego-depletion: The moderating role of autonomy'. *Personality and Social Psychology Bulletin*, 32(8): 1024–1036.

16 **Our need to belong...** Baumeister, R.F. & Leary, M.R. (1995). 'The need to belong: Desire for interpersonal attachments as a fundamental human motivation'. *Psychological Bulletin*, 117: 497–529.

17 **when they are accompanied by positive feedback...** Ryan, R.M., Mims, V. & Koestner, R. (1983). 'Relation of reward contingency and interpersonal context to intrinsic motivation: A review and test using cognitive evaluation theory'. *Journal of Personality and Social Psychology*, 45(4): 736–750.

18 **a small improvement in a person's relationship with their boss...** Helliwell, J.F. & Huang, H. (2008). 'Well-being and trust in the workplace'. NBER Working Paper No. 14589.

19 **the concept of 'relational autonomy'...** Christman, J. (2004). 'Relational autonomy, liberal individualism, and the social constitution of selves'. *Philosophical Studies*, 117: 143–164.

20 **'We have oversold carrot and stick motivators...'** Quoted by the author from his 2013 RSA talk, Pink, D.H. (2013). 'To sell is human'. *RSA Audio*. See also Pink, D.H. (2011) *Drive: The Surprising Truth About What Motivates Us*. Canongate Books Ltd.

21 **the resources we can bring to it...** This list is actually inspired by the work on stress of Stevan Hobfoll, such as in Hobfoll, S.E. (1989). 'Conservation of resources. A new attempt at conceptualizing stress'. *American Psychologist*, 44(3): 516. We propose that the 'perceived abilities' found in motivation

research are closely aligned to the concept of 'resources' in stress management, and that the two can be connected here for consistency and clarity. See Chapter 4 for how motivation and stress link up.

22 **self-efficacy, of doing something we are good at...** Bandura, A. (1977). 'Self-efficacy: Toward a unifying theory of behavioral change'. *Psychological Review*. 84(2): 191–215.

23 **people who attribute their successes to hard work...**Mueller, C.M & Dweck, C.S. (1998). 'Praise for intelligence can undermine children's motivation and performance'. *Journal of Personality and Social Psychology*, 75(1): 33–52. And for a good round-up of the research in this field, see Dweck, C.S. (2000). *Self-theories: Their Role in Motivation, Personality, and Development*. Psychology Press.

24 **New challenges tap into our desire for mastery...** Bandura, A. (1977). 'Self-efficacy: Toward a unifying theory of behavioral change'. *Psychological Review*, 84(2): 191–215.

25 **the more vigilant we need to be of stress...** See Chapter 4 for more on the effects of stress and how to manage it.

26 **Here are a few things you can try...** These tips are suggested in, or inferred from, the sources listed above.

27 **it is one of the best ways to boost your motivation...** Baard, P.P., Deci, E.L. & Ryan, R.M. (2004). 'Intrinsic need satisfaction: A motivational basis of performance and well-being in two work settings'. *Journal of Applied Social Psychology*, 34: 2045–2068.

28 **Psychologists describe three levels of internalisation...** Adapted from Ryan, R.M. & Deci, E.L. (2000). 'Self-determination theory and the facilitation of intrinsic motivation, social development, and well-being'. *American Psychologist*, 55: 68–78.

29 **One group was asked to write about how science related to their lives...** Hulleman, C.S. & Harackiewicz, J.M. (2009). 'Promoting interest and performance in high school science classes'. *Science*, 326(5958): 1410–1412.

30 **The goal of motivation is to reach a state of 'flow'...** Csikszentmihalyi, M. (1990). *Flow: The Psychology of Optimal Experience.* New York: Harper and Row. More recent models also suggest flow is not simply about feeling relaxed but occurs when challenges and skills are relatively in balance.

31 **'Motivation blossoms when you stay true to your beliefs and values.'** Yuhas, D. (2012). 'Three critical elements sustain motivation', *Scientific American*, 18 October 2012.

HANDLE PRESSURE

We all face pressure at some point in our lives. Whether personally or professionally, most of us know how it feels to have a lot to do and people depending on us.

A little pressure can be good for us, focussing our minds, motivating us to take action. However, pressure has a dark side. As far back as 1908, psychologists Yerkes and Dodson found that although increased urgency can boost our performance on simple, manual tasks, for more complex, intellectual activities, too much pressure actually reduces performance.[1]

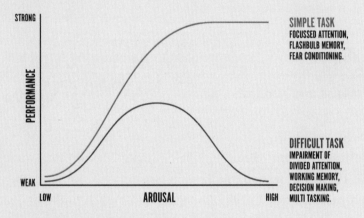

THE STRESS RESPONSE

This is because pressure we can't handle causes us stress, which makes us unwell and impedes our performance – the downward curve in the Yerkes-Dodson model.

The stress response is a natural part of how we all function, and not a disease or a weakness. It is our mind's emergency system, a primal response designed to keep us safe by enabling us to react swiftly to danger.

Imagine you are being attacked by a tiger. Your stress response is triggered, your heart beats faster, stimulants race around your system, and your mind focusses solely on the tiger. You are now equipped to 'fight' the tiger or 'fly' away – the 'fight or flight' response.

So far, so good. The problem arises when we transport this primal system into a modern environment. There aren't many actual tigers around these days. Instead we face metaphorical tigers, such as the prospect of letting others down, missing deadlines or failing in our work. These social threats can trigger the same, primal response.

Whilst it makes perfect sense that we can't sleep during a tiger attack, it's much less helpful when we're facing an angry boss or a presentation in the morning.[2]

THE IMPACT OF STRESS

Stress is a physical response, a form of temporary arousal stimulated by 'stress hormones' called glucocorticoids (cortisol being the most well-known). These hormones suppress immune functions and redirect resources normally used for basic maintenance.[3]

When we are stressed, our body redirects resources that it would normally use to keep us healthy, and channels them instead towards fighting the threat. In some situations this can be helpful. After all, who cares about catching a cold if they're being eaten by a tiger?

However, staying in this emergency state for a long time is hard on our bodies and this can cause long-term physical health issues, from coughs and colds to heart disease, musculoskeletal problems and organ damage.

Stress affects our minds too. It stops us thinking clearly and changes how we react to risks and opportunities. When we feel stressed, our attention narrows and we can become hyper-vigilant to threats. This is quite rational, because missing a threat is often worse than missing an opportunity. If a tiger and an ice cream van both appeared now, our attention would rightly be drawn to the tiger.

The trouble is that this increased vigilance distorts our perspective, causing us to be selective in our memories and affecting our perception of the world around us.[4]

Stress can also change how we see risks and rewards. Sometimes it can cause us to become more risk-averse, missing good things and focussing on potential threats. However, one particularly interesting study suggests that stress can also make us more pro-risk, causing us to forget about the potential negative consequences of our actions.[5]

When we get stressed, we remember the positive results of things we have done in the past. We find it harder to resist things that are bad for us when we are stressed, because at these moments only the pleasure associated with these activities comes to mind. We remember rewards (like feeling drunk) but forget punishments (like the hangover afterwards). The result is that we are more likely to do things that are potentially risky and bad for us.

These excessively risky behaviours are bad for business too. If you or your colleagues are stressed, you won't assess risks as accurately and may make errors of judgement, including on major decisions that affect the entire business. Risk management is about more than just good governance: it is also about stress management.

The effects seem to be different in men and women, at least on average. 'What we found is that under stress, males are more likely to make risky choices and...make their choices faster', says Mara Mather, the lead author of the study. 'Whereas females under stress become more conservative and actually make their choices slower'.

The study adds further evidence of the benefits of gender balance in teams, boards and committees. In situations where risk-taking pays off, men may do better, but when caution is needed women may be more likely to succeed, so the more diversity you have, the more chance you have of correcting for the biases that come from stress.

Stress affects each of us differently and it is difficult to tell exactly how our minds are being affected by stress. The important thing is to recognise that, when we feel stressed, we may not think clearly and this can affect our work. If you have important decisions to make and you feel stressed, it may be best to talk them through or delay them until you feel calmer, because things may look completely different once your mind calms down.

STRESS IS BAD FOR BUSINESS

You may hear people say that stress is good for you.

The argument goes that stress motivates us to work harder and reach our goals. In both ethical and psychological terms though, this is not true. Stress is a natural response and is useful in an emergency, but it is harmful to our health and performance.

Stress is when the pressure gets too much and you start to panic. It is extremely bad for us, particularly in the long term, and there are no beneficial effects of this stressed reaction on motivation or cognitive performance.

If people in your organisation are stressed, it is because they feel in danger. This is both ethically and commercially unwise: people who feel in danger do bad work. They forget things, take stupid risks and make costly – and sometimes disastrous – mistakes.

We wouldn't want to get rid of the stress response though, because we would lose our ability to respond in a crisis. However, a persistent state of crisis is very bad for our health, stops us working well, and needs to be managed.

Asking staff to be a little bit stressed is like asking them to be a little bit stupider and eat five burgers a day.

When people say a little bit of stress is good for us, what they really mean is pressure. Pressure is about the situation, stress is your reaction to it.

A little bit of external pressure can be motivating, but stress is a sign the pressure has got too much. We can respond to pressure, and feel motivated, without the need for stress.

WHAT MAKES US STRESSED?

Many situations can trigger this stress response, and understanding more about the causes of stress can be useful both in dealing with it and in preventing it before it occurs.

Researchers Lazarus and Folkman defined stress as:

'[a] relationship between the person and the environment that is...taxing or exceeding his or her resources and endangering his or her well-being'

Stress is a very personal response. What makes one person stressed may not affect someone else, and what we find stressful varies with our emotional state and life events. It's not just our minds making us stressed, nor the situations we face, but a combination of the two.[6]

That said, there are three particularly common factors that can make a situation feel more stressful:[7]

1 **Pursuit of a vital goal**
   Such as safety, social status or acquiring or protecting something that matters to you.
2 **Social evaluation**
   Failure would be seen negatively by others.
3 **Lack of control**
   Success seems difficult or beyond your power.

Having a goal you care about is very important. Situations are only stressful if they matter to us, so it is often when we are most motivated and enthusiastic about our work, or care most about our colleagues and clients, that we can find ourselves experiencing rising stress levels.

Our sense of control over the task at hand also matters. The more sense of control we feel over a task, the more manageable it feels. When the things that matter to us feel like they are slipping out of control, we can get stressed.

The extent to which we believe we can control the events in our lives is known as our 'locus of control'. Those of us with an external locus of control – the belief that our fate is controlled by external forces about which we can do little – are often more stressed and prone to clinical depression.[8]

This is about our perception of control though, rather than the reality. On an aeroplane, for example, we have very little practical control over our safety, and yet our experience of flying is one of complete control – from the button to call the steward, to the range of personalised in-flight entertainment, and even the safety card in the back of the seat, everything makes us feel like we are more in control than we actually are.

So feeling in control is usually good for us. Challenge can be motivating though: we like to stretch our abilities, so we have a tendency to push ourselves further to see what we can do.[9] If you like to work to the limit of your abilities, all it takes is one unexpected crisis and you can tip into stress.

Your moods and emotional state are important too. If you feel low or anxious that can make your mind more sensitive to potential threats. Worrying about stressful situations or ruminating on past failures can increase your chances of getting stressed, and staying stressed.[10]

The stress response is a natural survival mechanism though, so cutting it out of our everyday lives is tricky. If you didn't have a stress response, you wouldn't know how to react to a real emergency like a tiger. The question is what to do when you feel stressed, and there is no tiger.

SIGNS OF STRESS

If we can't just do away with stress, we must learn to identify it quickly and deal with it when it occurs.

The first step is to recognise when you are stressed, so that you can do something about it.

There are various signs that can tell you when you (or other people around you) are stressed.[11]

PHYSICAL		PSYCHOLOGICAL
Headaches		Short temper
Insomnia		Hyperactivity
Dry mouth		Risk taking
Exhaustion		Difficulty thinking
Pounding heart		Loss of perspective

Think about how you can tell you are stressed, and learn how to spot it quickly so that you can take action to manage it and avoid long-term stress.

Remember too that if you are experiencing one of these symptoms, you are probably experiencing others. So if you notice you are talking fast or struggling to sleep, you may want to check your decisions too because your judgement may be impaired without you even realising.

COPING WITH STRESS

Various activities can help with the physical symptoms of stress. **Exercise, sleep and leisure activities** can all reduce cortisol levels, and a **healthy diet** can keep your body going in its heightened state.[12] **Mindfulness** can also reduce stress.[13]

The problem is, when you are stressed, it is particularly hard to make time for actions that calm or nourish your mind. When we are stressed, we have less willpower, eat rubbish food, don't go to the gym and struggle to relax.

There's also another problem: stress is a feedback loop. As long as your mind believes it is still under threat it will keep pumping hormones around your body to ensure your survival – making you feel even more threatened.[14]

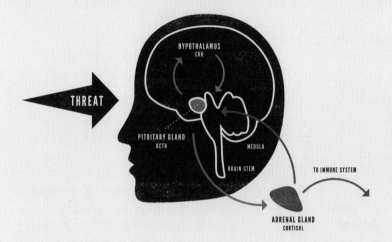

So whilst stress reduction techniques can help relieve symptoms during the 'emergency', unless you deal with the threat, the symptoms will keep coming back.

HANDLING PRESSURE

A more proactive approach is to look at how we respond to pressure. By changing our mindset about the situation, we can reduce stress in a more long-lasting way.

When we face a pressurised situation, our mind conducts a **'cognitive appraisal'** – a mental assessment of the situation that determines our response. We evaluate the situation, and also our resources to respond to it. It is this balancing act between pressures and resources that determines whether we see it as a potential challenge, or a potential threat.

Understanding this relationship between stress and resources is the key to handling pressure better, and cutting out stress from your life and work. In fact, stress researcher Stevan Hobfoll has even argued that *'resources...are the single unit necessary for understanding stress'.*[15]

PRESSURE AND RESOURCES

A more lasting way to reduce stress is therefore to **build and manage your resources** for handling pressure, and so turn your perception of threat into a sense of challenge.

Resources here mean more than just time and money – they mean anything we can use to accomplish a task. Stevan Hobfoll defined resources as *'those objects, personal characteristics, conditions, or energies that...serve as a means for attainment'.*[16] They can include:[17]

- **Knowledge, skills and abilities**
- **Self-belief and confidence**
- **Resourcefulness or adaptability**
- **Social status and supporting relationships**
- **Money and physical assets**

Mental resources are also important here too. You have more capacity to respond to challenges when your mind is healthy and rested, so maintaining your mental and physical wellbeing can help you handle pressure better.

The pressures we face may not always be under our control, but our resources can be – both in terms of our capacity to respond, and the help we can get from others.

Building and maintaining our resources then can enable us to take on more challenges in our lives safely. The more resources we have, the more likely we are to be able to handle the challenges life throws at us.

GETTING PERSPECTIVE

The trouble is that stress narrows our perspective. In a persistently stressful situation, we become less aware of our resources, blinding us to our own skills and the assets around us – and making us even more stressed.

Then, as our focus narrows, we focus more on the problem, and cling more desperately to the few resources we can still see – causing us to react defensively, and creating a vicious circle of rising stress and lost perspective.

Breaking this vicious circle of lost perspective and forgotten resources is fundamental to handling stressful situations in an effective and sustainable way.

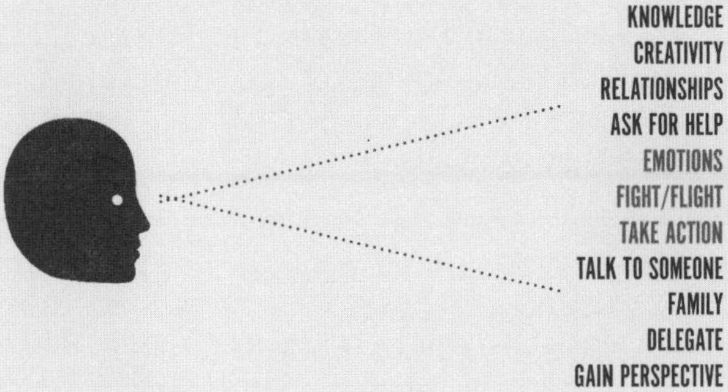

KNOWLEDGE
CREATIVITY
RELATIONSHIPS
ASK FOR HELP
EMOTIONS
FIGHT/FLIGHT
TAKE ACTION
TALK TO SOMEONE
FAMILY
DELEGATE
GAIN PERSPECTIVE

Reminding yourself what you are good at, and the people and assets you can call on to help you, can help you broaden out your perspective and start to find things more manageable.

One good way to do this is to take some time to **map out your own resources**. Make a list of your biggest strengths, the skills and assets you use to solve problems and get things done. Focus particularly on what you think you are really good at. It may seem challenging to think about yourself in such a positive way – we aren't used to talking ourselves up all the time – but it can help free your mind from the constraints of stressful 'fight or flight' thinking.

This exercise can be particularly challenging when you feel stressed, so you may want to do this with other people. Ask other people what they think are your key strengths to help you identify assets you might have missed. You can also ask them to tell you how they think you should tackle it, and what they could do to help. Managers, colleagues, friends and family can all remind you of your resources when you are under pressure. It's surprising how much easier it is to solve other people's problems than our own.

If you can identify a set of practical suggestions for how you can use your resources, you may find the pressures facing you more manageable and slowly coax your mind out of its stressed state.

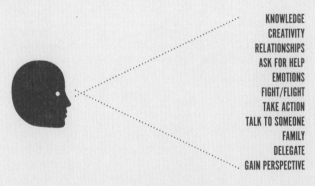

KNOWLEDGE
CREATIVITY
RELATIONSHIPS
ASK FOR HELP
EMOTIONS
FIGHT/FLIGHT
TAKE ACTION
TALK TO SOMEONE
FAMILY
DELEGATE
GAIN PERSPECTIVE

You won't eliminate stress in one simple exercise of course, but by continuing to remind yourself of the things you're good at, and of the people who might be able to help you, you can make broadening your perspective into a positive habit, and turn pressures into challenges.

RESILIENCE?

Resilience usually means the ability to handle the events facing us and find ways to 'bounce back' from setbacks. It is becoming an increasingly popular term as organisations seek to help staff cope better with increased pressures. So are some people more resilient to stress than others?

There may be some connection between personality traits and the impact of stress.[18] Whilst the stress response is natural, it may also trigger other negative emotions, which can pull us into longer-term problems. Feeling stress is a natural part of a healthy mind though, so selecting people who don't notice threats isn't a very sensible idea.

The other complication is that stress and motivation are linked: the more motivated we are, the more likely we are to feel stressed. If people care about their work, they are more like to become stressed. Our goal is not low stress, but high motivation combined with low stress.

Psychologist Kelly McGonigal argues that although stress is bad for our health, worrying about stress could be even worse. No one is arguing stress is good here, but mindset seems to matter. If we can see stress as a natural part of dealing with the adversity in our lives, we may find it easier to handle it, and even live longer. We may not be able to avoid stress, but at least we can try to avoid getting stressed about being stressed.[19]

Resilience should be approached with caution though. Asking people to be more 'resilient' can suggest that the problem is located in them rather than their environment, which may not be the case. It can imply individuals should feel a particular way, which can be intrusive and bad for their wellbeing. It can also be misinterpreted to mean we should feel less, which is not in itself a virtue.

RESOURCEFULNESS

When employers talk about 'resilience' they usually mean people's ability to handle pressure. Given how our minds actually respond to pressure though, perhaps a better term for this might be 'resourcefulness'.[20]

Resourcefulness is 'the ability to find quick and clever ways to overcome difficulties'.[21] It is a quality we can all aspire to have, and one from which businesses can clearly benefit. When businesses need to increase profits with fewer people and hit the same targets with less time and money, we need to be increasingly resourceful to survive.

The advantage of promoting resourcefulness is that it makes no judgement about how people should feel, but simply asks them to deploy their resources effectively to get things done. Rather than aspiring to be less sensitive or emotionally affected by setbacks, we can focus on how to protect and deploy our resources more effectively in dealing with pressure.

Learning how to use your resources to handle pressure is an essential part of staying mentally effective at work. If you feel stressed, remind yourself of your skills and abilities, and ask other people what you might have missed too. You can also use this approach to support other people, by reminding them of their strengths, spotting new approaches, and offering your resources.

However, teaching people new ways to cope is useful, but it is not a substitute for fixing the problems in a business, or for giving people proper support and realistic goals. Piling on the pressure and teaching people to cope is only a short-term solution. We can learn to be more resourceful and resilient, but we all have our breaking points.

BUILDING YOUR RESOURCES

Resources, then, are our tools for combatting stress and handling pressure successfully. If you want to reduce your stress levels, or take on more ambitious challenges, building your resources is essential.

Invest in your skills and your relationships: the more resources you have, the better you will do in your work. Just as businesses invest in their key assets, you can take the same approach yourself, building up a wide range of personal assets to handle future challenges.

Don't wait until you're under pressure to build your resources either. Barbara Fredrickson's 'broaden and build' theory suggests that building resources is much easier when we are in a positive state of mind. Building your resources is much easier during quieter times.[22]

So when things are good, take the opportunity to learn new skills and build new relationships, so that you can reduce stress and handle future pressures more easily.

Remember though that we have a natural motivation to test our skills and master new challenges. We may be tempted to keep on pushing our limits, leaving us still only one setback away from slipping back into stress.

Growing your resources, building supporting relationships and expanding your base of assets, both personally and professionally, can help you handle more pressure and take on more difficult projects and job roles. If you are really determined to cut stress from your life though, you may need to get comfortable saying no, and doing less. Working within your resources is the best way to keep calm, but it doesn't always make for an exciting life.

SUPPORTING PEOPLE

There is no one-size-fits-all solution for reducing stress. Stress is incredibly personal: what you find stressful is probably not what other people find stressful. For instance, many of us find public speaking terrifying, but others find it exciting and enjoyable. We hit our limits in different situations, because we each have different resources.

Managing stress is an ongoing process of balancing pressure against resources. The key to reducing stress then lies in listening to people about what they are worried about, and the resources they feel they need, and setting goals safely that are within their resources.[23]

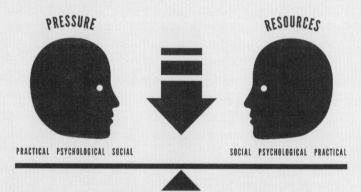

There are a number of practical things you can do to support people when they feel stressed.

First you need to **understand the situation** and why it feels so unmanageable for that person, because the source of stress will be different for each of us. Understanding this can help you both focus on the source of the problem.

The next is to **offer help** and share your resources. Very often something that feels impossible for a colleague may feel easy for you, so offer your own resources to help them, and connect them to other people with relevant skills too.

You can help people with the psychological impact of stress too. Quite often people have the solution but in their stressed state they can't see it, so if you **offer fresh perspectives**, you can often help them spot things they might have missed.

Sometimes **just being with someone** can reduce their stress too.[24] When we feel stressed we seek out other people to 'tend and befriend' and comfort us.[25] Good relationships with colleagues, managers, friends and family can all help reduce the physical and psychological effects of stress. Sometimes it isn't about what you say, it's about showing sympathy.

So the next time you are finding things stressful, don't cut yourself off: talk things through with other people, ask for their help and insights, and the situation may start to feel more manageable after all.

Other people still cause us stress of course. Social evaluation, lack of control, people letting us down – all these things stress us out at one time or another – but we would be much worse off without the people around us.

As a wise person nearly said:

> # Other people. The cause of, and solution to, all of life's problems.

HABIT 4
BUILD YOUR RESOURCES AND SUPPORTING RELATIONSHIPS TO TURN PRESSURES INTO CHALLENGES

HANDLE PRESSURE
IN A NUTSHELL

THE TWITTER VERSION

Pressure can be motivating but stress is not. Cut out the stress from your life by building your resources to turn pressure into challenge.

THE SUMMARY VERSION

A little bit of stress is not good for you. Pressure is motivating but stress is the sign the pressure has got too much and you start to panic. It affects your judgement and memory, makes you take stupid risks, and is bad for your long-term health.

Successful businesses motivate their staff without causing stress, by managing people's skills and resources to match the pressures they face. Whenever we face pressure, we ask ourselves whether we can find the resources to handle it. If we do, it feels like a challenge; if we don't, we get stressed.

You can reduce stress by building your resources: learning skills, acquiring essential assets to help you in your work, and building good supportive relationships. The more assets and people we can tap into, the more manageable things feel. Stress makes us forgetful though, so when you are stressed you also need to remind yourself of the resources you have.

Don't wait until you're already stressed to build your resources though: stress makes it harder to learn new things and develop good relationships. So plan ahead: build and broaden your mind to prepare yourself for future challenges.

NOTES

1 **However, pressure has a dark side...** Yerkes R.M. & Dodson J.D. (1908). 'The relation of strength of stimulus to rapidity of habit-formation'. *Journal of Comparative Neurology and Psychology*, 18: 459–482. However, see also this review of the various ways in which the original research has been reinterpreted over the years: Teigen, K.H. (1994). 'Yerkes-Dodson: A law for all seasons'. *Theory Psychology*, 4(4): 525–547.

2 **Imagine you are being attacked by a tiger...** I am very grateful to Dr David Matthews MB, BS, DRCOG, DOccMed, AFOM, FRCGP for first introducing me to this helpful, memorable and comical analogy for stress, and for helping me develop the narrative of stress in this chapter.

3 **this can cause long-term physical health issues...** For a review of some of the physical effects of stress, see McEwen, B.S (2008). 'Central effects of stress hormones in health and disease: Understanding the protective and damaging effects of stress and stress mediators'. *European Journal of Pharmacology*, 583(2–3): 174–185. See also the range of research on the health risks of stress by the Institute for Behavioral Medicine Research at Ohio State University: http://mindap.pl/1ppvpJl.

4 **causing us to be selective in our memories...** Lupien S.J., Maheu F., Tu M., Fiocco A. & Schramek, T. E. (2007). 'The effects of stress and stress hormones on human cognition: Implications for the field of brain and cognition'. *Brain and Cognition*, 65: 209–237.

5 **Stress can also change how we see risks and rewards...** Mather, M. & Lighthall, N.R. (2012). 'Both risk and reward are processed differently in decisions made under stress'. *Current Directions in Psychological Science*, 21(2): 36–41.

6 **Researchers Lazarus and Folkman defined stress as...** Lazarus, R.S. & Folkman, S. (1984). *Stress, Appraisal, and Coping*. Springer Publishing Co Inc. This book on cognitive evaluation and coping in stress remains a classic work on this subject.

7 **there are three common factors...** The situations that cause us stress are analysed in Dickerson, S.S. & Kemeny, M.E. (2004). 'Acute stressors and cortisol responses: A theoretical integration and synthesis of laboratory research'. *Psychological Bulletin*, 130: 355–391.

8 **Those of us with an external locus of control...** Benassi, V.A., Sweeney, P.D. & Dufour, C.L. (1988). 'Is there a relation between locus of control orientation and depression?' *Journal of Abnormal Psychology*, 97(3): 357–367.

9 **Challenge can be motivating though...** See Chapter 3 for the motivational effects of challenge and mastery.

10 **Your moods and emotional state are important too...** Stress is related to high energy and high tension states in the mood map described in Chapter 2. Some models of mood use 'arousal' rather than energy to link them to the heightened arousal experienced during periods of stress.

11 **There are various signs...** There are many signs of stress and the lists

can be extensive, such as the UK Health & Safety Executive's list here: http://mindap.pl/1IS9KVE The list we present here is drawn from the standard clinical lists, and particularly those that are most commonly identified by participants in Mindapples training sessions.

12 **Exercise, sleep and leisure activities...** The benefits of these and other activities for reducing cortisol are well known and documented in Chapter 1. Many wellbeing activities offer temporary relief from stress – if you can find the time.

13 **Mindfulness can also reduce stress...** See for example Khoury, B., Lecomte, T., Fortin, G., Masse, M., Therien, P., Bouchard, V., Chapleau M-A., Paquin, K. & Hofmann, S.G. (2013). 'Mindfulness-based therapy: A comprehensive meta-analysis'. *Clinical Psychology Review*, 33(6): 763–771.

14 **stress is a feedback loop...** For more on the recursive nature of stress, see Lazarus, R.S. & Folkman, S. (1984). *Stress, Appraisal, and Coping*. Springer Publishing Co; and Lovallo, W.R. & Thomas, T.L. (2000). 'Stress hormones in psychophysiological research: Emotional, behavioral, and cognitive implications'. In Cacioppo, J.T., Tassinary, L.G. & Berntson, G.G. (Eds.). *Handbook of Psychophysiology*. 2nd edn. Cambridge University Press, pp. 342–67.

15 **'resources...are the single unit necessary for understanding stress.'** Hobfoll, S.E. (1989). 'Conservation of resources. A new attempt at conceptualizing stress'. *American Psychologist*, 44(3): 516.

16 **Hobfoll defined resources as...** Hobfoll, S.E. (1989).'Conservation of Resources. A new attempt at conceptualizing stress'. *American Psychologist*, 44(3): 516. See also Hobfoll, S.E. (1988). *The Ecology of Stress*. Taylor & Francis.

17 **anything we can use to accomplish a task...** This list may look familiar from the previous chapter on motivation. Ability in motivation theory and the resource theory of stress management are not strictly synonymous but they are sufficiently similar to tentatively link them for our purposes here.

18 **There may be some connection between personality traits...** See Chapter 5 for more on how personality traits, particularly neuroticism, can make us more sensitive to stress and threats.

19 **Psychologist Kelly McGonigal argues that...**McGonigal, K. (2013). 'How to make stress your friend'. *TED Global*, June 2013: http://mindap.pl/1iGXIAl. The reference at the heart of the talk is Keller, A., Litzelman, K., Wisk, L.E., Maddox, T., Cheng, E.R., Creswell, P.D. & Witt, W.P. (2012). 'Does the perception that stress affects health matter? The association with health and mortality'. *Health Psychology*, 31(5): 677–84.

20 **a better term for this might be 'resourcefulness'...** Some psychologists do use 'resourcefulness' in place of 'resilience', but the topic has not yet perhaps received the attention it deserves. I am very grateful to Geoff McDonald at Unilever for introducing me to the concept.

21 **'the ability to find quick and clever ways to overcome difficulties'** Oxford British and World Dictionary, available online at http://mindap.pl/Y1qXqy.

22 **Don't wait until you're under pressure to build your resources...**
Fredrickson, B.L. (2001). 'The role of positive emotions in positive psychology: the broaden-and-build theory of positive emotions'. *American Psychologist*, 56: 218–226.

23 **balancing pressure against resources...** This helpful summary, and the diagram that follows, are drawn from the wellbeing work of Dodge, R., Daly, A., Huyton, J., & Sanders, L. (2012). 'The challenge of defining wellbeing'. *International Journal of Wellbeing*, 2(3): 222–235. Reproduced by permission of the authors.

24 **just being with people can be good for reducing stress...** Thoits, P.A. (1995). 'Stress, coping and social support processes: where are we now? What next?' *Journal of Health and Social Behaviour* (extra issue), 35: 53–79.

25 **we seek out other people to 'tend and befriend'...** Taylor, S.E. (2006). 'Tend and befriend. Biobehavioral bases of affiliation under stress'. *Current Directions in Psychological Science*, 15(6): 273–277.

CHAPTER 5
KNOW YOURSELF

How well do you know yourself? Most of us like to think that we are 'self-aware', that we know our strengths and could predict how we might react in different situations.

Indeed it is one of the defining characteristics of being human to be self-aware. We are one of only a handful of species that can reliably recognise themselves in a mirror.[1]

Self-awareness is very useful. It helps us identify our strengths, anticipate our reactions, understand the impact we have on other people, and assess our careers more accurately. In short, self-awareness enables us to be more in control of ourselves, and of our life and work.

Self-awareness can be uncomfortable though: it is often unpleasant to be aware of our bad qualities, especially if we can't easily change or manage them. The skill is to be able to examine yourself in a non-judgemental way and notice how you think, feel and act in a range of situations. And one of the best ways to do this is to study personality.

PERSONALITY PSYCHOLOGY

The study of personality is the study of our individual differences. Whereas most of psychology and neuroscience focusses on what is common to all of us, personality research studies what makes one person so different from another. Why do two very similar people react so differently in similar situations? Why does one person thrive whilst another struggles?

Since the early days of medicine, the study of humanity has been preoccupied by this question. In the fifth century BCE, Hippocrates, the founder of classical medicine, proposed that personality was the result of four 'humours' in our bodies. Excess blood or 'sanguine' made us passionate and impulsive; 'phlegm' made us content or lazy; bile or 'choler' made us ambitious or aggressive; and black bile – 'melancholer' – made us sad and introverted.[2]

The model is archaic of course – no psychiatrist would prescribe you a course of leeches to alter your mood these days – but the four humours still persist in our language today, when we describe sad people as 'melancholic' or cheerful people as 'sanguine'.

The emergence of personality psychology in the twentieth century inspired a search for the most robust, evidence-based model for measuring and predicting personality. Personality psychology examines the consistent lines in our thoughts, feelings and behaviour throughout our lives, to pin down what distinguishes us from the people around us.

Personality is one of the most popular ideas in business. Aside from being an interesting intellectual exercise, there are many benefits to achieving greater understanding of the personalities of yourself and your colleagues.

Personality studies are mainly used in business to predict and explain behaviour. Understanding someone's personality can help assign them suitable tasks and manage them effectively. Personality psychology can also help us select the right staff, develop talent and build successful teams.[3]

Understanding personality can help you:

- Maintain your health and **mental wellbeing**.
- Choose the **right career** and job role.
- **Collaborate** better with colleagues.
- Select, support and **manage staff** better.
- Build balanced and versatile **teams**.

With so much at stake, the study of personality has become a hot topic for psychologists, and an area of considerable debate over the past few decades.

Personality is big business.

TRAITS, NOT TYPES

One of the most popular theories of personality has been the Myers-Briggs Type Indicator (MBTI),[4] which has its roots in the work of the psychoanalyst Carl Jung.[5]

Many people find Myers-Briggs helpful for opening up conversations about the differences between people, but if you want a reliable and up-to-date model for predicting behaviour, it falls somewhat short.[6] People seem to retest differently on different occasions[7] and there are various problems with how it is measured.[8] The MBTI definitions have been questioned too, such as the distinction between 'thinkers' and 'feelers', which does not really fit with our modern understanding of the mind.[9] The descriptions can sound convincing, but they don't seem to be as consistent or meaningful as they might appear.[10]

The other problem with the MBTI is that it divides people into personality 'types'. Personality variations tend to follow a normal distribution curve, so most people score in the middle. By dividing subjects into types, the MBTI creates artificial divisions between people with very similar scores – so you can end up being classified as a completely different 'type' to someone very similar to you, because you happen to fall on either side of the line.[11]

In the past few decades, personality 'types' have given way to the study of 'traits'. Neuroscientist Colin DeYoung describes personality traits as *'relatively stable patterns of behaviour, motivation, emotion and cognition'.*[12]

Personality traits allow for much greater variation when measuring our personalities, and more complexity of combinations and variations between us. They also allow us to measure long-term trends and changes without having to reclassify someone as a different 'type' of person.

Traits are general and enduring trends in our behaviour, and are revealed by examining how we think, feel and act over a long period of time.

For example, if we frequently experience a 'state' of joy, this may indicate an underlying 'trait' of positivity.

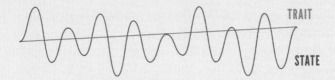

Of course, our individual identities are more than just these traits: we are a product of our cultural adaptations and life stories too. Nurture makes a difference as well as nature.[13] Personality traits don't tell you who you are, they just describe what comes naturally to you.

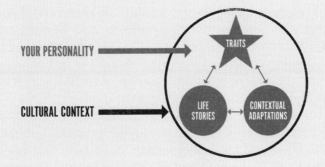

Personality traits can be very useful for revealing the underlying patterns in our behaviour though. They can show us our strengths and weaknesses, predict the situations we will find comfortable and uncomfortable, and help us make sense of why we are the way we are.

THE 'BIG FIVE' PERSONALITY TRAITS

The most extensively researched and widely used model of personality measurement is the so-called 'Big Five', also known as the 'five-factor model'.[14]

The Big Five brings together decades of personality research into one combined model in an attempt to identify the core, distinct and observable traits that define our basic personalities.[15]

There are still problems with the model. Psychologist Dan P. McAdams called the Big Five the *'psychology of the stranger'*, because it deals only with observable characteristics rather than deeper values.[16] The traits also may not be as unconnected as was once thought.[17]

Yet the Big Five remains, for now, our most reliable model for analysing and predicting behaviour, and it seems to fit reasonably well with the findings of modern neuroscience. If you want to work with a model that is backed by experimental evidence rather than anecdote and observation, the Big Five is the best system we have.[18]

Personality is usually measured through questionnaires. These rely on people answering honestly, and there are other methods such as inkblot tests and biometric measures of brain chemistry, but personality is a subjective business and questionnaires remain the best way to assess how someone thinks and feels in particular situations.

Tests for the Big Five are harder to find than some of the more traditional business psychology tests. You can do the proprietary five-factor model version, or you can find free basic versions of the Big Five test online.[19] The tests work best when you know least about the model being used, so you may want to consider taking a test yourself now, before you learn more.

Here are the 'Big Five' personality traits.[20]

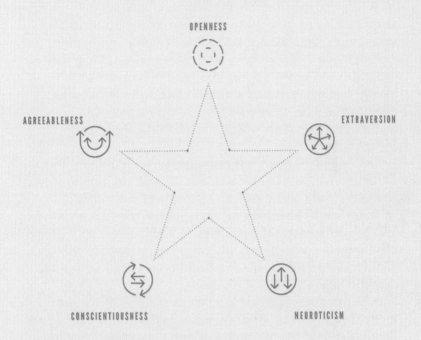

None of the traits are considered 'good' or 'bad': they just reveal the particular tasks and situations for which you are most suited. Your score in each of these traits shows your preferences for certain types of response. If you score low in any trait, that doesn't mean you lack personality: it means you display the opposite characteristics instead.[21]

Let's go through each of the five traits in turn. As we go through them, think about how strongly you think you display each one, and then afterwards you can see how your test results compare to your view of yourself.

OPENNESS

Openness is our capacity to find pleasure in new ideas and experiences, and willingness to listen to new information.

People high in openness tend to be curious, imaginative, insightful and often artistic, and tend to have broad intellectual interests and **unusual thought processes**. They can also be more aware of their own feelings and might have a tendency towards introspection and self-analysis.

People high in openness assimilate new ideas easily and are often changing their views, but can get lost in theory and abstraction and find it difficult to stick with one thing.

Those low in openness may tend to be more conservative and **prefer practical activities** to abstract concepts. They can be more conventional and are often resistant to change, and usually prefer the plain, straightforward and well-tested over the new, complex and subtle.

High openness is linked to intellect and the ability and motivation to learn,[22] and open people do well in training and discussions and tend to keep learning throughout their lives. They can also be good at spotting and harnessing complex patterns of information and experiences, making them very **creative and analytical**.[23]

Low openness can be a **steadying factor** and is useful for consistency, social bonding and conserving assets. High openness is associated with intelligence and creativity though, and is generally considered an asset at work.

CONSCIENTIOUSNESS

Conscientiousness is our desire to get things right.

In the Big Five, this implies an aspiration to do high quality work, but also self-discipline, forward planning, ability to focus and a **sense of duty**. Conscientiousness is strongly associated with being organised and systematic, and also with being ethically-motivated, principled and goal-orientated. Very high conscientiousness can become workaholic, perfectionist and compulsive.

Our level of conscientiousness reflects how well we can control and direct our natural impulses. Those of us low in conscientiousness can be disorganised and unreliable, but can also be **more spontaneous and better at handling uncertainty**. Conscientiousness should not be confused with a desire to please others (agreeableness), or sensitivity to failure (neuroticism), although they may be related since the serotonin system seems to be involved in all three traits. Conscientiousness combined with neuroticism can sometimes result in perfectionism.[24]

Conscientiousness seems to be the most reliable trait in the Big Five for predicting **success at work**.[25] Conscientious employees tend to be more reliable and hard-working, although they can also struggle in times of change and find it harder being unemployed.

Very low conscientiousness, conversely, is linked to a lack of self-control, antisocial behaviour, low academic attainment, and even reduced life expectancy.[26]

EXTRAVERSION

Extraversion is not just about being sociable: it is about our sensitivity to external rewards and gratification.

Extraversion is associated with the dopamine system and involves **seeking pleasure outside ourselves**, including in social situations. Extraverts can be energetic, enthusiastic, assertive, outgoing and talkative, but in extreme forms can be domineering and have difficulty being on their own.

Its opposite, **introversion**, is not the same as shyness; it describes enjoyment of solitary activities rather than fear of social situations.[27] Some commentators also argue that extraversion and introversion are not opposites but can co-exist together, and use the term 'ambivert' for this.[28]

Extraverts tend to be happier and can experience **strong positive feelings**, although it is not clear if that's due to a greater enjoyment of positive emotions and experiences, or because they find it easier to engage in today's society.[29] People high in extraversion and neuroticism may also find themselves on an 'emotional rollercoaster'.

The outgoing aspects of extraversion mean it is traditionally considered an asset in many management and sales roles, whilst introversion is more often associated with academic and skill-specific professions, since introverts enjoy working alone. However, extraverts may not be as good in teams as is often believed,[30] and Susan Cain has made an impassioned and convincing case for the **value of introversion** in her influential book, *Quiet*.[31]

AGREEABLENESS

Agreeableness is our desire to support others and find harmony in relationships.

High agreeableness is linked with being appreciative, forgiving, generous and sympathetic. Highly agreeable people tend towards altruism and **good relationships**. They are trusting and considerate, show compassionate concern for others, but can also be less critical of ideas.

Agreeable people tend to be **less assertive** than their peers, and so they may also score lower for extraversion. Some studies suggest this may be due to the influence of testosterone, which promotes assertiveness but can reduce some aspects of agreeableness. It's not clear why women often score higher in agreeableness than men though.[32]

Less agreeable people can be single-minded about their goals and **uncompromising in their work**, but they can also be suspicious, unfriendly and uncooperative. If they are also high in conscientiousness they may pursue high standards or principles even at the risk of upsetting others. They can also be more likely to give honest criticism of bad ideas, which can be an asset in decision-making and creativity, but probably won't make good peacemakers.

Agreeableness can be an **asset in teams** and can make you more likely to get a job and keep it, but also less likely to be promoted to leadership roles than your more assertive peers.[33] It seems the value agreeable people bring to their teams is often overlooked by their managers.

NEUROTICISM

Neuroticism is sensitivity to threats and negative emotions.

High neuroticism makes us **more cautious**, sensitive to criticism and punishment, and fearful of disappointing others. High neuroticism is also linked to mood swings, anxiety and depression, and neurotic people may need to manage their moods more to stay comfortable.[34]

Low neuroticism is linked with emotional stability, higher serotonin levels and **resilience to negative experiences**. That's not the same as feeling happy more often though – that's linked to extraversion – but about having lower sensitivity and feeling bad less often.

Neuroticism is unusual in the Big Five for being a trait that few people want to have. Indeed many psychologists have looked for alternative labels for this trait, as the word implies 'brain disorder' and is often seen as stigmatising.[35]

Yet neuroticism may serve some important purposes, particularly in teams. People high in neuroticism tend to be more cautious and are likely to steer away from dangerous risks, which can balance out an aggressive or risk-taking team dynamic. They may also empathise more with people who are having a tough time emotionally.[36]

Neuroticism has also been linked to **increased drive and productivity** due to this sensitivity to failure, and a strong desire not to let down colleagues can be an asset in teams.

PERSONALITY NEUROSCIENCE

Research into the neuroscience of personality is beginning to link personality traits to neurobiology.[37]

According to an emerging theoretical framework, two neurochemicals in particular appear to be important:

- **Dopamine** is the neurotransmitter linked to rewards and pleasure. Sensitivity to dopamine seems to be linked to **'plasticity'**, your capacity for exploration and seeking out new things. The dopamine system may be connected to openness and extraversion.
- **Serotonin** is the neurotransmitter linked to happiness and mood regulation. This seems to be connected to **'stability'**: your ability to regulate your thoughts, feelings and behaviour. Serotonin may be connected to conscientiousness, agreeableness and neuroticism.

It is early days in the study of personality neuroscience and there is little consensus on whether these chemicals cause our personalities, or simply facilitate them, but we are beginning to uncover the biological basis for who we are. It could be that our personalities are as dependent on chemistry as classical philosophers once believed.

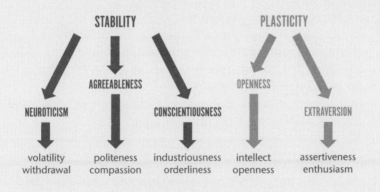

CAN YOU CHANGE YOUR PERSONALITY?

Genetics affects personality. One review concluded that all the five traits are broadly inherited, as follows:[38]

- **Openness**   57%
- **Conscientiousness** 49%
- **Extraversion**   54%
- **Agreeableness**   42%
- **Neuroticism**   48%

Yet personality traits do change naturally through our lives, and they can be changed by significant life events.[39] We may find it hard to imagine how different we will be in the future, but we actually change more than we think.[40]

- **To increase openness**
  Do crosswords and pattern-recognition puzzles, study logic and reasoning, and make time for music and art.[41]
- **To increase conscientiousness**
  Seek a fulfilling career and invest time in relationships.[42]
- **To increase extraversion**
  Spend enjoyable times with other people, try new things, and seek out work you find rewarding.[43]
- **To increase agreeableness**
  Try emotional intelligence training or loving-kindness meditation, and spend time with people you like.[44]
  (Alternatively, to decrease it, try assertiveness training.)
- **To decrease neuroticism**
  Manage your moods proactively and seek a fulfilling career and satisfying long-term relationships.[45]

Conscientiousness and **agreeableness** also tend to increase with age, whilst **extraversion** and **neuroticism** decrease.[46]

WORKING WITH PERSONALITY

Whatever your personality traits are, don't worry. None of the traits are good or bad in themselves: they just reveal your basic tendencies and the situations where you are likely to feel most comfortable.

Personality is not a constraint that prevents you from acting in a certain way, but a predictive framework that describes the common patterns in your behaviour, and the thoughts and activities that come most naturally to you.

Knowing your personality can help you choose the right job, develop your skills, maintain your wellbeing and improve your relationships. It can also help you avoid roles and situations you know you will find difficult.[47]

There are situations in which behaving against our personalities can be beneficial of course, whether we are trying to be more conscientious in our work or taking on new challenges. It is always possible to act contrary to your personality. Introverted people can still be excellent public speakers, and agreeable people still get cross if you push them too far. If there are aspects of your personality that do not serve you in a situation, you can override them.

If you can though, try to work with your personality, to maximise your strengths and minimise your weaknesses. Going against our personalities takes energy. If we are continually forced to act against our natural inclinations, the result can be cognitive fatigue – using up mental resources which could be better spent on the task itself.[48]

Act outside your personality whenever you need to, but bear in mind that the more time you and your colleagues spend in situations which suit your natural personality traits, the more energy you will have for your work.

A STRENGTH-BASED CULTURE

Personality psychology reveals that what worked for one person doesn't necessarily work for the next. The more we know about the personalities of the people who work for us, with us and above us, the more we can tailor our approach to work well with each of them.

Here are a few things to bear in mind:

- **Setting rewards**
  Extraverts are likely to be strongly motivated by praise and external rewards, but this may work less well on introverted or highly conscientious people, who may be more motivated by taking pride in their work. People high in agreeableness and neuroticism may be more motivated by a desire not to let people down.
- **Delivering criticism**
  People high in neuroticism are more sensitive to criticism and punishment and require gentler approaches, whilst extraverted people pay less attention to negative feedback. Agreeable people will tend to agree with you even if your criticisms are unfair.
- **Managing change**
  People high in neuroticism or conscientiousness may find change difficult and need support and certainty. Their more gung-ho counterparts will tend to handle change better, but may not be so good at planning for it.

Whether you are dealing with a manager, a client or a colleague, considering their personality traits can help you relate to them better. One-size-fits-all solutions won't work for managing and motivating people, because the same factors affect people in completely different ways.

Try to tailor your approach to match the individual. Fairness doesn't mean giving everyone the same thing.

RECRUITING BASED ON PERSONALITY

Many employers use personality tests to select people for job roles. There is considerable merit in doing this: a robust model like the Big Five can predict all kinds of things about a potential recruit, including their likely attention to detail, how they may respond to uncertainty, and how they prefer to be managed.[49]

There are some risks to bear in mind though. Personality tests aren't an exact science, and even in many of the best tests answers can still vary according to people's mood and the context. Candidates can also answer tests dishonestly, giving answers that sound like what an employer might want to hear.

The other problem lies in deciding what personality traits are desirable in the first place. There are many clichés in our culture about the type of person who would make a great leader, a great researcher and so on. If you are going to select for personality traits, think carefully about the assumptions you've made about what it takes to do the job. Introverts often make great leaders, and disagreeable people can be good for teams. People can surprise you.

We also tend to like people with similar temperaments to our own. If you are selecting for specific personality traits then be particularly careful not to fill your business with minds similar to yours or you may end up in a state of 'groupthink', stuck in narrow thinking and unable to relate to those who don't fit the group profile.[50]

If you want to understand your clients and staff, and generate a wide range of ideas, it is important to keep seeking out people who complement the natural traits of your team rather than simply reinforcing them.

NEURODIVERSITY

Neurodiversity is a relatively new term that is used to highlight the value of particular mental and neurological features. Some progressive businesses are now using the term to connect mental health and wellbeing to their policies on diversity and equality.

Although it has specific origins in the clinical realm, the term 'neurodiversity' might usefully be expanded to describe all the diverse personality traits and cognitive styles needed to get a genuine balance of minds in an organisation.[51]

We know that diversity of skills, experience, cultural background, age, gender and ethnicity can enhance the performance of a business,[52] so perhaps it's time we considered the neurodiversity of our businesses too.

For example, technical teams and professional firms may be heavy on introverts, and extraverted people may find it hard to fit in. Sales teams might be dominated by extraverted people who are good at dealing with uncertainty, and may struggle to make room for the quiet, conscientious people who can keep them organised.

Developing a wide diversity of personality traits in your business can help you plug gaps in your competencies, relate to a more diverse client base, and become a more attractive employer to talented people.

Journalist Harvey Blume has argued that neurodiversity might be as important to the human race as biodiversity. After all:[53]

> **Who can say what form of wiring will prove best at any given moment?**

HABIT 5
WORK WITHIN YOUR NATURAL PERSONALITY TO STAY COMFORTABLE AND CONSERVE YOUR MENTAL ENERGY

KNOW YOURSELF
IN A NUTSHELL

THE TWITTER VERSION

Learning about the Big Five personality traits can help you identify your strengths and focus your energy on what comes naturally to you.

THE SUMMARY VERSION

There are many models of personality but the most robust and widely used by psychologists is the Big Five, which can be used to identify the long-term trends in people's behaviour. Learning about personality can help you work better with other people, and identify your strengths and weaknesses.

Openness and extraversion are about being stimulated by the world around us. People high in openness are curious about new ideas, whilst extraverts seek out external rewards and gratification from other people.

Conscientiousness, agreeableness and neuroticism all relate to inner satisfaction. Conscientious people are motivated by doing things right, ethically and professionally. Agreeable people promote harmony in all their relationships. People high in neuroticism are more affected by negative emotions.

There is no correct personality to have though: all the traits have positive elements. However, acting outside your natural personality traits is tiring, so the most important thing is to identify where you feel most comfortable and focus your energies on your strengths to be successful in your work.

NOTES

1 **that can reliably recognise themselves in a mirror...** Gallup, G.G. Jr (1970). 'Chimpanzees: Self-recognition'. *Science*, 167(3914): 86–87. The validity of this test for assessing self-awareness is disputed, but it's still interesting. See also Povinelli, D.J. (1987). 'Monkeys, apes, mirrors and minds: The evolution of self-awareness in primates'. *Human Evolution*, 2(6): 493–507.

2 **four 'humours' in our bodies...** Hippocrates (c. 460–370 BCE). *Hippocratic Corpus: On The Sacred Disease*. The image dates from a book illustration in *Quinta Essentia* by Leonhart Thurneisser zum Thurn (1574), and shows the four humours in relation to the four elements and zodiacal signs (with thanks to Wikimedia Commons).

3 **mainly used in business to predict and explain behaviour...** Barrick, M.R. & Mount, M.K. (2005). 'Yes, personality matters: Moving on to more important matters'. *Human Performance*, 18(4): 359–372.

4 **the Myers-Briggs Type Indicator (MBTI)...** Myers-Briggs Type Indicator, Myers-Briggs, and MBTI® are trademarks of the MBTI Trust, Inc.

5 **has its roots in the work of the psychoanalyst Carl Jung...** In his 1921 book *Psychological Types*, Jung proposed that we make sense of the world through sensation, intuition, thinking and feeling, but this was not a full theory of personality and Myers-Briggs expands significantly on his ideas.

6 **it falls somewhat short...** Michael, J. (2003). 'Using the Myers-Briggs Type Indicator as a tool for leadership development? Apply with caution'. *Journal of Leadership and Organizational Studies*, 10: 68–81.

7 **People seem to retest differently...** Howes, R.J. & Carskadon, T.G. (1979). 'Test-retest reliabilities of the Myers-Briggs Type Indicator as a function of mood changes'. *Research in Psychological Type*, 2(1): 67–72.

8 **there are various problems...** Pittenger, D.J. (1993). 'Measuring the MBTI... and coming up short'. *Journal of Career Planning and Employment*, 54(1): 48–52.

9 **does not really fit with our modern understanding of the mind...** For more on the relationship between 'thinking' and 'feeling' in our minds, see Chapter 7. See also McCrae R.R. & Costa P.T. Jr. (1989). 'Reinterpreting the Myers-Briggs Type Indicator from the perspective of the five-factor model of personality'. *Journal of Personality*, 57(1): 17–40.

10 **The descriptions may sound convincing...** For an excellent example of why we need to look beyond subjective perceptions and take a more rigorous view of personality, see Forer, B.R. (1949). 'The fallacy of personal validation: A classroom demonstration of gullibility'. *Journal of Abnormal and Social Psychology*, 44(1): 118–123.

11 **the MBTI creates artificial divisions between people...** Stricker, L.J. & Ross, J. (1962). 'An assessment of some structural properties of the Jungian personality typology'. ETS Research Bulletin Series, (2): i–46.

12 **Neuroscientist Colin DeYoung describes personality traits as...** DeYoung, C.G. (2010). 'Personality neuroscience and the biology of traits'. *Social and Personality Psychology Compass*, 4(12): 1165–1180.

13 **our individual identities are more than just these traits...** This framework for understanding traits, adaptations, life narratives and culture is described in McAdams, D.P. & Pals, J.L. (2006). 'A new Big Five: Fundamental principles for an integrative science of personality'. *American Psychologist*, 61: 204–217.

14 **The most extensively researched and widely used...** The history of the five-factor model is summarised in McCrae, R.R., & John, O.P. (1992). 'An introduction to the five-factor model and its applications'. *Journal of Personality*, 60: 175–215.

15 **that define our basic personalities...** McCrae, R.R. & Costa, P.T (1997). 'Personality trait structure as a human universal'. *American Psychologist*, 52(5): 509–16.

16 **'psychology of the stranger'** McAdams, D. (1992). The five-factor model in personality: A critical appraisal'. *Journal of Personality*, 60(2): 329–361.

17 **The traits also may not be as unconnected...** Nevid, J. (2014). *Essentials of Psychology: Concepts and Applications*. Wadsworth, p.396.

18 **the Big Five is the best system we have...** For one endorsement of the Big Five, see Michael, J. (2003). 'Using the Myers-Briggs Type Indicator as a tool for leadership development? Apply with caution'. *Journal of Leadership and Organizational Studies*, 10: 168–81.

19 **you can find free basic versions...** See for example this free test from the BBC: http://mindap.pl/bbcbigfive.

20 **Here are the 'Big Five' personality traits...** What follows is drawn from the broad literature around the Big Five, and particularly the following sources. McCrae, R.R. & John, O.P. (1992). 'An introduction to the five-factor model and its applications'. *Journal of Personality*, 60: 175–215. McAdams, D.P. & Pals, J.L. (2006). 'A new Big Five: Fundamental principles for an integrative science of personality'. *American Psychologist*, 61: 204–17. Barrick, M.R. & Mount, M.K. (2005). 'Yes, personality matters: Moving on to more important matters'. *Human Performance*, 18(4): 359–72. DeYoung, C.G. (2010). 'Personality neuroscience and the biology of traits'. *Social and Personality Psychology Compass*, 4(12): 1165–80. Nettle, D. (2007). *Personality: What Makes You the Way You Are*. Oxford University Press.

21 **it means you display the opposite characteristics...** Much consideration has been given to labels of the traits and their opposites and no consensus has been reached. Some traits have established opposite terms, such as introversion and extraversion, whilst others do not have terms to describe their opposites. This can suggest that scoring highly in each trait is better, but this is not always the case.

22 **the ability and motivation to learn...** DeYoung, C.G., Peterson, J.B. & Higgins, D.M. (2005). 'Sources of openness/intellect: Cognitive and

neuropsychological correlates of the fifth factor of personality'. *Journal of Personality*, 73: 825–858.

23 **good at spotting and harnessing complex patterns...** DeYoung, C.G. (2010). 'Personality neuroscience and the biology of traits'. *Social and Personality Psychology Compass*, 4(12): 1165–1180.

24 **can sometimes result in perfectionism...** Hill, R.W., Huelsman, T.J., Furr, R.M., Kibler, J., Vicente, B.B. & Kennedy, C. (2004). 'A new measure of perfectionism: The perfectionism inventory'. *Journal of Personality Assessment*, 82(1): 80–91.

25 **for predicting success at work...** See Barrick, M.R. & Mount, M.K. (2005). 'Yes, personality matters: Moving on to more important matters'. *Human Performance*, 18(4): 359–372.

26 **low academic attainment...** See for example Conard, M. (2006). 'Aptitude is not enough: How personality and behavior predict academic performance'. *Journal of Research in Personality*, 40(3): 339–346.

27 **Introversion is not the same as shyness...** Briggs, S.R. (1988). 'Shyness: Introversion or neuroticism?' *Journal of Research in Personality*, 22(3): 290–307.

28 **extraversion and introversion are not opposites...** Grant, A.M. (2013). 'Rethinking the extraverted sales ideal: The ambivert advantage'. *Psychological Science*, 24(6): 1024–1030.

29 **Extraverts tend to be happier...** Stafford, L., Ng, W., Moore, R. & Bard, K. (2010). 'Bolder, happier, smarter: the role of extraversion in positive mood and cognition'. *Personality and Individual Differences*, 48(7): 827–832. See also Srivastava, S., Angelo, K.M. & Vallereux, S.R. (2008). 'Extraversion and positive affect: A day reconstruction study of person-environment transactions'. *Journal of Research in Personality*, 42: 1613–1618. And Lucas, R.E. & Diener, E. (2001). 'Understanding extraverts' enjoyment of social situations: The importance of pleasantness'. *Journal of Personality and Social Psychology*, 81: 343–356.

30 **Extraverts may not be as good in teams...** Bendersky, C. & Shah, N.P. (2013). 'The downfall of extraverts and rise of neurotics: the dynamic process of status allocation in task groups'. *Academy of Management Journal*, 56(2): 387–406.

31 **the value of introversion...** Cain, S. (2013). *Quiet*. Penguin.

32 **the influence of testosterone...** On average, women do tend to score higher for agreeableness than men, but there is some dispute as to whether this is the result of biological differences or our cultural attitudes. See for example Costa, P.T., Terracciano, A. & McCrae, R.R. (2001). 'Gender differences in personality traits across cultures: Robust and surprising findings'. *Journal of Personality and Social Psychology*, 81: 322–331.

33 **more likely to get a job and keep it...** Grewal, D. (2012). 'When nice guys finish first'. *Scientific American Mind*, 23: 62–65.

34 **neurotic people may need to manage their moods...** For more on how to do this, see Chapter 2.

35 **the word implies 'brain disorder' and is often seen as stigmatising...** There have been many attempts to rename neuroticism but few have stuck; 'emotional stability' is perhaps the closest so far, but this doesn't quite fit as neuroticism only relates to negative emotions, not positive ones. The closest related term in popular language is perhaps 'resilience', but resilience is often regarded in psychology as a set of techniques rather than as a trait of personality, so this label brings further problems.

36 **neuroticism may serve some important purposes...** Bendersky, C. & Shah, N.P. (2013). 'The downfall of extraverts and rise of neurotics: the dynamic process of status allocation in task groups'. *Academy of Management Journal*, 56(2): 387–406. There is also an interesting discussion of neuroticism in Nettle, D. (2007). *Personality: What Makes You the Way You Are.* Oxford University Press.

37 **beginning to link personality traits to neurobiology...** For more on the biological basis of personality see DeYoung, C.G. (2010). 'Personality neuroscience and the biology of traits'. *Social and Personality Psychology Compass*, 4(12): 1165–1180.

38 **the five traits are broadly inherited...** Bouchard, T.J. Jr & McGue, M. (2003). 'Genetic and environmental influences on human psychological differences'. *Journal of Neurobiology*, 54(1): 4–45.

39 **While personality traits do show consistency over time, they also change...** For the contrasting views of this, see Terracciano, A., Costa, P.T. Jr & McCrae, R.R. (2006). 'Personality plasticity after age 30'. *Personality Society Psychology Bulletin*, 32(8): 999–1009. See also Srivastava, S., John, O.P., Gosling, S.D. & Potter, J. (2003). 'Development of personality in early and middle adulthood: Set like plaster or persistent change?' *Journal of Personality and Social Psychology*, 84(5): 1041–1053. See also Boyce, C.J., Wood, A.M. & Powdthavee, N. (2013). 'Is personality fixed? Personality changes as much as "variable" economic factors and more strongly predicts changes to life satisfaction'. *Social Indicators Research*, 111: 287–305.

40 **we may find it hard to imagine how different we will be...** Although we are aware that we change a lot over the course of our lives, we seem to find it surprisingly hard to imagine that we might one day be different. See Quoidbach, J., Gilbert, D.T. & Wilson, T.D. (2013). 'The end of history illusion'. *Science*, 339: 96–98.

41 **To increase openness...** Jackson, J.J., Hill, P.L., Payne, B.R., Roberts, B.W. & Stine-Morrow, E.A.L. (2012). 'Can an old dog learn (and want to experience) new tricks? Cognitive training increases openness to experience in older adults'. *Psychology and Aging*, 27(2): 286–292.

42 **To increase conscientiousness...** Scollon, C.N. & Diener, E. (2006). 'Love, work, and changes in extraversion and neuroticism over time'. *Journal of Personality and Social Psychology*, 91: 1152–1165.

43 **To increase extraversion...** Scollon, C.N. & Diener, E. (2006). 'Love, work, and changes in extraversion and neuroticism over time'. *Journal of Personality*

and Social Psychology, 91: 1152–1165. See also Fleeson, W., Malanos, A.B. & Achille, N.M. (2002). 'An intraindividual process approach to the relationship between extraversion and positive affect: Is acting extraverted as "good" as being extraverted?' *Journal of Personality and Social Psychology*, 83(6): 1409–1422.

44 **To increase agreeableness...** Lutz A., Brefczynski-Lewis J., Johnstone, T. & Davidson, R.J. (2008). 'Regulation of the neural circuitry of emotion by compassion meditation: Effects of the meditative expertise'. *Public Library of ONE*, 3: 1–5.

45 **To decrease neuroticism...** Scollon, C.N. & Diener, E. (2006). 'Love, work, and changes in extraversion and neuroticism over time'. *Journal of Personality and Social Psychology*, 91: 1152–1165. Many positive psychology tools, wellbeing activities and therapeutic treatments, if viewed through the lens of personality research, could be argued to reduce neuroticism. See Chapter 1 for more on these activities – although whether these activities actually shift long-term traits or just manage short-term states is disputed. See for example Diener, E., Lucas, R.E. & Scollon, C.N. (2006). 'Beyond the hedonic treadmill: Revising the adaptation theory of well-being'. *American Psychologist*, 61(4): 305–314.

46 **tend to increase with age...** Roberts, B.W., Walton, K.E. & Viechtbauer, W. (2006). 'Patterns of mean-level change in personality traits across the life course: a meta-analysis of longitudinal studies'. *Psychological Bulletin*, 132(1): 1.

47 **Knowing your personality can help you...** For more on using the Big Five at work, see Barrick, M.R. & Mount, M.K. (2005). 'Yes, personality matters: Moving on to more important matters'. *Human Performance,* 18(4): 359–372.

48 **using up mental energy...** Baumeister, R.F.; Bratslavsky, E.; Muraven, M. & Tice, D.M. (1998). 'Ego depletion: Is the active self a limited resource?' *Journal of Personality and Social Psychology*, 74(5): 1252–1265.

49 **the Big Five can predict all kinds of things about a potential recruit...** For more on personality and recruitment, see for example Hogan, R., Hogan, J. & Roberts, B.W. (1996). 'Personality measurement and employment decisions: Questions and answers'. *American Psychologist*, 51(5): 469.

50 **you may end up in a state of 'groupthink'...** See Chapter 9 for more on what this is and how to avoid it.

51 **the term 'neurodiversity' might usefully be expanded...** Neurodiversity is a thorny subject with a lot of sensitivities around it, but the word is too good to pass up. A review of how it has been used in clinical and disability circles can be seen in Jaarsma P. & Welin S. (2011). 'Autism as a natural human variation: Reflections on the claims of the neurodiversity movement'. *Health Care Analysis* 20(1): 20–30. Here I propose that the term 'neurodiversity' could usefully be broadened to encompass a general spirit of neurological variation, much like workplace diversity or biodiversity, rather than as a tool to describe people with particular neurological features.

52 **can enhance the performance of a business...** See for example Pieterse, A.N., van Knippenberg, D. & van Dierendonck, D (2013). 'Cultural diversity and team performance: The role of team member goal orientation'. *Academy of Management Journal*, 56(3), 782–804.

53 **'Who can say what form of wiring will prove best...'** Blume, H. (1998). 'Neurodiversity. On the neurological underpinnings of geekdom'. *The Atlantic*. http://mindap.pl/ViiddB.

TRAIN YOUR MIND

The human mind is the most advanced biological system ever evolved, and you have been put in charge of one. Yet sometimes it can feel like your mind is in charge of you. If it is sharp and capable, you can achieve more in your life and work; if it is slow and limited, it could hold you back.

No wonder then that we invest so much time and money in improving our minds. We go to school, learn new skills, work on our habits and take on new challenges. Businesses invest in training for their staff and managers, and we invest in our personal and professional growth too. Training our minds is one of our most popular pastimes.

It is also something humans are particularly good at. Our capacity to learn and adapt to change is why we have risen to the top of the evolutionary game. From memory champions to concert pianists, history is filled with examples of the remarkable things our minds can do.

Nevertheless, there are limits. One of the biggest debates in neuropsychology is how, and how far, we can train ourselves to be smarter.

BRAINPOWER

In the last century it was widely believed that our brains were fixed from childhood and would struggle to learn and adapt past a certain point. Now we know differently: genetics and upbringing shape our neural development, but our brains keep changing throughout our lives.[1]

However, some aspects of our mental capacity still seem to be fixed. The closest thing we have to a word for this is 'intelligence' – our underlying ability to recall and process information and acquire knowledge and skills.

Many studies suggest that intelligence is a good predictor of success in education and work, particularly for more complex roles. A review of intelligence research by the American Psychological Association concluded that intelligence tests seem to be effective and have value in predicting intellectual capability and future success.[2]

Intelligence can be a sensitive topic though. Like personality, it describes something quite fundamental to us, and can seem to limit what we are capable of doing. Many of us – well, particularly men – tend to overestimate our intelligence too,[3] so learning the truth can be a bit dispiriting.

This is perhaps why it is so hard to get everyone to agree on how to measure it. Roger Highfield of London's Science Museum argues *'it would be absurd to use an "athletics quotient" to compare a long-distance runner with a sprinter.'*[4] The Medical Research Council has devised new IQ tests that they claim improve on standard measures.[5]

Even in the early days of intelligence testing, psychologist Edwin Boring argued that intelligence is *'what the tests of intelligence test'*.[6]

One of the most popular critiques of intelligence has come from psychologist Howard Gardner, who proposed that we have seven types of intelligence: musical–rhythmic, visual–spatial, verbal–linguistic, logical–mathematical, bodily–kinesthetic, interpersonal and intrapersonal (he later added naturalistic and moral too).[7]

Gardner clearly has a point: after all, we all know people who are, let's say, brilliant at art but terrible at maths. However, his theory has been widely criticised, particularly for its failure to explain why people who are intelligent in one area tend to be intelligent in the others too.[8]

In fact, the whole idea behind intelligence tests is that people who score highly in one type of skill will tend to score highly in the others too – suggesting the presence of an underlying 'brainpower' or 'general intelligence'.[9]

For example, one intelligence test is the Wechsler Adult Intelligence Scale,[10] which tests a range of skills:

- **Verbal comprehension**
  Defining and connecting words, general knowledge and remembering facts.
- **Perceptual organisation**
  Spotting patterns and sequences, and remembering differences.
- **Working memory**
  The number of things you can hold in your mind at the same time (more on this later).
- **Processing speed**
  How quickly your mind can recall information and analyse problems.

The tests seem separate, but people who test highly on one tend to score highly on the others. Whatever you're trying to do, having a high intelligence seems to help.

This is the theory of general intelligence. Just as a computer can have a powerful graphics card but a slow central processor, we can train our minds for particular skills, but we still have a basic mental capacity that facilitates or limits everything we do.[11]

INCREASING YOUR INTELLIGENCE

The bad news is that increasing your intelligence seems to be quite hard. Intelligence is partly inherited,[12] and it may reflect the physical size and structure of the brain too.[13] Nevertheless, increasing intelligence has become a huge field of study, and one that still provokes heated debate.

One example of this is 'brain training' games. Their theory is that basic mental tasks like maths problems and memory games can train your mind like a muscle, making you smarter just like lifting weights can make you stronger.

Despite their popularity though, there is very little evidence yet that most brain training games make you smarter. Dr

Adrian Owen of the BBC's *Brain Test Britain* project even concluded that: *'The result is crystal clear. Brain training is only as good as spending six weeks using the internet.'*[14]

This type of training helps you improve at a particular skill, but the benefits don't seem to transfer to other activities. Doing crosswords makes you better at doing crosswords but it won't make you better at anything else, any more than learning Italian makes you better at playing the piano.

There are exceptions emerging though. For example, the free 'Dual N-Back Task', available online, does seem to be showing increases in fluid intelligence.[15] There is also growing evidence that mindfulness helps people perform better in intelligence and memory tasks.[16]

It's not clear whether these activities actually increase our mental capacity though, or just harness it more effectively. It is early days in the quest to train intelligence, so we may still have individual limits. For now at least, the jury is still out on whether intelligence can be increased.

HOW WE LEARN

There's more to our minds than intelligence though. Our minds are brilliant at adapting to change and acquiring new skills. We call this process of neural adaptation 'learning'.[17] If you want to train your mind, the best way to do it is learning.

There are many different aspects to learning, and each relies on a different part of your mind.[18] So if you want to improve how you learn, there are various ways to go about it.

- **Working memory**
  This holds whatever you're doing right now. Make the most of it by maintaining your mental energy, learning things in small chunks and paying mindful attention.
- **Explicit memory**
  This holds knowledge and experiences for future recall.

Improve it by concentrating better, recalling and reflecting on memories and building up knowledge.

* **Implicit memory**
This holds skills and habits, things you do without thinking. Practise new skills intensively and regularly, and identify your cues and rewards to build new habits.

MENTAL BOTTLENECKS

Working memory is our capacity to hold many things in our conscious mind at the same time. Anything you remember for less than a minute, like a sum in your head or a postcode to look up, is stored in working memory.

Working memory is what enables you to remember the start of this sentence by the time you reach the end of it.[19]

Working memory is probably the most noticeable aspect of our underlying 'brainpower'. It is used for all conscious thought and is involved in learning new skills, weighing up decisions and explaining our ideas. In fact it is virtually impossible to do anything in your mind without it.

Working memory is finite and is easily overloaded so it creates a bottleneck, making it harder to learn new things. If you are struggling to follow the thread of a conversation, or to remember all the different factors in a decision, chances are it is your working memory holding you back.[20]

You can make the most of your working memory by maintaining your mental energy levels and freeing your mind from stress, worry, multitasking and other distractions.[21] It is hard to increase your working memory beyond a certain point though, and we all naturally have limits – classic studies suggest most of us can only hold around seven things in our minds at a time. Intelligence varies, but all our minds have bottlenecks.[22]

This concept of a 'mental bottleneck' is useful for understanding how intelligence works. If you have high intelligence, you can hold more ideas in your mind, learn things faster and synthesise more complex information – but it doesn't describe what you have put into your mind or what you've trained it to do. It's useful for handling lots of information, but it doesn't make you right all the time.[23]

EASING THE BOTTLENECK

The way we cope with the limitations of working memory is through 'chunking'. Chunking means breaking up complex patterns into smaller patterns to help us process them. We remember most things by dividing them into smaller chunks and then connecting them together.[24]

For example, try to memorise this sequence of letters:

---

heietoraeobqtsuontnthiobteostt

It is really difficult to remember a random sequence of letters like this. They have no meaning, no connections between them, and so all you can do is try to hold them all in your mind and hope you have remembered them right.

Now try memorising this sequence of letters:

'To be or not to be, that is the question'

Both sequences contain exactly the same letters, but because the second version is divided into words and has grammatical structure, and because it means something to you, it is much easier to remember, and know that you've remembered it correctly. This is how our minds remember. We make things meaningful to make them memorable.

Words and phrases, chords and scales, mnemonics, 'mind palaces' and even stories are all examples of 'chunks'. By learning things in small chunks, then connecting them together, you can learn far more than first seemed possible. It's easy to do, and useful for everyone. Chunking is a very powerful technique for training your mind.

MEMORIES (ARE MADE OF THIS)

Chunking makes it easier to get information into your long-term memory. Anything you remember for more than a minute is long-term memory.

Knowledge and experience is held in **explicit memory**.

There are two branches of explicit memory: semantic memory, which handles knowledge of facts, places and ideas, and episodic memory, which stores memories of events and things that have happened to you.[25]

The two are closely related. This book, for example, trains your semantic memory by giving you concepts to make sense of the world. If you apply these principles to your business, you will remember what happened as episodic memory.

Long-term memory is much more than a data archive: it is the mental framework of experiences and associations that we use to interpret and explain the world.[26] We organise our thoughts through our memories, building up 'mental categories' from our past experiences which we use to make sense of the events in our lives.[27]

Chess Grand Masters, for example, have seen the positions on a chess board so many times they automatically know what is likely to come next. They have trained their minds to remember the board positions so well that it actually changes how they see the game.[28] As one writer puts it, *'learners construct their sense of the world by applying their old understanding to new experiences and ideas'.*[29]

When you learn something, you see the world differently. One study even suggested that *'long-term memory is now viewed as the central, dominant structure of human cognition. Everything we see, hear, and think about is critically dependent on and influenced by our long-term memory.'*[30] If you want to change your mind, change your memory.

IMPROVING YOUR MEMORY

Some researchers believe that our memories are infinite, and that we remember everything we ever experience.[31] We certainly appear to know things that we cannot easily recall. If you were asked to write down all the section titles in this book you might struggle, but if you flick back through the book most will look vaguely familiar to you.

We can't always recall things as accurately as we might like though.[32] Frequently-recalled memories change over time, we remember things that didn't happen[33] and we can be selective in our memories too, ignoring things that don't fit with our version of events. As the eminent psychologist Daniel Kahneman observed, *'when there is no coherent story about what happened we tend to think that it didn't happen'.*[34] Human memory doesn't appear to work like a computer.

Free recall is very hard, so a better way to recall memories is by finding a **memory cue**, like a starting fact that helps you think of others, or a piece of music that you associate with a particular time in our lives. Sensory cues like taste and smell seem to be particularly effective.[35] Emotions can act as memory cues too, so particularly intense emotional experiences – good and bad – tend to be harder to forget.[36]

Since memories can be linked to other memories, one memory can help you recall others. We use our existing knowledge to organise new knowledge.[37] So the more you **learn and connect your knowledge**, the easier it becomes to recall what you know.[38] Our memories may even specialise too.[39] Think about the areas you need to know well and invest time in learning more about them to improve your recall of them.

As one author put it, *'The most important single factor influencing learning is what the learner already knows.'*[40]

Another way to improve your recall is to **keep recalling memories**. Every time you recall a memory, you make it stronger, so if you keep explaining a fact or retelling a story, this helps you consolidate the memory and makes it easier to recall. This is not about mindless repetition, but thoughtful repetition, explaining and reflecting on memories.[41] So if you want to learn something, teach it.[42]

According to Maria Konnikova, we can improve our memories by **paying attention better**. We keep track of what's in our memories through memory encoding – a bit like a library index. If memories are not encoded properly, they are harder to find when you need them. The more you pay attention, the better you encode memories.[43] Anything that stops you from concentrating or drains your mind of energy stops you encoding memories effectively.

This means that many actions to **maintain your wellbeing** are also good for improving memory. Sleeping after learning something can increase how much you can recall later[44] and looking at nature seems to aid recall too.[45] Managing your moods is important too: positive moods can help us absorb new ideas and experiences, whilst negative moods can make us less open to learning.[46]

Stress is particularly bad for learning, because it diverts people's attention during the memory encoding process. An experiment by German cognitive psychologists showed that people under stress recalled thirty per cent fewer words than those in a calmer state of mind.[47]

To learn things effectively, you need to reach **a state of flow**, in which action feels easy and tasks are immersive.[48] The more time you spend in this state of deep activity, the more effectively you will learn and remember information. Improving your memory is all about paying attention.

LEARNING TO CONCENTRATE

Concentration frees up your working memory for the task at hand. If your mind is free from distractions, you can focus more 'brainpower' on what you are doing.

Concentration is complex because it relates to consciousness. When we say 'concentrate', we usually mean putting our conscious attention on something, such as listening to a talk or analysing a problem. When we can't focus, or forget what someone has just said, we say we need to concentrate better.

External distractions such as noise and interruptions from other people can affect concentration. So too can **internal distractions** such as rumination and worry. Positive moods can make it easier to deal with these disruptions, so mood management is again important.[49]

Motivation affects concentration too: if we are motivated by an activity, we find it easier to give our attention to it. So if you are sat in a dull meeting, you will need more energy to stay focussed than if you are listening to an inspiring talk about something you care about.[50]

The best way we know to train attention is **mindfulness meditation**. Mindfulness seems to help us concentrate better in all situations. Interestingly, mindful people tend to notice more in their surroundings, not less, but they seem to be less distracted by them and better at choosing their focus.[51]

However, this type of conscious attention is hard work. Our minds naturally wander half the time,[52] and we filter out much of what we see too[53] – so forcing ourselves to focus takes effort and can't be sustained indefinitely. Your mind is often working without you noticing.[54]

If you are finding it hard to concentrate, don't panic: this is a natural part of how your mind works. Simply learn to notice what affects your concentration and when you can focus well, and make the most of these times to do your best work.

LEARNING STYLES?

One of the more popular theories in education is 'learning styles', the idea that some people are naturally better at learning through one type of communication or another. The theory goes that some people prefer, for example, 'auditory' learning – listening to information – whilst others prefer 'visual' learning, and so on. Find the right style, and people will take on information better and remember more.

There is a lot to be said for acknowledging that we are all different in how we learn: no two minds are the same and learning theories need to account for our individual differences. However, there is surprisingly little experimental evidence that learning styles are the best model for achieving this, or that teaching according to learning styles gives better learning outcomes. A recent study concluded that *'there is no adequate evidence base to justify incorporating learning-styles assessments into general educational practice'.*[55]

People still say they prefer learning in one way or another though, so it could be that there is more to learning styles than the current evidence suggests. Varying the ways in which we take on information seems like a sensible strategy.

For now though – as with the theories of multiple intelligences – it seems that although we prefer some forms of learning to others, this does not correspond to any underlying physical variation, or affect how successfully we learn. As long as there is enough variety of interaction to keep us interested, the specific style of learning doesn't seem to matter.

What is much more important is establishing whether you are trying to gain knowledge and experience, or trying to learn a skill. The processes for the two are quite different.

PRACTICE MAKES PERFECT

Not all the things we learn require conscious attention. One of the cleverest things about our minds is that we can use our conscious minds to train our unconscious minds.

If you are a regular driver, driving probably feels so natural to you now that it is hard to remember when you couldn't do it. Yet there will have been a time when you could only drive by concentrating very deliberately on the pedals, the mirrors, the steering wheel, and so on. Doing it for the first time was hard, but doing it now feels like second nature.

These automatic patterns are held in our **implicit memory**, where we remember skills and habits.[56] Riding a bike, driving a car, entering a PIN number – these memories pop into our minds naturally when we need them, and they are surprisingly hard to forget.

They are stored separately to our knowledge and experiences – so if you were worried you might learn the capital of Finland and then forget how to walk, don't worry: that's a whole different type of memory. Unlike knowledge and experiences, skills and habits can be acquired without you even noticing. Learning skills takes practice, but not necessarily understanding.

Many skills do move from conscious learning to unconscious habit over time though. Take, for instance, London taxi drivers who do 'the Knowledge' – every major driving route through central London. They begin by learning each route explicitly, such as *'leave by Montague Street, right Great Russell Street, set down on right,'* but over time they learn to do it without thinking.[57]

This process is known as adaptive learning. Conscious learning leads to unconscious ability.

Learning new skills takes effort, but once they are automated your mind stores these new patterns so you can do them without needing to concentrate – freeing your conscious minds up for new tasks.

We begin by being blissfully unaware of our limitations (**unconscious incompetence**); then we realise how hard the task is and how bad we are at it (**conscious incompetence**); then we practise it by doing it deliberately (**conscious competence**); until finally, we can do it without thinking (**unconscious competence**).

By the end of the process we feel like we have always been able to do it. This is why teaching can be so challenging: once you've got there, it's hard to remember how you got there.[58]

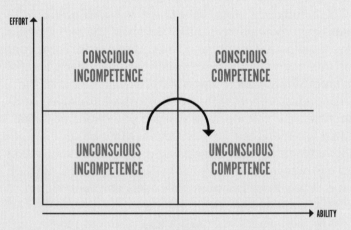

You can use this model to improve your mind and adapt to new situations. Think about the skills and behaviours you need for your current job, and for the job you want next, and work towards them. Set aside regular slots in your week to focus on practising these skills, and after long enough you will find yourself doing them naturally.[59]

Our minds aren't infinitely adaptable of course – there are natural limits to mental and physical capabilities – but if there is anything we can conclude from the lives of top athletes, musicians, dancers and brain surgeons – and taxi drivers – it is that practice makes perfect.[60]

FEEDING THE SEAHORSE

Intensive learning physically changes us. When we learn a skill, our brains establish specialised pathways to make these actions more efficient. They are wrapped in a fatty tissue called myelin, which speeds up the signals and makes that action up to three thousand times quicker.[61]

Areas of your brain can also grow or shrink with training too. For example, the brains of professional musicians develop significant physical differences to non-musicians, with more grey matter for key skills like motor control.[62]

One intriguing example of this is the hippocampus, a small, seahorse-shaped area of your brain (the name really means seahorse) that plays an important role in learning and memory.[63] London taxi drivers doing the Knowledge seem to develop much larger hippocampi in the training.[64] The more you learn the bigger your hippocampus grows. Some researchers even believe that training to increase the volume of the hippocampus might combat dementia.[65]

Bigger isn't always better though – as activities get easier they can actually take less 'brainpower' – but it's a useful image. If you want to train your mind, feed the seahorse.

THE POWER OF HABIT

Not everything in our implicit memories gets there on purpose. Sometimes our minds are being trained without us even realising.

Whenever we do something regularly, intensively and for a long time, it can become a habit.[66] Despite their negative associations, habits are really useful.

We create habits to conserve mental energy. Once we have done something a few times, we automate it so we can do it without thinking.[67] They are essential to how our minds work. Without them, we would be overloaded with choices and wouldn't even make it to the office. From brushing our teeth to checking our phones, habits keep us moving along and allow to focus on the world around us.

You can habituate yourself to almost anything. Whatever you do, your mind will adapt to do it more efficiently. Some of these habits are helpful, but some are harmful.[68]

So the question is not whether you should train your mind, but what are you training your mind to do? What are you doing regularly and intensively? Do you spend your days practising the skills you need to succeed, or conditioning yourself to fail? Think about what you need to be good at and what you don't, and try to build your routine to practise positive actions and avoid negative ones. Otherwise you may end up with a mind that is perfectly adapted to a life you don't want to have.

The truth can be sobering. Most of us are not training our minds for the things we really need, particularly at work. As productivity writer Cal Newport puts it, whilst chess players practise chess and violinists practise scales, *'if you're a veteran knowledge worker, you'll spend most of your day answering e-mail'.*[69]

YOUR MIND ON EMAIL

If we can train our minds for pretty much anything, then we should consider the impact of technology on our minds. It is probably too early to say how digital tools are affecting us – and they often move on too quickly to be researched – but they are certainly having an impact. As Jack Lewis and Adrian Webster put it in *Sort Your Brain Out*: *'Your malleable brain...*

will accommodate the demands of any environment...physical or virtual.'[70]

The main impact of technology is more information, which makes it much easier for us to learn more and connect our knowledge, but it can also make it much easier for us to get interrupted and distracted.

Often this is due to social pressure – the need to respond to messages – but we may be conditioning our minds to seek out distractions more generally, so that even when we do get time to focus, we find ourselves checking our messages anyway.[71] We take this habit home too. Studies of television habits showed that when we watch a show, we tend to check our phones or tablets every fifteen seconds.[72] We are training our minds to be constantly interrupted.

This process of constant attention switching uses up our mental resources and affects our cognitive performance. Heavy multitaskers seem to have less willpower and score lower in intelligence tests.[73] We may be spending our days draining our minds of the energy they need to work.

Email in particular may be quite addictive. Tom Stafford of *Mind Hacks* argues this is because email produces unpredictable rewards. Sometimes, checking your email gives you some good news, or an amusing web link, but because you can never tell when it will produce the reward, you have to keep checking all the time, just in case.[74] Checking your email becomes a habit.

CHANGING YOUR HABITS

So can we retrain our minds once they have adapted like this? How do we forget all these bad habits we've learned?

In his excellent book *The Power of Habit*, Charles Duhigg explores the findings from a whole range of experiments about how habits work and how to change them.[75] He describes the process of habit-forming as a 'habit loop'. The 'habit loop' contains a cue, a routine, and a reward.

A **cue**, says Duhigg, is *'a trigger that tells your brain to go into automatic mode'*. This starts a **routine** – a response to the cue – which could be a physical action, a thought process, or an emotional response. This routine then leads to a **reward**, which *'helps your brain figure out if this particular loop is worth remembering for the future'*.[76]

For example, you feel stressed (the cue), so you eat cake (the routine), and feel more energised (the reward).

According to Duhigg, the *'golden rule of habit change'* is very simple: if you keep the same cue and the same reward, you can change the routine in the middle.

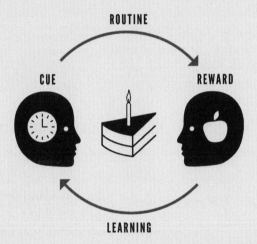

Maybe you want to break your addiction to checking your phone, or perhaps you just want to eat less cake. Whatever habit you want to change, here's how the process works:

1 Identify the cues
What triggers you to do this routine? Cues can be internal, like feeling tired in the middle of the afternoon, or external, like a friend offering you some cake.

2 Identify the reward
Why does this particular habit satisfy you? Is it improving how you feel physically or psychologically? What do you like about how things feel after you've done it?

3 Practise a new routine
Interrupt the cue and practise a new routine instead that gives you the same reward. For instance, if you eat cake when you're stressed, find healthier ways to give yourself a treat. Instead of checking your phone, find something else to do when your date goes to the bathroom.

All this takes effort of course. Old habits die hard and there will be times when you fall back into old patterns. This is most likely to happen when you are tired and lack mental energy, since this is when you have the least willpower.[77] It gets easier though. Doing anything for the first time is tiring, but the more you practise the less energy it takes. There's even some evidence that exercising self-discipline is itself a habit – so the more you change your habits, the better you get at it.[78]

Don't just rely on habits though. Knowledge and experiences change your behaviour too, and can also make it easier to see *why* you are doing things, helping you stick at them when they get hard. Not everything can be fixed through mindless repetition. Sometimes you need to consciously learn new things and change how you see the world, and other times you just need to practise a skill until you can do it. Telling the difference can help you train your mind more effectively.

SHARPENING THE AXE
So our minds are being trained all the time then, dealing with new experiences, learning new skills, building new habits and adapting to our ever-changing environment.

If you want to train your mind, ask yourself what you are trying to achieve. If you want to apply your knowledge and experiences to complex problems more effectively, then recalling and connecting what you know will help. If you want to change your habits and build new skills, then identify the cues, and practice makes perfect. If you just want to be smarter, look after your mental wellbeing and train your attention to make the most of what you've got.

Try not to obsess about improving your mind though, or worry too much about the impact the world is having on it. We can obsess about trying to improve ourselves, but despite their quirks our minds are truly remarkable things. Whilst we might wish we were calmer or cleverer, there is much more to celebrate in our minds than there is to fear.

Just keep an eye on how your mind is performing. If you notice particular times when you feel sharp and capable, consider why that is; if you feel flat and stupid, ask yourself what you might be doing to your brain to cause that.

Invest in your mind, because it is the tool of your trade, and if you take care of it, it will take care of you.

As the old woodsmen's saying goes:[79]

> **If I had five minutes to chop down a tree, I would spend three of them sharpening the axe.**

HABIT 6
LEARN THINGS IN SMALL CHUNKS AND DESIGN YOUR DAILY ROUTINE TO TRAIN YOUR MIND

TRAIN YOUR MIND
IN A NUTSHELL

THE TWITTER VERSION
Your mind adapts to everything you do, so focus on what you're learning and the skills you're practising and design your day accordingly.

THE SUMMARY VERSION
Despite all our efforts to increase our brainpower, it is actually quite hard to increase our natural intelligence. We can improve how we use our minds though, and train them for particular activities.

Training your attention and breaking up knowledge into small chunks can help you do more with your mind. Your existing knowledge makes it easier to acquire more knowledge too. Learning seems to be a habit: the more you learn, the more your brain adapts to learning.

Sometimes you need to remember information better, so connecting knowledge together and recalling what you know can help to embed memories. For skills and habits though, practice makes perfect, so keep training yourself to do things until you can do them without thinking.

Your mind picks up habits all the time though, so watch what you are training your mind to do. Anything you do regularly intensively and for a long time can become a habit, so watch your daily routine or you could end up with a mind that is perfectly suited for a life you don't want to have.

NOTES

1 **our brains keep changing throughout our lives...** For an enlightening introduction into neuroplasticity, see Doidge, N. (2008). *The Brain that Changes Itself: Stories of Personal Triumph from the Frontiers of Brain Science.* Penguin.

2 **A review of intelligence research by the American Psychological Association...** Neisser, U., Boodoo, G., Bouchard, T.J., Boykin, A.W., Brody, N., Ceci, S.J., Halpern, D.F., Loehlin, J.C., Perloff, R., Sternberg, R.J & Urbina, S. (1996). Intelligence: Knowns and Unknowns. *American Psychologist.* 51: 77–101.

3 **tend to overestimate our intelligence...** Furnham, A. (2001). 'Self-estimates of intelligence: culture and gender difference in self and other estimates of both general (g) and multiple intelligences'. *Personality and Individual Differences,* 31(8): 1381–1405.

4 **'it would be absurd to use an 'athletics quotient'...** Highfield, R. (2012). 'It takes more than an IQ to describe how our brains work'. *The Telegraph,* 20 December 2012. http://mindap.pl/1I2bp0j.

5 **The Medical Research Council has devised new IQ tests...** You can take their new style of IQ test online at http://mindap.pl/newIQtest.

6 **intelligence is 'what the tests of intelligence test'** Boring, E.G. (1923). 'Intelligence as the Tests Test It'. *New Republic,* 36: 35-37.

7 **proposed in 1983 that we have seven types of intelligence...** Gardner, H. (1983). *Frames of Mind: The Theory of Multiple Intelligences.* Basic Books.

8 **his theory has been criticised...** Visser, B.A., Ashton, M.C. & Vernon, P.A. (2006). 'Beyond g: Putting multiple intelligences theory to the test'. *Intelligence,* 34(5): 487–502.

9 **an underlying 'brainpower' or 'general intelligence'...** Spearman, C.E. (1904). '"General intelligence", objectively determined and measured'. *American Journal of Psychology,* 15: 201–293.

10 **the Wechsler Adult Intelligence Scale...** The original WAIS, released by psychologist David Wechsler in 1955 is now in its fourth edition and available online: http://mindap.pl/1Ad8ips.

11 **that facilitates or limits everything we do...** For a fine introduction to intelligence and what it means, see Freeman, D. & Freeman, J. (2010). *Use Your Head: The Inside Track on the Way We Think.* John Murray.

12 **it seems to be at least partly inherited...** Bouchard, T.J. (2004). 'Genetic influence on human psychological traits: A survey'. *Current Directions in Psychological Science,* 13(4): 148–151.

13 **it may reflect the physical size and structure of the brain...** McDaniel, M. (2005). 'Big-brained people are smarter'. *Intelligence,* 33: 337–346.

14 **Dr Adrian Owen of the BBC's *Brain Test Britain*...**Quoted online on BBC Lab UK: http://mindap.pl/1p5frUA.

15 **the free 'Dual N-Back Task'...** See Jaeggi, S.M., Buschkuehl M., Jonides, J. & Perrig, W.J. (2008). 'Improving fluid intelligence with training on working

memory'. *Proceedings of the National Academy of Sciences of the USA*, 105(19): 6829–6833. The test is available free online at http://mindap.pl/N-Back.

16 **evidence that mindfulness improves intelligence...** Mrazek, M.D., Franklin, M.S., Phillips, D.T., Baird, B. & Schooler, J.W. (2013). 'Mindfulness training improves working memory capacity and GRE performance while reducing mind wandering'. *Psychological Science*, 24(5): 776–781.

17 **we call this process of neural adaptation 'learning'...** For an example of this view of learning, see Dennis Coon, who defined learning as 'a relatively permanent change in behaviour due to past experience'. Coon, D. (1983) *Introduction to Psychology,* 3rd edn. St Paul, MN: West Publishing Co.

18 **each relies on a different part of your mind...** How our memory actually works is still something of a mystery. For a more detailed look at memory and learning, see for example Kolb, B. & Whishaw, I.Q. (2008). *Fundamentals of Human Neuropsychology*, 6th edn. (Worth Publishers), Chapter 18.

19 **Working memory...** See Broadbent, D.E. (1958). *Perception and Communication*. New York: Pergamon Press. See also Atkinson, R.C. & Shiffrin, R.M. (1968). 'Human memory: A proposed system and its control processes'. In Spence, K.W. & Spence, J.T. *The Psychology of Learning and Motivation (Volume 2)*. New York: Academic Press. Baddeley, A. (1986). *Working Memory*. Clarendon Press.

20 **working memory is a small bottleneck...** Miller G.A. (1956). 'The magical number seven, plus or minus two: Some limits on our capacity for processing information'. *Psychological Review*, 63: 81–97.

21 **You can make the most of your working memory...** See the previous sections on increasing intelligence, and also the material on mental resources and mindfulness in Chapters 1 and 7.

22 **most of us can only hold around seven things in our minds...** Miller G.A. (1956). 'The magical number seven, plus or minus two: Some limits on our capacity for processing information'. *Psychological Review*, 63: 81–97. Naturally the precision of this figure has been widely questioned though.

23 **it doesn't make you right all the time...** For more on how to be right, see Chapter 7.

24 **a better way to get around it is through 'chunking'...** Miller G.A. (1956). 'The magical number seven, plus or minus two: Some limits on our capacity for processing information'. *Psychological Review*, 63: 81–97.

25 **There are two branches of explicit memory...** Tulving, E. (1972). 'Episodic and semantic memory'. In Tulving, E. and Donaldson, W. (Eds.). *Organization of Memory*. New York: Academic Press.

26 **the mental framework of experiences and associations...** Daniel Kahneman's term for this is 'associative coherence', and there is more on this in Chapter 7. See Morewedge, C.K. & Kahneman, D. (2010). 'Associative processes in intuitive judgment'. *Trends in Cognitive Sciences*, 14(10): 435–40.

27 **We organise our thoughts through our memories...** Schapiro, A.C,

Rogers, T.T., Cordova, N.I., Turk-Browne, N.B. & Botvinick, M.M. (2013). 'Neural representations of events arise from temporal community structure'. *Nature Neuroscience*, 16(4): 486. (And see also this helpful article on Science Daily: http://mindap.pl/1AdNspK).

28 **Chess Grand Masters, for example...** De Groot, A.D. & Gobet, F. (1996) *Perception and Memory in Chess. Heuristics of the Professional Eye*. Van Gorcum, Assen.

29 **'learners construct their sense of the world by applying their old understanding...'** Schulman, L. (1999). 'Taking learning seriously'. *Change*, 31(4).

30 **'long-term memory is now viewed as the central, dominant structure of human cognition...'** Kirschner, P.A., Sweller, J. & Clark, R.E (2006). 'Why minimal guidance during instruction does not work: an analysis of the failure of constructivist, discovery, problem-based, experiential, and inquiry-based teaching'. *Educational Psychologist*, 41(2): 75–86.

31 **Some people believe that our memories are infinite...** Standing, L. (1973). 'Learning 10000 pictures', *Quarterly Journal of Experimental Psychology*, 25(2): 207–222.

32 **We can't always recall things as accurately...** See for example this influential review of the ways in which our memories get things wrong: Schacter, D.L. (1999). 'The seven sins of memory: Insights from psychology and cognitive neuroscience'. *American Psychologist*, 54(3).

33 **we remember things that didn't happen...** See for example Loftus, E.F. & Pickrell, J.E. (1995). 'The formation of false memories'. *Psychiatric Annals*, 25: 720–725. This applies to semantic memory as well: see for example the often-repeated 'word list' tests created by James Deese in the 1950s and popularised in Roediger, H.L., & McDermott, K.B. (1995). 'Creating false memories: Remembering words not presented in lists'. *Journal of Experimental Psychology: Learning, Memory and Cognition*, 21(4): 803–814.

34 **'when there is no coherent story about what happened...'** Quoted by the author from his 2014 lecture: Kahneman, D. (2014). *How To: Thinking, Fast and Slow*. Methodist Hall, 18 March 2014.

35 **Sensory cues like taste and smell...** See for example Yeshurun, Y., Lapid, H., Dudai, Y. & Sobel, N. (2009). 'The privileged brain representation of first olfactory associations'. *Current Biology*, 19(21): 1869–1874.

36 **Emotions can act as memory cues too...** Heuer, F. & Reisberg, D. (1990). 'Vivid memories of emotional events: The accuracy of remembered minutiae'. *Memory & Cognition*, 18(5): 496–506.

37 **We use our existing knowledge to organise new knowledge...** Schulman, L. (1999). 'Taking learning seriously'. *Change*, 31(4): 12.

38 **the more you learn and connect your knowledge...** See for example Recht, D.R. & Leslie, L. (1988). 'Effect of prior knowledge on good and poor readers' memory of text'. *Journal of Educational Psychology*, 80(1): 16–20. And Van Overschelde, J.P. & Healy, A.F. (2001). 'Learning of non-domain facts

in high- and low-knowledge domains'. *Journal of Experimental Psychology: Learning, Memory, and Cognition*, 27(5): 1160–1171.

39 **Our memories may even specialise...** Woollett, K. & Maguire E.A. (2011). 'Acquiring "the Knowledge" of London's layout drives structural brain changes'. *Current Biology*, 21: 2109–2114.

40 **'The most important single factor influencing learning is what the learner already knows'** Ausubel, D., Novak, J. & Hanesian, H. (1978). *Educational Psychology: A Cognitive View*. Holt, Rinehart and Winston.

41 **Every time you recall a memory, you make it stronger...** Craik, F.I., & Watkins, M.J. (1973). 'The role of rehearsal in short-term memory'. *Journal of Verbal Learning and Verbal Behavior*, 12(6): 599–607. And see also Tronson, N.C., Taylor, J.R. (2007). 'Molecular mechanisms of memory reconsolidation'. *Nature Reviews Neuroscience*, 8(4): 262–275.

42 **if you want to learn something, teach it...** This is something my father, Peter Gibson, a teacher all his life, told me many times when I was younger. It is nice to be able to confirm his advice now via modern neuroscience. Thanks neuroscience.

43 **The more you pay attention, the better you encode memories...** Konnikova, M. (2013). *Mastermind*. Canongate Books.

44 **Sleeping after learning something...** Gais, S., Lucas, B. & Born J. (2006). 'Sleep after learning aids memory recall'. *Learning & Memory*, 13(3): 259–62.

45 **looking at nature seems to aid recall too...** Berman, M.G., Jonides, J. & Kaplan, S. (2008). 'The cognitive benefits of interacting with nature'. *Psychological Science*, 19(12): 1207–1212.

46 **Positive moods can help us absorb new ideas and experiences...** Fredrickson, B.L. (2001). 'The role of positive emotions in positive psychology: The broaden-and-build theory of positive emotions'. *American Psychologist*, 56: 218–226.

47 **Stress is particularly bad for learning...** Schwabe, L. & Wolf, O.T. (2010). 'Learning under stress impairs memory formation'. *Neurobiology of Learning and Memory*, 93(2): 183–188.

48 **you need to reach a state of flow...** Csikszentmihalyi, M. (1990). *Flow: The Psychology of Optimal Experience*. New York: Harper and Row.

49 **Internal distractions...** See Chapters 1 and 2 for more on how to manage your moods and deal with the effect of your environment and internal state on your mind.

50 **Motivation affects concentration...** See Chapter 3 for how to motivate yourself genuinely rather than using up mental energy forcing yourself to focus.

51 **The best way we know to train attention is mindfulness...** See for example Hodgins, H.S. & Adair, K.C. (2010). 'Attentional processes and meditation'. *Consciousness and Cognition* 19(4): 872–8. MacLean, K.A. et al (2010). 'Intensive meditation training improves perceptual discrimination and sustained attention'. *Psychological Science* 21: 829–839. Lutz, A., Slagter, H.A.,

Rawlings, N.B., Francis, A.D., Greischar, L.L. & Davidson, R.J. (2009). 'Mental training enhances attentional stability: Neural and behavioral evidence'. *The Journal of Neuroscience* 29(42): 13418–13427.

52 **Our minds naturally wander...** Killingsworth, M.A. & Gilbert, D.T. (2010). 'A wandering mind is an unhappy mind'. *Science* 330(6006): 932.

53 **we filter out much of what we see...** See for example the classic gorilla experiments of Simons, D.J. & Chabris, C.F. (1999). 'Gorillas in our midst: Sustained inattentional blindness for dynamic events'. *Perception*, 28: 1059–1074.

54 **Your mind is often working without you noticing...** See Chapter 10 for more on the benefits of not concentrating and how your automatic, unconscious mind makes creative associations when you are distracted.

55 **'there is no adequate evidence base to justify incorporating learning-styles...'** Pashler, H., McDaniel, M., Rohrer, D. & Bjork, R. 'Learning styles: concepts and evidence'. *Psychological Science in the Public Interest*, 9(3): 105–119.

56 **These automatic patterns are held in our implicit memory...** What follows is strictly a discussion of procedural memory, which is only one aspect of implicit memory. For a better summary of implicit memory, see amongst others Kolb, B. & Whishaw, I.Q. (2008) *Fundamentals of Human Neuropsychology*. Worth Publishers, Chapter 18.

57 **London taxi drivers who do 'the Knowledge'...** Transport for London, London Taxi and Private Hire (2011). *The Knowledge of London.*

58 **At first we are unaware of our limitations...** The 'four stages of competence' model of learning is often credited to Noel Burch and Gordon Training International, but its origins may go back further than that. For the online debate see http://mindap.pl/1t3ISd2 and http://mindap.pl/1qCBTSh.

59 **You can use this model to improve your mind...** For more on this approach to training your mind, see Lewis J. & Webster A. (2014). *Sort Your Brain Out.* Capstone.

60 **practice makes perfect...** See for example Syed, M. (2011). *Bounce: The Myth of Talent and the Power of Practice.* Fourth Estate.

61 **They are wrapped in a fatty tissue called myelin...** Hartline, D.K. & Colman, D.R. (2007). 'Rapid conduction and the evolution of giant axons and myelinated fibers'. *Current Biology* 17(1): R29–35. Bengtsson, S.L., Nagy, Z., Skare, S., Forsman, L., Forssberg, H. & Ullén, F. (2005). 'Extensive piano practicing has regionally specific effects on white matter development'. *Nature Neuroscience*, 8(9):1148–50.

62 **The brains of professional musicians...** Croom, A.M. (2011). 'Music, neuroscience, and the psychology of well-being: A précis'. *Frontiers in Psychology*, 2: 393.

63 **a small, seahorse-shaped area of your brain...** There are many theories as to the exact role of the hippocampus, from storing or consolidating memories to performing a 'librarian' function of tagging and retrieval. For

a brief introduction, see Kolb, B. & Whishaw, I.Q. (2008) *Fundamentals of Human Neuropsychology* (6th ed., Worth Publishers), Chapter 18.

64 **London taxi drivers doing the Knowledge...** Woollett K. & Maguire E.A. (2011). 'Acquiring "the Knowledge" of London's layout drives structural brain changes'. *Current Biology*, 21: 2109–2114.

65 **training to increase the volume of the hippocampus might combat dementia...** Erickson K.I. et al (2011). 'Exercise training increases size of hippocampus and improves memory'. *Proceedings of the National Academy of Sciences of the USA*, 108: 3017–3022.

66 **Whenever we do something regularly, intensively and for a long time...** I am grateful to Dr Jack Lewis for this helpful summary of the three ingredients of building new skills and habits.

67 **we automate it so we can do it without thinking...** This is actually a form of 'chunking', our system for reducing the load on our working memories. See for example Graybiel, A.M. (1998). 'The basal ganglia and chunking of action repertoires'. *Neurobiology of Learning and Memory*, 70: 119–136.

68 **You can habituate yourself to almost anything...** Research into habituation and 'conditioning' is extensive, from Pavlov's dogs in 1927 to Martin Seligman's 'learned helplessness' experiments in the 1950s and Langer & Rodin's studies of nursing homes in 1976. For a good introduction to this topic see Gross, R. (2010). *Psychology. The Science of Mind and Behaviour*. 6th ed. Hodder Education, chapter 11.

69 **'if you're a veteran knowledge worker, you'll spend most of your day answering e-mail'** Newport, C. (2012). 'Knowledge workers are bad at working (and here's what to do about it...)'. *Study Hacks Blog*, 21 November 2012. http://mindap.pl/1lpImUz.

70 **'Your malleable brain... will accommodate the demands of any environment... physical or virtual'** Lewis J. & Webster A. (2014) *Sort Your Brain Out*. Capstone. p. 42.

71 **conditioning our minds to seek out distractions...** Cain, M.S., Mitroff, S.R. (2011). 'Distractor filtering in media multitaskers'. *Perception*, 40: 1183–1192.

72 **Studies of television habits...** Brasel, S.A. & Gips, J. (2011). 'Media multitasking behavior: concurrent television and computer usage'. *Cyberpsychology, Behavior and Social Networking*, 14(9): 527–534.

73 **Heavy multitaskers seem to have less willpower and score lower in intelligence tests...** Minear, M., Brasher, F., McCurdy, M, Lewis, J. & Younggren, A. (2013). 'Working memory, fluid intelligence, and impulsiveness in heavy media multitaskers'. *Psychonomic Bulletin & Review*, 20: 1274–1281.

74 **Email in particular may be quite addictive...** Stafford, T. (2006). 'Why email is addictive (and what to do about it)'. *Mind Hacks Blog*, 19 September 2006. http://mindap.pl/1pV2cqt.

75 **a whole range of experiments about how habits work...** There are

many studies on habit forming in the brain, all covered brilliantly in Duhigg, C. (2012). *The Power of Habit*. Random House.

76 **The 'habit loop' contains a cue, a routine, and a reward...** Duhigg, C. (2012). *The Power of Habit: Why We Do What We Do And How To Change*. Random House, p. 19. Illustration based on the original by Anton Ioukhnovets.

77 **this is when you have the least willpower...** Baumeister, R.F.; Bratslavsky, E.; Muraven, M.; Tice, D.M. (1998). ,Ego depletion: Is the active self a limited resource?' *Journal of Personality and Social Psychology*, 74: 1252–1265.

78 **exercising self-discipline is itself a habit...** See for example Baumeister, R.F., Gailliot, M., DeWall. C.N. & Oaten, M. (2006). 'Self-regulation and personality: how interventions increase regulatory success and how depletion moderates the effects of traits on behaviour'. *Journal of Personality*, 74: 1773–1801.

79 **'If I had five minutes to chop down a tree, I would spend three of them sharpening the axe.'** This quote is often attributed to Abraham Lincoln, perhaps due to a 1960 advert, but there is no reference to it in his public writings and speeches and it appears as an anonymous quote before it was attributed to him – so sadly it probably originates elsewhere: http://mindap.pl/1vaQGu8.

CHAPTER 7
MAKE SMARTER DECISIONS

We like to think of ourselves as rational and objective, but the reality is a bit more complicated.

Imagine you are choosing lunch from a menu in a café. You may try to weigh up the options logically – but how big are the portions? Does the chef cook steak well? Suppose the fish has been in the fridge for a week? And are your blood sugar levels too high to have that orange juice?

The problem with logical, objective decision-making is that you can never know enough. By the time you have done all the necessary research, lunch is over.

All our decisions are limited by context. Our minds have evolved to make best-guess decisions with limited information, take action, and move on. As the Zen Buddhist teacher Gudo Wafu Nishijima reportedly put it:[1]

> *'If you have to make a decision, it's because you don't have enough information. If you have all the information, there's no decision to make.'*

YOUR EMOTIONAL MIND

Decision-making is not, in fact, an intellectual process but an emotional one. A decision is the point at which we feel we can stop thinking and take action. And since we never know what we don't know, somewhere along the line we need to put our analysis away and act. Contrary to popular belief, decisions are not intellectual: they are emotional.

French philosopher Jean Buridan summarised this problem in the fourteenth century by imagining a perfectly logical donkey which is placed exactly equidistant between two identical piles of hay – and starves to death. With no reason to pick one pile over the other, the donkey cannot decide, and chooses neither.

This philosophical conundrum, affectionately known as 'Buridan's Ass', highlights the limitations of pure logic in decision-making. The truly rational thing for the donkey to do is to take action, of any kind. Making a decision, even the wrong decision, is often better than doing nothing.

Patients suffering from brain damage can experience Buridan's hypothetical problem in real life. People whose emotional systems have been damaged may report feeling less anxious and more clear-thinking, but place a lunch menu in their hands and they are incapable of deciding what to eat. They can weigh up the options rationally, but without emotions, they struggle to take action.[2]

Feelings can be very helpful in decisions, giving us valuable information by combining our prior knowledge, immediate information and learned experience to help guide our choices. Often we aren't even aware of how our minds are doing this: we just follow our instincts.

The importance of emotions in decisions means that our moods and emotional states can profoundly influence our decisions though, often without us even realising it. You may think you make decisions based on evidence, but in fact your opinions are quite likely to change with your moods – no matter how intelligent you are.

How well we manage these feelings determines whether our emotions end up helping us, or ruling us. The former means smart, informed decisions that incorporate all our wisdom and experience; the latter means making rash, ill-informed choices, without even knowing why. Angry people take stupid risks, fearful people miss opportunities, happy people think everything will work out fine – our emotional states change how we think, and so influence what we do.[3]

Accepting the role of emotions in our business thinking can be challenging for some people, particularly in very evidence-based, analytic industries. The idea conflicts with our view of ourselves as the rational 'rider' planning ahead and thinking things through. Yet we ignore our emotions at our peril, even in the most rational of occupations.

As Naomi Shragai put it in the *Financial Times*:[4]

'Whatever we think, emotions always play a part in our decisions. Understanding this can help business people make better choices and achieve better results.'

ONE MIND, TWO SYSTEMS

We are clearly quite good at making decisions though, or we would never have got this far. So how do we decide? We make hundreds of decisions every day, some trivial and some very important. Most we hardly think about whilst others we agonise over for a long time. How do our minds handle this constant flow of choices and information?

When psychologists Stanovich and West conducted a review of decision-making theories, they proposed a unified model of thought which has now been popularised by Nobel Prize-winning psychologist Daniel Kahneman in his remarkable book, *Thinking, Fast and Slow*.

This model, known as 'dual process theory', proposes that the mind uses two distinct types of thinking to make decisions: **'System 1'**, sometimes called the **automatic system**, and **'System 2'**, the **controlled system**.[5]

System 1 is fast and intuitive and comes to conclusions quickly, but tends towards 'best guess' answers and is sometimes wrong. System 2 is better at accurate, linear thinking and breaking down problems, but it is slower.

1 AUTOMATIC	**2** CONTROLLED
Fast	Slow
Unconscious	Conscious
Emotional	Analytical
Intuitive	Deliberate
Biased	Laborious

For Kahneman, System 1 represents 'normal' decision-making, with System 2 only involved in very important decisions. We rely on System 1 to make the thousands of little decisions our minds are faced with every day, and use System 2 for thinking about key decisions in more detail.

The automatic 'System 1' is much more than a set of instinctive loops: it plays an important role in analytic thought too. Our unconscious minds can hold multiple factors together and assess their relative value and importance – a process called the 'integration of value'.[6]

In fact we will often spot things intuitively first, and struggle to explain our reactions on a conscious level. In experiments at the University of Iowa, participants played a gambling game in which they chose from two different decks of cards – one high risk, the other much safer. Participants soon realised the difference between the decks and switched their play accordingly – but interestingly, they showed unconscious stress responses when reaching for the high-risk deck several rounds before they realised the difference. Their unconscious minds had figured out the game before their conscious minds had caught up.[7]

Most of our decisions never make it to our conscious awareness. Even when we choose to think things through in a more controlled manner, our automatic reactions are still there in the background, bringing hidden influences into our decisions – some useful, and some less useful.

This is the power of your automatic system: it draws together all your memories and experiences and uses them to make sense of the world, in what Kahneman calls 'associative coherence'.[8] Your automatic system is harder to control, but it is remarkably well-informed. We have to rely on our unconscious minds to weigh up our choices, because they can hold so much more information.

Making smart decisions, then, is not just about rational deduction, but about knowing how and when to trust your automatic reactions.

AUTOMATIC REACTIONS

Before you can think consciously about a decision, your automatic system has already formed an opinion about it.

Your mind is just being helpful, presenting you with a default choice in case you don't want to think about it. As Kahneman puts it, System 1 *'is never dumbfounded: if it doesn't know the answer, it makes one up'*.[9]

It doesn't do this in isolation though: it draws on previous knowledge to interpret the world, enabling you to navigate situations better and guess in ways that are more likely to be right. We develop implicit associations, good and bad, based on our experiences and the culture around us.[10]

We bring these automatic reactions into almost every decision that we make. Most of the time, these signals are useful, channelling our past experiences to help us respond appropriately. However, some can throw us off course and lead us to bad decisions. Telling the difference, or even recognising them when they occur, can be tricky.

The sensitivity of our automatic system means we need to be careful what we put into it, or it can lead us into prejudice. Harvard's Project Implicit has been tracking the assumptions we make about people and situations.[11] These 'implicit associations' help us navigate unfamiliar situations, but they can also lead to sexism, racism and other prejudices – sometimes without us even realising it.[12]

We can use our controlled system to consciously correct for these associations if we are aware of them, but they are still there under the surface, influencing our decisions. This is why we go to so much effort to ensure diversity in the workplace and representation in the media, not simply to counter present inequality, but to retrain our minds and set more positive implicit associations for the future.

WHY WE MAKE MISTAKES

We also have inbuilt biases in our automatic systems that help us navigate common situations quickly but can also cause predictable errors in how we assess decisions and weigh up risks and opportunities – a phenomenon that Dan Ariely calls predictable irrationality.[13]

For one thing, our minds can be **a little negative**, a hangover from our evolutionary past.[14] We tend to go for middle values and safer choices,[15] and we prefer safe, familiar choices to risky, unfamiliar ones. For example, we tend to favour objects on our dominant side, simply because we are familiar with the action required to pick them up.[16]

One very bizarre example of this **'familiarity bias'** is that we may prefer things that remind us of our own names. The result is that, statistically, people named Dennis or Denise are more likely to become dentists, Laurie or Lawrence to become lawyers, and so on. Something about it just feels right.[17]

Positivity isn't always great either though. We are also prone to **'optimism bias'**, a tendency to be overly positive about the future. We underestimate potential risks, ignore crucial realities and imagine that good outcomes are more likely than they really are. This seemingly innocent trait is actually why we smoke, drink and play the lottery.[18]

There are a great many of these 'cognitive biases' influencing our thinking. Some can be consciously overruled, whilst others can only be managed. The more we are aware of the limitations to our automatic system, and the more energy we have for our controlled system, the more chance we have to correct for common mistakes.[19]

If we have a strong automatic reaction to a situation though, we can end up using our controlled system to **invent plausible arguments** for that choice, rather than appraising and perhaps overruling our first instinct.[20] As Kahneman puts it, *'we are wrong in a coherent way'*.[21]

BLIND SPOTS

Sometimes, it's not our analysis that is flawed, but the information we select in the first place. Many bad decisions are the result of missed information, not poor reasoning.

Our minds are bombarded with information all the time, only some of which will be relevant. We can only focus consciously on one information stream at a time though, so our automatic system filters it all for us. This means that before we even start consciously analysing a choice, we may already have missed some important information.[22]

The result of this can be **'confirmation bias'**, where we unconsciously select information that confirms our automatic reactions.[23] We become more critical of evidence that doesn't support our theories, and more accepting of evidence that confirms our intuition. We also feel more positive about an option after we've chosen it.[24] For this reason it can be useful to step back and ask whether we have selected our opinion based on the evidence, or vice versa.

We also tend not to notice when information is missing – a trait known as **'omission neglect'**. In the Sherlock Holmes story *Silver Blaze*, Holmes calls Detective Gregory's attention to the *'curious incident of the dog in the night-time'*. *'The dog did nothing in the night-time,'* replied Gregory. *'That was the* *curious incident,'* said Holmes. Holmes realised that if the dog did not bark, it must have known the killer. Unfortunately though, most of the time these omissions slip past our minds unnoticed.[25]

Emotions affect these filters. When we are in a negative mood, we can miss positive elements of a situation. When we are in a positive mood we notice more, and so make more informed choices.[26] **Stress** distorts our perspective too, blinding us to possibilities and making us take irrational risks or chase unrealistic opportunities.[27]

IMPROVING DECISION-MAKING

There are so many unconscious biases that it can sometimes feel impossible to make good decisions. No matter how much we try to think things through, we end up being predictably irrational.

There are still a few things you can do to make your decisions smarter though. One thing is to **build up relevant knowledge and experience**, such as learning how to assess an interview candidate, or getting to know the property market. Training your mind can improve your intuition for that task and make your 'gut feel' more accurate.[28]

The more knowledge you have of a subject, the better your decisions are likely to be about it, because you notice more about the situation and have more experience to call on. Very often, this experience is hard to pin down, and you end up experiencing it as an intuitive sense, but the more experience you have of an area, the more likely your instincts are leading you in the right direction.

For instance, Malcolm Gladwell in his book *Blink* relates the story of the Getty Kouros, an archaic Greek statue purchased by the Getty Museum as a significant find but now believed to be a nineteenth-century fake. Initial tests seemed to show the statue was genuine but several independent experts said it felt wrong. One even said: *'Anyone who has ever seen a sculpture coming out of the ground could tell that that thing has never been in the ground.'* Having seen so many sculptures, their automatic reactions could spot what the scientific tests could not.[29]

Learned experience only works for each specific area of decision-making though: it won't make your decisions better in general. Familiarity with ancient statues won't make you better at buying a house or choosing a career.

MENTAL RESOURCES

Using your controlled system takes energy, so the best thing you can do to improve your general decision-making is to **conserve your mental resources**, to give your mind the best chance possible of recalling and considering all the relevant factors and overriding your automatic reactions.

When we lack mental energy, we find it harder to use our controlled system to interrupt and overrule our automatic reactions – leaving us more vulnerable to unconscious bias and errors of judgement.[30]

In one particularly alarming study, of judges conducting appeal rulings, researchers found that the normal rate of overturning convictions (around 67 per cent) dropped to close to zero the longer a judge went without eating or taking a break. Hungry, tired judges were more likely to stick with the status quo because they lacked the mental energy to think deeply about the case.[31]

Maintaining your mental energy is very important for making smart decisions. Keep your mind **well-fed, healthy and rested** to give yourself energy for thinking through decisions and choosing your responses.

The process of making decisions depletes our mental resources too, so try to **make important decisions first** rather than leaving them until last.[32] Even minor choices add up, so if you have an important decision to make, try to avoid making unnecessary decisions during the day and save your energy for what really matters.

Barack Obama even applied these findings to his presidency, sticking with routines and wearing similar suits every day to conserve his mental resources for more important decisions. As he put it in a *Vanity Fair* interview:

> **'You need to focus your decision-making energy. You need to routinize yourself.'**[33]

AVOID MULTITASKING

There is no such thing as conscious multitasking.

The controlled system can only **focus on one thing** at a time, so what we call multitasking is actually rapidly cycling our attention between tasks, which drains our mental energy and hampers our concentration in each.

It can feel exciting to juggle all those plates, but when we 'multitask', we think less clearly, remember less accurately, and are more likely to be influenced by irrelevant factors.[34]

There is another reason for avoiding multitasking in decision-making though. When we do more than one thing at once, these **parallel processes** can interfere with each other, meaning that what happens in one can affect how we feel about the other. This means that sometimes very important decisions are affected by unrelated events and experiences that are happening alongside them.

In one study, participants were asked to hold either a hot drink or a cold drink for a short time. Afterwards, they were asked to give their reactions to a standard description of a person they didn't know. The people who had been holding a warm drink felt more warmly towards this stranger; those who had held the cold drink felt cooler towards them. The unrelated action they were doing at the same time interfered with their judgement.[35]

So when making important decisions, try to **do one thing at a time** and avoid switching between seemingly unconnected tasks – because you never know quite how your mind is being affected.

PAY ATTENTION

Maria Konnikova, in her book *Mastermind: How to think like Sherlock Holmes*,[36] studied many different ways in which we can improve our decision-making and deduction skills.

She argues that the key to good decision-making is **being present and attentive** to information and experiences – not just when you are making a decision, but all the time.

You may remember (or perhaps you won't) that when you aren't paying attention, memories are not encoded properly. The result of this is that you can't tap into the value of your knowledge and experiences, making it more likely that you will evaluate situations incorrectly and make poorer, less-informed decisions as a result.[37]

The more you can be present and focussed when taking in new information and experiences, the better you will **process and store memories** for future use. A more accurate, organised recall of information enables you to use your knowledge more effectively in your decisions.

Konnikova is a fan of **mindfulness meditation** for achieving this. Mindfulness does seem to help us make more accurate, objective observations about situations. One study proposed that people who practise mindfulness are able to assess their personalities more accurately, perhaps because they notice more, and also because they are more able to accept the truth about themselves even if it is upsetting or disappointing.[38] Another showed that mindfulness can help people overcome some forms of cognitive bias.[39]

Control of your attention, and of your emotions, leads to **more accurate observations**, better recall of information and experiences, and hence better decisions.

KEEP PERSPECTIVE

Many errors of judgement occur because we get stuck in one particular view of a situation, so **talk things through** with other people to get perspective on your thoughts and actions. They don't have to be experts: even discussing things with people who know nothing about your situation can help you decide whether your assumptions are reasonable and identify any biases in your thinking.

Beware though: groups are just as susceptible to unconscious biases as individuals, and will tend to agree with each other and ignore contrary evidence. Group leaders can influence the rest of the group to agree with them, and group members will tend to give more weight to information the group already knows, rather than prioritising new information.[40]

To be really sure that your decisions are smart, seek out opinions from **a diverse range of people**, particularly people with different skills and life experiences, and different personalities. Checking your decisions with people who think differently to you can help you question your assumptions and spot what you have missed.[41]

Of course, once a decision has been taken, everyone needs to stick to it in order to get things done. Learn when to listen to dissenting voices and correct your thinking, and when to **stop thinking** and swing into action.

SMARTER DECISIONS

We may not be perfectly rational creatures, but for all our faults, we do make good decisions most of the time.

Decision-making is not an exact science of course, but here are a few things you can do to give yourself the best possible chance of making smart decisions:[42]

- **Rest and nutrition matter**
  A well-rested, well-fed brain makes better decisions.
- **Take major decisions first**
  Don't wait till you've made lots of minor choices.
- **Avoid distractions and multitasking**
  Parallel processes can affect your decisions and stop you encoding memories accurately.
- **Manage your moods and stress levels**
  Stay calm to avoid blind spots and narrow thinking.
- **Seek out diverse opinions**
  They can test your assumptions and identify blind spots.

Smart decisions aren't perfect decisions though, so try not to obsess over every choice you make. Over-thinking things, second-guessing ourselves and 'analysis paralysis' can all get in the way of us being successful. Just like the logical donkey, sometimes the best thing to do is to do something.

The most important thing is just to make the best decision you can and then take action. As a wise person once said:[43]

> **It's better to regret something you have done than to regret something you haven't done.**

HABIT 7
CONSERVE YOUR MENTAL RESOURCES AND AVOID MULTITASKING TO MAKE SMARTER DECISIONS

MAKE SMART DECISIONS
IN A NUTSHELL

THE TWITTER VERSION
All your decisions rely on your unconscious mind, so maintain your mental resources, watch for bias and avoid multitasking to stay smart.

THE SUMMARY VERSION
We like to think of ourselves as rational and objective but in fact we make surprisingly predictable mistakes in our decisions. This is because decision-making is emotional. We rely on unconscious, automatic systems in our minds to weigh up alternatives and stop thinking and take action.

In fact, most of our decision-making happens without us even noticing. We bring automatic reactions into every decision we make, and they shape our choices and influence our thinking, and even the information we consider. Unless we are aware of these unconscious biases, they can run our lives.

We can use our controlled system to correct for bias, but this takes energy so the best way to improve your decisions is to conserve your mental resources. Avoid multitasking too: it can confuse our minds and make us forget things. Decisions also tire our minds out, so make important decisions first.

Decision-making isn't an exact science. Keep your mind healthy and rested, watch for bias, but don't overthink things. Often the best thing is just to do something.

NOTES

1 **'If you have to make a decision, it's because you don't have enough information...'** Nishijima, G. & Bailey, J. (2009). *To Meet the Real Dragon*. Dogen Sangha Publications, Fourth Revised Edition. He may not actually have said this though, but it still makes a great point.

2 **Patients suffering from brain damage...** Bechara, A., Tranel, D. & Damasio, H. (2000). 'Characterization of the decision-making deficit of patients with ventromedial prefrontal cortex lesions'. *Brain* 123(11): 2189–2202. See also Bechara, A. & Damasio, A.R. (2005). 'The somatic marker hypothesis: A neural theory of economic decision'. *Games and Economic Behavior*, 52(2): 336–372.

3 **our emotional states change how we think...** See Chapter 2 for more on how moods and emotions influence cognition.

4 **'Whatever we think, emotions always play a part in our decisions...'** Shragai, N. (2014). 'Emotions at work in finance'. *Financial Times*, 15 January 2014.

5 **the mind uses two distinct types of thinking to make decisions...** The terms 'System 1' and 'System 2' were proposed in Stanovich, K.E. & West, R.F. (2000). 'Individual differences in reasoning: Implications for the rationality debate?' *Behavioral and Brain Sciences*, 23: 645–726. They were then expanded and popularised in what is now the definitive introduction to this topic, Kahneman, D. (2012). *Thinking, Fast and Slow*. Penguin.

6 **a process called the 'integration of value'...** Tsetsos, K., Chater, N. & Usher, M. (2012). 'Salience driven value integration explains decision biases and preference reversal'. *Proceedings of the National Academy of Sciences USA*, 109(24): 9659–9664.

7 **participants played a gambling game...** Bechara, A., Damasio, H., Tranel, D. & Damasio, A.R. (1997). 'Deciding advantageously before knowing the advantageous strategy'. *Science*, 275(5304): 1293–1295.

8 **'associative coherence'...** Morewedge, C.K. & Kahneman, D. (2010). 'Associative processes in intuitive judgment'. *Trends in Cognitive Sciences*, 14(10): 435-40.

9 **'[System 1] is never dumbfounded...'** Quoted by the author from his 2014 lecture: Kahneman, D. (2014). *How To: Thinking, Fast and Slow*. Methodist Hall, 18 March 2014.

10 **We develop implicit associations...** These associations are extremely useful to us most of the time: we build up associations in our long-term memories, and they are essential to how we build up knowledge and navigate the world.

11 **Harvard's Project Implicit has been tracking the assumptions we make...** Greenwald, A.G., McGhee, D.E., & Schwartz, J. L. (1998). 'Measuring individual differences in implicit cognition: the implicit association test'. *Journal of Personality and Social Psychology*, 74(6), 1464. For more on Harvard's research into our implicit associations, see www.projectimplicit.org.

12 **they can also lead to sexism, racism and other prejudices...** For a chilling example of how easy it is to train our minds to be prejudiced, see the famous 'black doll, white doll' tests. Clark, K.B. & Clark, M.P. (1947). 'Racial identification and preference among negro children'. In E.L. Hartley (Ed.) *Readings in Social Psychology.* http://mindap.pl/blackdollwhitedoll.

13 **a phenomenon that Dan Ariely calls...** Ariely, D. (2009) *Predictably Irrational. The Hidden Forces That Shape Our Decisions.* New York: HarperCollins.

14 **our minds can be a little negative...** Taylor, S.E. (1991). 'Asymmetrical effects of positive and negative events: The mobilization-minimization hypothesis'. *Psychological Bulletin*, 110(l): 67–85. And Carretié, L., Mercado, F., Tapia, M., & Hinojosa, J. A. (2001). 'Emotion, attention, and the "negativity bias", studied through event-related potentials'. *International Journal of Psychophysiology*, 41(1): 75–85.

15 **We tend to go for middle values...** Rodway, P., Schepman, A. & Lambert, J. (2012). 'Preferring the one in the middle: Further Evidence for the Centre-stage Effect. *Applied Cognitive Psychology*, 26 (2): 215–222.

16 **we tend to favour objects on our dominant side...** Casasanto, D. (2009). 'Embodiment of abstract concepts: Good and bad in right- and left-handers'. *Journal of Experimental Psychology: General*, 138(3): 351–367.

17 **we often like things that remind us of our own names...** There is some controversy around the validity of these findings, but they are at the very least somewhat unnerving. See Pelham, B.W., Carvallo, M., DeHart, T. & Jones, J.T. (2003). 'Assessing the validity of implicit egotism: A reply to Gallucci'. *Journal of Personality and Social Psychology*, 85(5): 800–807.

18 **a tendency to be overly positive about the future...** Sharot, T. (2011). *The Optimism Bias: A Tour of the Irrationally Positive Brain.* Pantheon.

19 **Some can be consciously overruled...** Daniel Kahneman has explored a range of ways that this can happen, from adjusting the initial view, to overruling it completely. See for instance Kahneman, D. (2003). 'A perspective on judgement and choice'. *American Psychologist*, 58: 697–720.

20 **we can end up using our controlled system to invent plausible arguments...** The work of Gazzaniga on split-brain patients demonstrated this confabulation, and see also Festinger, L. (1957). *A Theory of Cognitive Dissonance.* Stanford University Press. We also overestimate how much we know about familiar subjects, thinking we understand them when we really don't. See Rozenblit, L. & Keil, F. (2002). 'The misunderstood limits of folk science: An illusion of explanatory depth'. *Cognitive Science*, 26(5): 521–62.

21 **'We are wrong in a coherent way.'** Quoted by the author from his 2014 lecture. Kahneman, D. (2014). *How To: Thinking, Fast and Slow.* Methodist Hall, 18 March 2014.

22 **our automatic system filters it all for us...** Schmitz, T.W., De Rosa, E. & Anderson, A.K. (2009). 'Opposing influences of affective state valence on visual cortical encoding'. *Journal of Neuroscience*, 29: 7199–7207.

23 **to select information more if it supports our automatic reactions...** Nickerson, R.S. (1998). 'Confirmation bias: A ubiquitous phenomenon in many guises'. *Review of General Psychology*, 2(2): 175.

24 **feel more positive about an option after we've chosen it...** Sharot, T., De Martino, B. & Dolan, R.J. (2009). 'How choice reveals and shapes expected hedonic outcome'. *Journal of Neuroscience*, 29(12): 3760–3765. Brehm, J. (1956). 'Postdecision changes in the desirability of alternatives'. *Journal of Abnormal and Social Psychology*, 52(3): 384–389.

25 **'curious incident of the dog in the night-time'** The original story is of course by Arthur Conan Doyle, but this example is quoted in many places including Gilbert, D. (2006). *Stumbling on Happiness*. Harper Press.

26 **we notice more...** Schmitz, T.W., De Rosa, E. & Anderson, A.K. (2009). 'Opposing influences of affective state valence on visual cortical encoding'. *Journal of Neuroscience*, 29: 7199–7207.

27 **Stress distorts our perspective too...** Mather, M. & Lighthall, N.R. (2012). 'Both risk and reward are processed differently in decisions made under stress'. *Current Directions in Psychological Science*, 21(2): 36–41.

28 **Training your mind can improve your intuition...** See Chapter 6 for more on how we learn and how to train the mind to remember information and automate tasks.

29 **the story of the Getty Kouros...** Gladwell, M. (2006). *Blink: The Power of Thinking Without Thinking*. Penguin.

30 **When we lack mental energy, we find it harder to use our controlled system...** Pocheptsova, A., Amir, O., Dhar, R. & Baumeister, R. (2009). 'Deciding without resources: Resource depletion and choice in context. *Journal of Marketing Research*, 46(3): 344–355. And see also the detailed discussion of this in Kahneman, D. (2012). *Thinking, Fast and Slow*. Penguin, chapter 3.

31 **Hungry, tired judges were more likely to stick with the status quo...** Danzinger, S., Levav, J. & Avnaim-Pesso, L. (2011). 'Extraneous factors in judicial decisions'. *PNAS*, 108: 6889–6892.

32 **making decisions depletes our mental resources...** One of the major conclusions of the judge study is that making decisions reduces our capacity to make decisions. Danzinger, S., Levav, J. & Anaim-Pesso, L. (2011). 'Extraneous factors in judicial decisions'. *PNAS*, 108: 6889–6892.

33 **'You need to focus your decision-making energy. You need to routinize yourself.'** President Barack Obama, quoted in Lewis, M. (2012). 'Obama's way'. *Vanity Fair*, October 2012. http://mindap.pl/obamaroutine.

34 **what we call multitasking is actually rapidly cycling our attention...** See Chapter 6 for more on the cognitive effects of multitasking.

35 **participants were asked to hold either a hot drink or a cold drink...** Williams, L.E. & Bargh, J.A. (2008). 'Experiencing physical warmth promotes interpersonal warmth. *Science*, 322: 606.

36 **Maria Konnikova, in her book *Mastermind*...** Konnikova, M. (2013).

Mastermind: How to think like Sherlock Holmes. Canongate Books. See also Konnikova's RSA lecture, 'The scientific method of the mind' (2008). http://mindap.pl/rsamasterminda.

37 **when you aren't paying attention, memories are not encoded properly...** You may remember this point from Chapter 6 – if you were paying attention of course.

38 **are able to assess their personalities more accurately...** Carlson, E.N. (2013). 'Overcoming the barriers to self-knowledge. Mindfulness as a path to seeing yourself as you really are'. *Perspectives on Psychological Science*, 8(2): 173–186.

39 **mindfulness can help people overcome some forms of cognitive bias...** Hafenbrack, A.C., Kinias, Z. & Barsade, S.G. (2014). 'Debiasing the mind through meditation. Mindfulness and the sunk-cost bias'. *Psychological Science*, 25(2): 369–376.

40 **groups are just as susceptible to unconscious biases as individuals...** More on this in Chapter 9.

41 **Checking your decisions with people who think differently to you...** People of a similar background or who have similar information can reinforce each other's biases though, as discussed in Chapter 9.

42 **here are a few things you can do...** This list focusses on the psychological process of decision-making. For a more practical list of ways to engage with analysing a decision, see Myatt, M. (2012). 'Six tips for making better decisions'. *Forbes*, 28 March 2012. http://mindap.pl/1BxAQL5.

43 **'It's better to regret something you have done...'** Many people have said this, but I first heard it in the intro to Orbital's 1996 single, *Satan*.

CHAPTER 8
INFLUENCE PEOPLE

We all like being influential. Being listened to, having our opinions taken seriously, feeling we are having an impact on other people – these things are good for our self-esteem and our ability to achieve our goals at work and in life.

Many books on influence focus on sales though. They offer 'secret tricks' for persuading people to buy things and do what we want. The result is that 'influencing skills' have got rather a bad press over the years.

There is much more to influence than that. Influence is our capacity to produce effects on others, usually through intangible or indirect means. It refers to the ways in which we pick up thoughts and behaviours from the people around us, often without even realising it.

Influencing people is not something we can choose to do or not do. We all influence each other all the time, whether we like it or not. Understanding and managing our unintentional impact on other people is the first step towards using our influence intentionally, and being more influential and successful at work.

MIRROR NEURONS

A good starting point for exploring our unintentional influence on other people is the study of mirror neurons.

In the 1990s, Giacomo Rizzolatti and his colleagues at the University of Parma were studying premotor neurons in primates, when they stumbled on an unexpected discovery. They were measuring the brain activity of a group of monkeys as they picked up peanuts, when one of the neuroscientists got peckish and ate a peanut himself.

As the monkey watched, to the scientists' surprise, its neurons fired in just the same way as when it had picked up the peanut itself. The monkey hadn't moved, but it seemed that merely watching the act was enough to elicit the same response in the brain.

This unexpected observation led to the discovery of mirror neurons, neurons in our brains that imitate the experiences we see around us. Rizzolatti and his colleagues found that these neurons fire in sympathy when someone performs an action – enabling us to experience a part of that person's experience through our own observation.[1]

Mirror neurons are a fundamental social system in the brain. They connect us to the people around us, help us communicate, and enable us to learn by watching others. They also underpin our ability to understand and empathise with others – our emotional intelligence.

When we see someone experiencing an emotion, our brains tune into them and we experience part of that emotion ourselves. When a friend is sad, we feel sad too. When we see someone experiencing great joy or excitement, such as an Olympic athlete winning a gold medal, we experience a slice of that excitement too.

Even simple facial expressions can have a big impact: experiments have shown that simply seeing someone smile or frown creates a similar effect in the brain as actually smiling or frowning ourselves.[2]

The response is uncontrollable: even when we try not to react, we still experience the mirror neuron response in our brains. Whether we like it or not, our emotions affect how other people feel, and vice versa.

This unconscious 'mirroring' of others can affect our own moods, for better or worse. Stressed people can make you feel stressed too, whilst someone smiling at you is likely to put you in a good mood. People laughing, an angry passer-by

– they all affect your mind and influence your mood, often without you even noticing.

Furthermore, when we experience these emotions we often find ourselves copying the other person physically, taking on their emotional state. Our emotions are affected by feedback from our facial expressions, posture, voice and physical movements, so the more we tune into the people around us, the more we converge with them emotionally.[3]

Influencing people comes naturally to us. We are hard-wired to care. When you feel down, you can bring other people down too. Laugh, and the world laughs with you – psychologically speaking at least.

EMOTIONAL CONTAGION

The set of processes by which we share moods and emotions is known collectively as 'emotional contagion'. Researchers Hatfield, Cacioppo and Rapson described emotional contagion as:[4]

> 'The tendency to automatically mimic and synchronize expressions, vocalizations, postures, and movements with those of another person and, consequently, to converge emotionally'.

Many research studies have shown this effect in practice. People in meetings together end up sharing moods, and the moods of teams track together, with members feeling low one week and cheerful the next.[5] Classic studies have even shown that if three people sit in a room together, facing each other, in total silence, the most emotionally expressive can transfer their mood onto the other two in just two minutes.[6]

Everyone has an influence on the emotional state of the people around them, no matter how junior. So if you were worried that you had no influence, think again.

Once you begin to notice the impact other people have on your moods, you can manage your own mental state more successfully. You can also use this knowledge to influence the moods of the people around you.

Dan Siegel of the Mindsight Institute sums this up nicely:[7]

'This inner sensation that we call 'mind' is profoundly social. What I do influences how you feel.'

EMOTIONS AT WORK

Whether we like it or not, our emotional states affect the mood and performance of those around us, and vice versa. If we are more conscious of the impact other people have on us, we can manage our own moods better, and use this knowledge positively to influence the moods of the people around us and improve our organisations.

Negative emotions can spread through a team, and that team may influence others in the business, creating a negative feedback loop. Positive emotions are contagious too, creating positive loops. When we consider the impact of these moods on our performance, emotional contagion represents a huge risk – and opportunity – for businesses.[8]

Tuning into the moods of others can help you build positive relationships with customers and colleagues. By consciously creating an environment in which people can spread positive emotions at work, and establishing a calm, positive emotional tone, you can lift the entire workforce and significantly increase the wellbeing and productivity of your business.[9]

Leaders have a particular responsibility here. Inspirational leaders can set an emotional tone for their teams by visibly expressing the emotions they want to see in their business. Good leaders stay emotionally connected to the people around them and manage their emotional impact to get the best from their teams.[10]

Employers ignore these powerful subconscious triggers at their peril. Emotionally repressed firms leave themselves vulnerable to the negative effects of unmanaged emotional contagion in the workplace, whilst businesses that can harness their 'emotional intelligence' are more likely to thrive over their less socially adept competitors.

MANAGING YOUR INFLUENCE

So we all have more influence than we might think, as colleagues and as leaders. Often we don't realise the effect we are having, whether positive or negative, and this subconscious influence can interfere with what we are trying to achieve, and damage our relationships.

We like to spread positive feelings. If someone we know is feeling upset, we will try to calm them or cheer them up. We often want to share when we are in a good mood too, and we like it when other people are happy for us or excited about the same things as we are.

The flip side though is that when we feel upset or down, we may also seek to share this with the people around us so that they can understand us better. When we are stressed, we exhibit signs of stress to others, pulling people into our stressed state with us. Shouting, complaining, starting arguments, can all be signs that a person is trying to share their feelings with others to feel less isolated in their uncomfortable state.

Once you start to notice the impact you are having on other people, it is hard to ignore. Everyone can affect the mood of a room through their actions and behaviour. Even very junior members of a team can have a big impact on the moods of their colleagues.

Learning how to manage the emotional impact you have, and be a positive influence on the people around you, is very useful for getting things done at work, and can help you get along better with people too. Managing your emotional impact is quite simple, but it takes practice. There are a few key skills that you need to master: reading your context; building rapport; and expressing emotions appropriately.

MENTALISING

First you need to be **aware of your emotional context**. This is about more than just noticing how people are feeling: it is also about understanding the reasons behind the feelings. To be influential, you need to know what is going through people's minds.

Psychologists refer to this process as **'mentalising'**: the skill of imagining what is going through someone's mind and relating that to their behaviour.[11] It involves more than just facial expressions or physical cues:[12] it requires the whole context, your knowledge of that person's situation, your experience with people and your insights into your own mind too.

This is a separate skill to **'empathising'**, which is feeling another person's emotions and being connected to their experiences. Mentalising is how we make sense of those feelings and decide what action to take. For example, children often empathise with the moods of adults, but often don't understand the reasons behind the feelings.

Mentalising is a very important skill for relating to others, and one worth practising. The more accurately we observe people, the better we become at understanding and predicting their behaviour and responding appropriately.

Mentalising is hard. A lot of arguments stem from our incorrect guesses about what is happening in other people's heads. Take note of the assumptions you make about what goes on in other people's minds, and ask yourself what ideas and theories might be driving their behaviour. People aren't always thinking what you think they're thinking.

Don't jump to conclusions, but train yourself to observe more accurately. By really putting yourself in someone else's shoes and thinking about what lies behind their actions, you can often gain valuable insights into how to relate to them.

BUILDING RAPPORT

Next you need to **tune in to other people** emotionally. Your influence on others is much greater when you are in a similar physical and psychological state to them.

When we interact with others, we tend to match their behaviour. If we are with happy people, we laugh and smile more, we breathe faster around anxious people, and so on. Two people having a good conversation will have very similar physiological profiles in a few minutes.[13]

We call this process of tuning in **'rapport'**. Rapport is built unconsciously through non-verbal cues and instinctive actions, and we can learn to be better at it.[14]

There are lots of things you can do to build rapport:

- **Match gestures and facial expressions**
- **Control energy levels and interaction tempo**
- **Share tone of voice and speed of speech**
- **Observe and adjust your posture**

You can also reinforce this cognitively by talking about areas of mutual interest and emphasising what you have in common.[15]

The next time you speak to someone, think about the non-verbal signals you are giving them. Notice how they are mirroring you too, and adjust your behaviour to show them you are in tune with their state of mind. Don't overcomplicate it though: if you are genuinely paying attention to someone, you will naturally find yourself building rapport with them.

EXPRESSING EMOTIONS

Once you have tuned into the moods of the people around you, you can start to **express your own emotions**.

Influential people excel at setting the emotional tone. Learning how and when to **express your emotions** is an important tool for influencing people.[16]

To express your emotions appropriately, you need to be able to **manage your own emotional state**. You can suppress your feelings and act in spite of how you feel, but this is tiring and uses up mental energy. Genuinely managing your feelings to be in tune with your context is more effective and less tiring.[17]

This isn't about what you say, but more **how you say it**. Body language and other non-verbal cues reveal your feelings and can support or distract from what you are saying, so think about the emotional tone that is most appropriate for your situation. Match your posture, movements and interaction tempo to your audience and think about how to lead them into a receptive mood so your messages land well.

This is not just about being perpetually cheerful either: sometimes positive emotions aren't appropriate!

EMOTIONAL LEADERSHIP

Reading your context, tuning into people, expressing your emotions – these techniques sound simple enough, but the trick is to put them all together in a natural and effective way.

Here's a practical example of how you might use this model to influence someone's mood.

Imagine you are driving in a car and accidentally get in the way of a cyclist. You are both unharmed, and you barely noticed what happened – but the cyclist is quite shaken up.

If you take the time to **read the situation**, you have a fair idea what is going through their mind, so you can guess that if you step out of the car in a calm state, the cyclist is likely to react badly.

So your first instinct is probably to **build rapport** by pacing your emotions to theirs, through mimicry and feedback. You talk faster, match their gestures and energy levels and so on. This shows them that you are sensitive to how they feel.

Once you have matched their state, you can then **lead them into a calmer mood** by consciously changing your own behaviour and physical state. By gently slowing your breathing down, calming your voice, slowing your tempo, you can bring them out of their stressed state. Sometimes, what you say is less important than how you say it.

This skill is useful in all kinds of situations – from dealing with an angry client to comforting a stressed out colleague.

Influencing other people emotionally is not a simple matter of acting in a certain way and hoping others will follow suit though: it is only by having empathy for other people, and following their lead first, that you can have a genuine influence on them. If you want to influence people, you have to **take an interest** in them.

BEING PERSUASIVE

So what about when we really need to be heard, or convince someone of something important? How can we make ourselves, and our messages, more influential?

One good place to start is with how you come across personally. The judgements other people make about us can impact on the influence we have. These small cues may seem silly but they can make the difference between someone listening to you, or ignoring you. In fact, sometimes we base our whole judgement of a person on one single feature.[18]

Physical appearance does matter.[19] We are more likely to be influenced by someone we find physically attractive, even though we usually believe we are not.[20] However, we are also more influenced by people whom we think look like us, so the key is to look and dress appropriately for your context, not simply to look good.[21]

Taking a position of **authority**, intellectually or practically, can be useful for getting people to listen. Highlight your knowledge and experience, show your credentials if you have them, and gain the support of authority figures to underline what you're saying.[22]

Be careful with **boasting** though. One study found that you should never talk about your successes if you've raised the topic yourself.[23] Avoid name-dropping as well: another study showed it gives people a very bad first impression of you.[24] Highlight your authority, but never so much as to alienate you from your peers.

Talking about yourself can be boring for others. We are more likely to pay attention to someone who is actually interested in us. If you **take an interest** in the people you speak to, they will do the same. You can also reinforce your connection to other people by highlighting areas of similarity and **mutual interest**.

Put your phone away: the mere presence of a nearby phone can reduce social intimacy and harms rapport.[25]

Finally, **confident body language** tends to get people's attention more than muted, closed postures.

Very confident postures are known as **'power poses'**. The effects of these poses are surprisingly physical. Holding a 'power pose' for two minutes can lower cortisol, elevate testosterone and increase your tolerance for risk.[26] Try it before an important meeting and see if it boosts your confidence and makes people take more notice of you (although maybe don't try it in the meeting itself).

MUTED POSES   POWER POSES

MENTAL SHORTCUTS

Influence isn't just about being confident and charismatic:
what you say matters too. Think carefully about the messages
you are sending to other people, not just on a conscious level,
but unconsciously too.

When you put an argument to someone, they can process
it in two different ways. The **peripheral route** involves
less conscious attention, and relies on mental shortcuts. The
central route involves consciously hearing and processing
arguments deliberately. These two routes are similar to the
System 1 and **System 2** model of dual-process thinking,
though the research is separate.[27]

1 AUTOMATIC	**2** CONTROLLED
'Peripheral'	'Central'
Mental shortcuts	Reason and argument
Low attention	Requires thought
Quick decisions	Lasting decisions
Short-term impact	Long-term impact

Most of the time – particularly when we are distracted or tired – we tend to give only peripheral attention to things, and so we rely on quick cognitive rules of thumb to help us navigate the world more efficiently.

You can use these 'mental shortcuts' to influence people's thinking and persuade them to listen to you. This is a delicate process – people don't like to feel manipulated – but a few rules are worth remembering so you can use them appropriately in the right context.[28]

CONFORMITY

The first is conformity. We instinctively look to other people for clues on how to act, especially in unfamiliar situations, and we are more likely to do something if we see it as normal.[29] Consider, for example, how you react to a sign saying 'keep off the grass'. This is sometimes known as 'social proof', and is typified by the *'eight out of ten customers prefer our product'* approach to marketing.

You can tap into this by **sharing testimonials** from other people who have worked with you, **highlighting past successes** of businesses and products like yours, and showing **statistics** about the number of people who agree with you or support your product or service. This is also the principle at the heart of 'social norm marketing' which works to influence our default choices by sharing what other people do.[30]

RECIPROCITY

The second is reciprocity. We are naturally inclined to do favours for people who have helped us and will usually try to repay what others give to us. If you've ever been to a free 'taster event' or drinks reception and then felt obliged to buy something, that's reciprocity in action.[31]

Give people your **time, attention and help**, give away useful information, and **offer things for free** where you can afford it. Be the first to **offer concessions** and favours, and people will tend to repay you in kind. Being nice really does pay: if you are helpful and supportive to others, you will have more influence on them.[32]

CONSISTENCY

A slightly less obvious factor is consistency. Many people like to maintain a consistent self-image, so we are more likely to support something if it fits with things we have previously supported, or that we believe we have supported.[33] We do things repeatedly, even if they are wrong, and act in line with what we believe about ourselves. If you don't think you do this either, this may be because you see yourself as a rational person and want to behave that way in everything you do.

Consider how your message relates to the previous **public commitments** people have made, and try to avoid challenging their **past choices** unnecessarily. Our need for consistency also underpins the well-known 'foot in the door' technique: getting people to agree to **something small first** makes them more likely to agree to something bigger later.[34] One small yes now can lead to a bigger yes later.

SCARCITY

The final shortcut that influences our thinking is scarcity. We attribute greater value to that which is rare or not widely available. If we fear we might be missing out, or that something is in short supply, we are more likely to act quickly rather than waiting. If you have ever attended an event or bought a book with the word 'secret' in the title, you have probably fallen for this one.[35]

When constructing your messages, highlight anything that is genuinely **rare or exclusive**, and remember to say what is **unique** about your offering or experience. These rare or unusual ingredients tend to catch people's attention and make what you are offering more memorable.

A CENTRAL MESSAGE

People aren't stupid though. They're just not always paying attention. Don't imagine that if you simply fill your messages with these factors you can bend people to your will. A lot of persuasion training focuses on piling up the unconscious cues, but a person who is interested in your message may be unimpressed by 'all sizzle and no steak'.

Peripheral cues can get people to listen to you in the first place, but once they start to engage their 'central route' it is important to have a convincing argument.

Which route people use to process your argument depends on their willingness and ability to think about what you are saying. This is affected by their mental energy levels, rapport with you, distracting noises, emotional preoccupations and other contextual factors.[36] The more mental resources people have, the less they need to rely on mental shortcuts.

Sometimes you need to use all the tricks you can muster just to get people to listen. Other times, simply explaining yourself clearly can be enough. If you want to convince people in the long term, rather than just for a brief time, you have to back up your message with convincing arguments.[37]

So, pay attention to your practical and emotional context, and find the right moment to approach people. Include some of these persuasive elements in your message – but always tailor what you are saying to your audience, and make sure that if people really pay attention to your message, they will find enough in it to really convince them.[38]

BEING A POSITIVE INFLUENCE

There is a lot more to influencing people than simply saying the magic word or hitting the right unconscious button. The influence we have on others is complex, subtle, and difficult to predict with precision.

Mirror neurons, emotional contagion, rapport – all these are tools that you can use to increase your influence on other people, but they are also cues to tell others how you really feel. Our natural capacity for influence means we find it hard to pretend to feel things we don't, and our influence we have on each other means that, like it or not, we're in this together.

So when you are seeking to influence other people, remember that how they feel affects how you feel. Think about the emotional impact you have on other people, because they are influencing you too. These unconscious influences are everywhere, all the time, and they affect us all far more than we realise.

In the words of the poet Maya Angelou:[39]

> **People will forget what you said, people will forget what you did, but people will never forget how you made them feel.**

HABIT 8
NOTICE THE MOODS OF PEOPLE AROUND YOU AND TAKE CHARGE OF YOUR EMOTIONAL IMPACT

INFLUENCE PEOPLE
IN A NUTSHELL

THE TWITTER VERSION
We influence each other all the time, so tune into people's moods and express your emotions appropriately to have a positive influence.

THE SUMMARY VERSION
We are very social animals. Our minds have evolved to pay close attention to the moods of others and share in their experiences, through mirror neurons and other elements of 'emotional contagion'. Rather than being naturally selfish and competitive, we are hard-wired to care.

The result is that moods and emotions travel through teams and must be managed. You can influence the moods of the people around you through your facial expressions, body language, tone of voice and other cues. What you say often matters less than how you say it. Tune into the moods of people around you and lead them into a better state of mind.

You can also use unconscious cues to influence people's decisions. Natural generosity, a desire to appear consistent, an inclination to follow the herd and fear of missing out all guide our decisions and make us do things without thinking.

Be careful of focussing too much on unconscious cues though: if people are paying attention you will need a strong message to convince them – and remember that they will be influencing you too...

NOTES

1   **the discovery of mirror neurons...** Rizzolatti, G. & Fabbri-Destro, M. (2009). 'Mirror neurons: from discovery to autism'. *Experimental Brain Research*, 200(3–4): 223–37. See also this PBS video introducing mirror neurons and the experiments that shaped our understanding of them: http://mindap.pl/1g85zHz.

2   **facial expressions can have a big impact...** Dimberg, U, Thunberg, M. & Grunedal, S. (2002). 'Facial reactions to emotional stimuli: Automatically controlled emotional responses'. *Cognition and Emotion*, 16(4): 449–471.

3   **we often find ourselves copying the other person physically...** Dimberg, U., Thunberg, M. & Grunedal, S. (2002). 'Facial reactions to emotional stimuli: Automatically controlled emotional responses'. *Cognition and Emotion*, 16(4): 449–471.

4   **'The tendency to automatically mimic and synchronize...'** Hatfield, E., Cacioppo, J.T. & Rapson, R.L. (1993). 'Emotional contagion'. *Current Directions in Psychological Science*, 2: 96–99.

5   **The moods of teams track together...** Bartel, C.A. & Saavedra, R. (2000). 'The collective construction of work group moods'. *Administrative Science Quarterly*, 45(2): 197–231.

6   **if three people sit in a room together...** Friedman, H.S. & Riggio, R. (1981). 'Effect of individual differences in nonverbal expressiveness on transmission of emotion'. *Journal of Nonverbal Behavior*, 6: 96–104.

7   **'This inner sensation that we call 'mind' is profoundly social...'** Siegel, D. (2012). 'The emerging mind: How relationships and the embodied brain shape who we are. RSA Events, 11 July 2012, 18 mins. http://mindap.pl/rsasiegel.

8   **the impact of these moods on our performance...** See Chapter 2 for the impact of moods and emotions on our mental and professional performance.

9   **you can lift the entire workforce...** A review of various studies into emotional contagion at work can be found in Goleman, D., Boyatzis, R. & McKee, A. (2001). 'Primal leadership: The hidden driver of great performance'. *Harvard Business Review*, December 2001. http://mindap.pl/M3hFo2.

10 **Leaders have a particular responsibility...** Volmer, J. (2012). 'Catching leaders' mood: contagion effects in teams'. *Administrative Sciences*, 2(3): 203–220. And for a great introduction to the emotional side of leadership, see Goleman, D., Boyatzis, R. & McKee, A. (2001). 'Primal leadership: The hidden driver of great performance'. *Harvard Business Review*, December 2001. http://mindap.pl/M3hFo2.

11 **Psychologists refer to this process as 'mentalisation'...** Fonagy, P., Gergely, G., & Jurist, E. L. (Eds.) (2004). *Affect Regulation, Mentalization, and the Development of the Self*. Karnac Books.

12 **It involves more than just facial expressions...** Hassin, R.R., Aviezer, H. & Bentin, S. (2013). 'Inherently ambiguous: Facial expressions of emotions, in context. *Emotion Review*, 5(1): 60–65.

13 **Two people having a good conversation...** Friedman, H.S. & Riggio, R.E. (1981). 'Effect of individual differences in nonverbal expressiveness on transmission of emotion'. *Journal of Nonverbal Behavior*, 6(2): 96–104.

14 **Rapport is built unconsciously...** Levenson, R.W. & Ruef, A.M. (1997). 'Physiological aspects of emotional knowledge and rapport'. In Ickes, W. (ed.) *Empathic Accuracy*. Guilford Press, pp. 44–72.

15 **You can also reinforce this cognitively...** See for example the concept of 'dialogue involvement' as an influencing tool, as in Dolinski, D., Nawrat, M. & Rudak, I. (2001). 'Dialogue involvement as a social influence technique'. *Personal & Social Psychology Bulletin*, 27: 1395–406.

16 **Learning how and when to express your emotions...** Côté, S. & Hideg, I. (2011). 'The ability to influence others via emotion displays: A new dimension of emotional intelligence'. *Organizational Psychology Review*, 1: 53–71.

17 **You can suppress your feelings...** For a recap of surface and deep acting to control your emotions, and the mental cost of these, see Chapter 2.

18 **we base our whole judgement of a person on one single feature...** Nisbett, R.E. & Wilson, T.D. (1977). 'The halo effect: Evidence for unconscious alteration of judgments'. *Journal of Personality and Social Psychology*, 35(4): 250–256.

19 **Physical appearance does matter...** There are a great many studies on how and when attractiveness and similarity to us affects our judgement of people, all excellently summarised in Cialdini, R.B. (2007). *Influence: The Psychology of Persuasion*. HarperBusiness, chapter 5.

20 **someone we find physically attractive...** Mack, D. & Rainey, D. (1990). 'Female applicants' grooming and personnel selection'. *Journal of Social Behavior & Personality*, 5(5): 399–407.

21 **people whom we think look like us...** See for example Emswiller, T., Deaux, K. & Willits, J.E. (1971). 'Similarity, sex, and requests for small favors'. *Journal of Applied Social Psychology*, 1(3): 284–291. And see Suedfeld, P., Bochner, S. & Matas, C. (1971). 'Petitioner's attire and petition signing by peace demonstrators: A field experiment'. *Journal of Applied Social Psychology*, 1(3): 278–283.

22 **Taking a position of authority...** For a good introduction to the research into authority and obedience, see Cialdini, R.B. & Goldstein, N.J. (2004). 'Social influence: Compliance and conformity'. *Annual Review of Psychology*, 55: 591–621. The oft-cited experiments by Stanley Milgram on instinctive obedience to authority may have been misinterpreted though, as discussed in Haslam, S.A., Reicher, S.D., Millard, K. & McDonald, R. (2014), 'Happy to have been of service: The Yale archive as a window into the engaged followership of participants in Milgram's "obedience" experiments'. *British Journal of Social Psychology* (in press).

23 **Be careful with boasting though...** Tal-Or, N. (2010). 'Bragging in the right context: Impressions formed of self-promoters who create a context for their boast'. *Social Influence*, 5(1): 23–39.

24 **Avoid name-dropping as well...** Lebherz, C., Jonas, K. & Tomljenovic, B. (2009). 'Are we known by the company we keep? Effects of name-dropping on first impressions'. *Social Influence*, 4(1): 62–79.

25 **Put your phone away too...** Przybylski, A.K. & Weinstein, N. (2012). 'Can you connect with me now? How the presence of mobile communication technology influences face-to-face conversation quality'. *Journal of Social and Personal Relationships*, 30(3): 237–246. See also Misra, S., Cheng, L., Genevie, J. & Yuan, M. (2014). 'The iPhone effect. The quality of in-person social interactions in the presence of mobile devices'. *Environment and Behavior*, July 2014.

26 **Holding a 'power pose' for two minutes...** This research, and the original versions of the images that follow, are from Carney, D.R., Cuddy, A.J.C. & Yap, A.J. (2010). 'Power posing: Brief nonverbal displays affect neuroendocrine levels and risk tolerance'. *Psychological Science*, 21(10): 1363–1368.

27 **they can process it in two different ways...** Petty, R.E. & Cacioppo, J.T. (1986). 'The elaboration likelihood model of persuasion'. *Advances in experimental social psychology*, 19: 123-205. And also Petty, R.E. & Cacioppo, J.T. (1986). *Communication and Persuasion: Central and Peripheral Routes to Attitude Change*. New York: Springer-Verlag. Their work predates the 'System 1' and 'System 2' model of Kahneman, Stanovich & West (see Chapter 7), but seems to be fairly consistent with it.

28 **You can use these 'mental shortcuts' to influence people's thinking...** What follows is based on Cialdini, R.B. (2007). *Influence: The Psychology of Persuasion*. HarperBusiness. In it he outlines six types of influence: 'authority' and 'liking' we have already covered earlier in this chapter, so what follows is the remaining four components in Cialdini's framework.

29 **We instinctively look to other people...** See for example the famous experiments in the 1950s by Solomon Asch in which participants were influenced to give obviously false answers to easy questions through peer pressure. Asch, S.E. (1956). 'Studies of independence and conformity. A minority of one against a unanimous majority'. *Psychological Monographs*, 70(9): 1–70.

30 **'social norm marketing' which works to influence our default choices...** Wechsler, H., Nelson, T.F., Lee, J.E., Seibring, M., Lewis, C. & Keeling, R.P. (2003). 'Perception and reality: A national evaluation of social norms marketing interventions to reduce college students' heavy alcohol use'. *Journal of Studies on Alcohol*, 64: 484–494. For some of the other positive benefits of social norms see also Basu, K. (1983). 'On why we do not try to walk off without paying after a taxi ride'. *Economic and Political Weekly*, 18(48).

31 **We are naturally inclined to do favours for other people...** One classic study of this tendency to reciprocate favours is Regan, R.T. (1971). 'Effects of a favor and liking on compliance'. *Journal of Experimental Social Psychology*, 7:

627–639. The effects seem to diminish over time though, as seen in Burger, J.M., Horita, M., Kinoshita, L., Roberts, K. & Vera, C. (1997). 'Effects of time on the norm of reciprocity'. *Basic and Applied Social Psychology*, 19: 91–100.

32 **if you are helpful and supportive...** For more on how we instinctively work together, and why reciprocity actually works better than competition, see Chapter 9.

33 **Many people like to maintain a consistent self-image...** Guadagno, R.E. & Cialdini, R.B. (2010). 'Preference for consistency and social influence: A review of current research findings'. *Social Influence*, 5(3): 152–163.

34 **the well-known 'foot in the door' technique...** Freedman, J.L. & Fraser, S.C. (1966). 'Compliance without pressure: The foot-in-the-door technique'. *Journal of Personality and Social Psychology*, 4: 195–202.

35 **If we fear we might be missing out...** For one classic study on scarcity, see Worchel, S., Lee, J. & Adewole, A. (1975). 'Effects of supply and demand on ratings of object value'. *Journal of Personality and Social Psychology*, 32: 906–914.

36 **their willingness and ability to think...** Petty, R. & Cacioppo, J. (1986). *Communication and Persuasion: Central and Peripheral Routes to Attitude Change.* New York: Springer-Verlag.

37 **Sometimes you need to use all the tricks...** For a nice overview of which influencing tactics seem to be most effective at work, see Higgins, C.A., Judge, T.A. & Ferris, G.R. (2003). 'Influence tactics and work outcomes: a meta-analysis'. *Journal of Organizational Behavior*, 24: 89–106.

38 **if people really pay attention to your message, they will find enough in it...** If you are reading these footnotes, for example, you are probably quite engaged in the messages in this chapter, and will be less swayed by rhetoric and nice graphics. However, the graphics and the rhetoric may have been why you thought these footnotes were worth reading in the first place...

39 **'people will never forget how you made them feel'** Maya Angelou, quoted in Kelly, B. (2003). *Worth Repeating: More Than 5,000 Classic and Contemporary Quotes*, p. 263. http://mindap.pl/1ztBJRM.

CHAPTER 9
WORK COLLABORATIVELY

Working with other people can be very annoying. They misunderstand us, they ignore our advice, they don't do what we need them to do and they just will not stop sending us emails. Most of us spend our lives navigating office politics, making business cases, negotiating deals and resolving conflict. No wonder Jean-Paul Sartre once wrote that *'hell is other people'.*[1]

We put up with all this, though, because we know we can achieve far more collectively than we can as individuals. The better we cooperate, the better we get at advancing our interests and progressing our goals.

Most biologists now regard cooperation as a cornerstone of our evolutionary development, because it allows for the development of more complex structures and processes. As biologist Martin Nowak put it, *'without co-operation there is no construction'.*[2] In the complexities of the knowledge economy, good collaboration is vital to good business.

THE EVOLUTION OF COOPERATION

In the early 1980s, political scientist Robert Axelrod held tournaments to test the social mechanics of evolution.[3] Participants played the 'prisoner's dilemma', a classic puzzle in which two people must collaborate to win the game, but either side can also sell the other out.

The results of his experiments were surprising. Rather than the classic Darwinian principle of selfish competition, *'red in tooth and claw'*,[4] the strategy that actually proved most competitive was being generous and forgiving. This was particularly true when errors are introduced into the model. Human collaboration is not a perfect system – we forget our promises, mistake the intentions of others and believe people are competing with us when they are not – so we compensate for this by being 'generous, hopeful and forgiving'.[5]

We are told a story about evolution that it is a selfish competition in which the strongest survive, yet in fact we are living proof to the contrary. Remember that our young have to be born some nine months premature so their brains can keep growing.[6] We won the evolutionary game by learning to work together so we could take care of our young and grow these amazing brains.[7]

We are told a similar story about business too; that it is a selfish competition that pits us against each other in the jungle of the market. Yet what is a company if not a gift economy in which everyone agrees to share resources freely in their collective interest? The power of someone in a business lies in their ability to pick up the phone to someone else in the business and ask for a favour. Most managers know that efficiency depends on the goodwill of employees. Trust and loyalty are essential to good business.[8]

FROM ONE MIND TO ANOTHER

In order to collaborate, we need to share our ideas and experiences with each other, to explain our needs, pool our knowledge and work together for collective benefit. We call this process of passing information from one mind to another communication.

Communication is common throughout nature. Bird song, bee dances, ant trails – all of these are systems for transferring ideas from one creature's mind to another. Humans are not unique – even some types of fungus communicate[9] – but we are much better at it than other animals, particularly for sharing complex and abstract ideas. This is because we have evolved language.

Language is second nature to most of us and that can blind us to how clever it is. We convert our ideas into words and share these with someone else, and they gain an insight into what we are thinking or feeling.

We have a thought or feeling in mind, we 'encode' it as a message and transmit it to the other person. The recipient then 'decodes' our message and, hopefully, understands what we mean.[10]

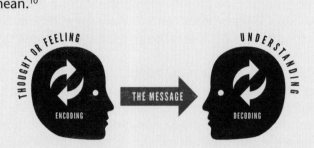

The trouble is that this process of encoding and decoding is difficult and often goes wrong. The action of putting thoughts into language inevitably distorts them, leaving out essential elements that are hard to express in words.

You can have a very clear set of images in your mind...

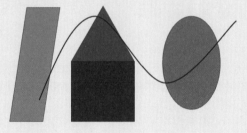

...but how people understand them may be a little different:[11]

Language is almost always an approximation of what is really going on in our heads. There is a difference between what you mean and what your words mean. No wonder, then, that we so often misunderstand each other.

READING BETWEEN THE LINES

To overcome the limitations of language, our minds have adapted to fill in the gaps in what people say, plugging them with our own knowledge to get a general sense of what things roughly mean.

The philosopher Slavoj Žižek gives a nice example of this from a scene in the film *Brassed Off*. A female character invites a man in for a coffee, but he says innocently that he doesn't like coffee. Her reply – that he doesn't have any coffee anyway – makes no sense on a literal level, but if we bring in our own experiences and cultural associations to it, the meaning becomes comically obvious.[12] There is more to this exchange than the literal meanings of the words. We make it more meaningful by the knowledge we bring to it, filling in the gaps ourselves.

In fact our minds are excellent at filling in the blanks. For instance, you can otefn siwcth the oderr of the lterets in a wrod, and as lnog as the frsit and lsat ltteer are in the rhgit pclae, you can sitll raed it whoutit a pboerlm.[13]

Our minds aren't designed to be literal, but to infer connections and find meaning in the world. As Daniel Kahneman puts it: *'The world makes more sense than it should, because we force it to make sense.'*[14]

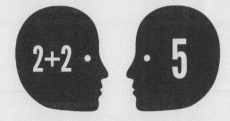

SIGNS AND SYMBOLS

To speed up this process, we rely on symbols. A cup of coffee, a house, a wedding ring – these ideas all signify something familiar to us. Signs and symbols help us get past basic concepts and share more advanced ideas.

If you were asked to draw a square with a triangle on top and four rectangles inside it, who knows what you might draw? But if you were asked to draw a house, you might very well draw something like this:

This is the power of symbols: they move ideas from one mind to another quicker than anything else.

We see the world as a series of symbols. We build up a conceptual map of reality and use it to communicate with each other. It isn't reality, but it works better.[15]

ON THE SAME WAVELENGTH

The meanings we make from other people's messages are shaped by our cultural assumptions and experiences.

If we have a similar view of the world, we understand each other better. If we lack common cultural reference points, we have to work harder to be understood.[16] Building a shared view of the world helps us communicate.

The language we speak can even affect how we think. English speakers, who tend to say *'John broke the vase'*, remember who caused accidents better than Spanish or Japanese speakers who might say *'the vase was broken'*.[17] The Pormpuraaw people in Australia who refer to directions as compass points, not left and right, excel at navigation.[18] The structure of our language shapes how we see the world.[19]

Studies of the neuroscience of communication even show that the process of sharing what is in our minds is quite physical. The brain patterns of people listening intently to a story seem to track those of the storyteller almost exactly. As one study put it, *'The more similar our brain patterns during a conversation, the better we understand each other'*.[20]

This is the power of communication. When we understand each other, our minds seem to synchronise – giving a literal meaning to the phrase 'on the same wavelength'.

MIXED MESSAGES

We rarely just say one thing. Alongside ideas and concepts, we also tell each other how we feel about each other, express status and social roles, and reinforce our relationships. If we aren't aware of this, we may communicate things we don't mean to, or that contradict what we're trying to say.

We can't always predict how our messages will be received, but we can be mindful of our language. There are many communication models around[21] but most of them boil down to a few key ingredients:

- **Use I statements**
  Rather than talking about the other person ('you're not making sense'), talk about yourself ('I don't understand'). It's harder to disagree with someone speaking from their own experience.
- **Separate facts from judgements**
  Rather than making claims like 'you're not listening', say 'I feel like you're not listening'. Learn to separate out what happened, and what you made it mean.
- **Ask open questions**
  Rather than closed questions ('are you going to reply to my email?') ask open questions that engage people's minds ('what did you think of my idea?').
- **Listen**
  Communication is a two-way street you know.

Many sources of misunderstanding and conflict stem from messy use of language. Good communication involves being mindful of the ideas, feelings, judgements and other messages you send out to others, and how they are being interpreted. This goes for non-verbal communication too.

NON-VERBAL COMMUNICATION

People often say that body language and other non-verbal cues make up most of our communication. This idea comes from a 1967 study by Albert Mehrabian which proposed the '7–38–55 rule', for the relative percentage impact of words, tone of voice and body language in communication.[22]

However, the original study related to feelings, not meaning. It found that non-verbal cues have a large impact on whether we like someone or not, and whether we believe what they're saying – but not on their underlying meaning. Mehrabian has often tried to correct the misinterpretation of his work.[23]

Non-verbal cues show us the feelings behind the words. Gestures show how you feel about your cashflow projections, but they won't explain how you arrived at them.

Our movements and actions often give away information about our state of mind and body. Physical cues are easiest, such as if someone appears tense or tired. If someone looks exhausted but says they have lots of energy, or says they are relaxed but is constantly biting their nails, this is telling you a lot about them.

Tone of voice and speed of speech are important too. Often people will say that it's not what you said that annoyed them, but how you said it. If you say things that don't match your tone, people may not believe you.

Beyond that though, it gets complicated: non-verbal cues can't be read like a book. Try to make sure what you say is supported and reinforced by your tone of voice and body language, but don't obsess over the details.

THE TROUBLE WITH EMAIL

Most modern businesses are drowning in email, and most of us have had emails misinterpreted at some point. Email has increased the speed of our communications, but also the frequency of our miscommunications.

The trouble is email misses out the non-verbal cues.[24]

In face-to-face communication, we rely heavily on these cues to gauge how people are feeling. We smile when we see them, sound interested when they speak, gauge their mood and reactions, and generally reinforce our relationship. Without these non-verbal cues, our minds have to fill in the blanks about the sender's feelings and intentions, leading to misunderstandings and damaged relationships.

We need to compensate for the lack of non-verbal cues in digital messages by showing how we feel in words:

- Open with a **social comment** to show you are interested in the person, not just the message.
- Err on the side of **positivity and friendliness** to compensate for the social distance of email.
- Remember that the recipient might be in a very **different mood** to you, so be sensitive to that.
- Tailor your tone to suit your relationship with the recipient and **show you remember them**.

New tools are being developed all the time – University of Washington scientists now claim to have created a wireless brain-to-brain interface[25] – but for now at least, we are limited to our current, imperfect forms of communication. There are no hard and fast rules for how to use technology: the most important thing is just to try to remain human.

CLEAR COMMUNICATION

Here are a few reminders to bear in mind when communicating with others, face-to-face or via technology.

Since your audience may not have the same set of shared assumptions as you, you may need to work harder to get some concepts across. Think about the knowledge and cultural background of your audience and tailor your message accordingly.

Define important words and explain unusual concepts so that everyone has a shared understanding. Sometimes what's obvious to you isn't obvious to anyone else. We learn things in small 'chunks' though, so make sure you **don't overwhelm people** with too many new concepts at once.[26]

Sometimes the words you say can trigger things in your audience that you didn't expect too. Identify and address any beliefs or assumptions that are stopping people from accepting your argument, and **avoid loaded terms** that could be misinterpreted by the listener.

Remember that people are busy too. Each communication is **a request for investment**. If you remember that every time you communicate you are asking for attention, you'll do it more carefully.

Sometimes people may just not like you of course, perhaps because of who you are or something you have done. So **be nice:** people will go to great lengths to avoid listening to someone they don't like.

Most of our problems communicating are not due to a lack of effort, but because communication is hard. Packaging up our thoughts into neat bundles of symbols and passing them between us inevitably leads to misunderstandings and lost messages. But when it works, it is wonderful.

DEALING WITH CONFLICT

Conflict is a natural part of collaboration. Whenever we work together, we are balancing our own needs with those of the people around us, and sometimes those needs clash.

Many conflicts arise from misunderstandings, so one way to resolve conflict is to gain a shared understanding of the situation. There may be differences in beliefs and experiences, unequal awareness of the current situation, or flawed logic leading people to different conclusions. Unravelling these can often cause the underlying conflict to unravel with it.

Sometimes, though, conflicts arise from a clash of needs or values and it is not practically possible for everyone to get what they want. In these situations careful communication is required to negotiate a solution.

It can be helpful to establish the reasons for disagreement, and to identify any unshared information and unconscious assumptions. Information is power. For example, some research suggests that the best strategy in an argument is not to argue back, but to ask the other person to explain how their idea would work.[27]

There are no hard and fast rules for conflict negotiation – every situation is different – but one popular framework is the Thomas-Kilmann Conflict Mode Instrument.[28] It proposes conflict and collaboration come from two opposing drivers:

- **Assertiveness**
  Pushing for your own needs
- **Cooperativeness**
  Satisfying the needs of others

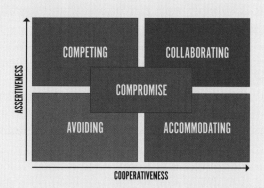

The Thomas-Kilmann model argues that we all have natural preferences for resolving conflict. If you are naturally accommodating, you may want to practise being more assertive about your needs. If you are naturally competitive, you may want to remind yourself about other people's needs.

The goal for both parties is collaboration, where both sides get their needs met, but in practice we spend a lot of our time in a state of compromise. You can't always get what you want, in life or in work, but if you try sometimes, so the saying goes, you might get what you need.

The best collaborations involve people being clear about their own needs, and supportive of others. As collaboration guru Khoi Tu put it, '*[teamwork] has to offer its members the best means for achieving their own ambitions.*'[29]

Think about what you want from your colleagues and work towards that. It's much easier for other people to collaborate with you if they know what you want.

WORKING IN GROUPS

When we work together we have the potential to be more than the sum of our parts.

Generally speaking, we are pretty good at working together. Most crowds are pretty good at self-organising, from drivers observing the rules of the road to strangers sitting quietly together in a cinema. When teams work, they combine the knowledge and skills of participants and work together smoothly to achieve more.

In some situations, groups can be wiser than individual experts. In his book *The Wisdom of Crowds*, James Surowiecki cites many examples where groups of people get things right that individual experts did not – from guessing the weight of a joint of beef to rescuing a lost submarine.[30] Scott Page also argues in *The Difference* that a diverse group outperforms experts.[31]

Sometimes, though, teams are much less wise than the individuals in them. They can be worse at answering factual questions than their members, and often reinforce members' prejudices and polarise in opinions rather than inspiring reasoned debate.[32]

Groups are prone to all the same biases as individual minds. Group members give more weight to their own positions and those that are similar to theirs.[33] They ignore information, dismiss challenges and refuse to go back on decisions, even in the face of overwhelming evidence.[34]

If they aren't properly managed, groups can end up being less than the sum of their parts. A person is smart, but people can be stupid. If groups aren't properly managed, they can end up being less than the sum of their parts.

AVOIDING GROUPTHINK

One of the biggest obstacles to collaboration is groupthink.

Groupthink is when a group prioritises consensus and won't tolerate dissent, resulting in decisions being made too quickly and without considering all the facts. Groups take on a life of their own, ignoring information and doing things that their individual members don't support privately. It has been blamed for some of the worst collective mistakes in history[35] and is why otherwise smart businesses ignore new trends, fail to adapt to changing markets and go out of business.

Groupthink stems partly from our natural adherence to social norms. Our instinct to follow the group consensus is often helpful – after all, no-one wants to go to a bar and have a two-hour argument about the best way to order a drink.[36] However, if everyone in a group has the same information, or is in a similar state of mind, they can all come to the same conclusions, and then gain confidence because they all agree.

We have fierce instincts to defend the group too. Members will tend to give preferential treatment to people in their group, which means anyone who is seen as an outsider is automatically at a disadvantage.[37] This keeps the group safe – except when the information being ignored is critical for their survival. This tribal instinct even seems to hold true if groups are completely random.[38]

Groups are more prone to groupthink if they have a forceful, dominant leader, are dealing with very stressful situations, or are isolated from external influences.[39]

Groupthink is the strength and the weakness of human groups: we form tight bonds, but this can get in the way of objective analysis. Groupthink happens because we prioritise getting along over getting it right.

It is possible to correct for groupthink, but only if the group is prepared to accept challenge. Groups that actively encourage free-thinking and dissent are less prone to groupthink.

Diversity is the enemy of groupthink. Diversity in a group improves its chances of making good decisions, particularly interdisciplinary groups with a diversity of knowledge and experience. If everyone in a group is bringing different perspectives, the chances of groupthink are reduced.[40]

However, diversity is only beneficial if we are also **open-minded** and interested in new perspectives. Sharing information, particularly unfamiliar information, is key. When someone in a group presents challenging ideas, they can often be ignored or excluded, so it is important to pay attention to the informed minority.[41] Successful groups incorporate novel, unfamiliar input in to their decisions.

Leaders play an important role here, and good leaders must create space for people to share information and disagree safely. Good leaders need to consider every perspective, and also decide whether the group has considered all the relevant information.[42]

External advisors can help too. The skill of influencing a group is to challenge its views without threatening the group or becoming seen as an outsider. Many consultants and thought leaders are experts in walking this delicate line and can help broaden the thinking of a group that has become stuck.

Stress and pressure make things worse of course. If the whole group is stressed, negative emotions can spread, narrowing everyone's thinking and making it harder to correct for bias or consider new views – so **keep people calm** if you can.

Often groupthink is the result of a pressure to 'get on with it'. **Take the time** to think about how you have arrived at decisions, and whether you have considered all the facts: if a few of you have a nagging sense you are missing something, you probably are, and someone needs to speak up.

HAVING BETTER MEETINGS

Pretty much everyone in business has to go to meetings, and most of us end up running them sometimes too – yet few of us are taught the basic principles of how they work. Perhaps this is why so many meetings are a waste of time.

One reason for this is that we have an unfortunate tendency to discuss things that everyone already knows rather than new material. When we share information others already know, we look more competent, credible and knowledgeable, and we tend to prefer to share, and hear, information that we already know and endorse.[43] This bonds the group together, but also wastes a lot of time.

Fear of getting it wrong is the enemy of collaboration. If people don't feel able to say what they really think in your meeting, you may be missing valuable insights that could help you. Remember that everyone's different too. People high in agreeableness or neuroticism may prefer consensus at the expense of criticism and debate, whilst people low in openness may be less willing to consider dissenting or contradictory views.[44]

Group size can make a difference too. When groups get too large – more than 16 people according to one practitioner[45] – it can be difficult for everyone to have their turn, which can hamper the flow of debate and mean people's ideas get wasted.[46] Extraverts may start to dominate, and quiet voices get lost in the crowd.

Remember too that people's mental energy levels affect their thoughts. The more people talk and make decisions in a meeting the more tired they will become. All too often meetings are full of good intentions, but let down because people are tired or distracted at the important moment.[47]

Here are a few principles for running better meetings.

- **Establish psychological safety**
  For instance, many organisations ask junior staff to give their opinions first in meetings, so that they can speak freely without fear of contradicting a more senior colleague. In his excellent book on creativity, *Zig Zag*, Keith Sawyer tells how Jon Citrin, CEO of the Citrin Group, even assigns someone in every meeting to disagree with everything he says. The result is deeper debate and serious consideration of the issues.[48]
- **Share new information**
  Sharing information can make groups wiser and more productive.[49] Groups that are specifically asked to pool information prior to reaching a decision are more likely to discuss previously unshared information.[50] Be explicit about the information and perspectives round the table and make sure all are considered in the meeting.
- **Manage the energy levels**
  Build in regular breaks, change the scenery and ensure everyone is fed and watered. Put the most difficult and important items first, when people have the most mental energy, and leave approving the minutes and reviewing paperclip expenditure to the end.
- **Have a clear purpose**
  Many meetings are a waste of time simply because we have them when we don't really need them. In fact, many meetings are just excuses to meet because people haven't sat down together for a while. We go along because we are afraid of being left out of the group.

So have fewer meetings, and invest time in getting them right. Focus on building relationships in your team and find ways for everyone to spend time together, and then you won't need to invent reasons to see each other.

GETTING ALONG

Much of what we say and do in groups is not about sharing knowledge, but about tending to relationships.

Groupthink and collective bias occur because we prioritise getting along over getting it right. The central importance of relationships to human collaboration explains why we sometimes favour consensus over reasoned debate, but also why we back up our colleagues and help strangers when they're lost.[51]

Much of our communication is about tending to our relationships. This isn't time-wasting, but an essential part of maintaining the neural connections between us. We keep the lines of communication open so that we are on the same wavelength when we have something important to say. Invest time in building relationships, and you may find communication and collaboration much easier.

Most of our collaboration problems come not from a lack of effort, but from the fact that collaboration is hard. Packaging up our thoughts into neat bundles of symbols and passing them between us is inevitably an imperfect process, and what we are thinking is unlikely to be the same as what everyone else is thinking. But when it works, it can transform the way we do business.

So have faith. Collaboration is messy but we get there in the end. As the movie producer Robert Evans once put it:[52]

> **There are three sides to every story: your side, my side, and the truth. And no one is lying.**

HABIT 9
INVEST TIME IN
RELATIONSHIPS AND SEEK OUT
DIVERSE OPINIONS TO AVOID
GROUPTHINK

WORK COLLABORATIVELY
IN A NUTSHELL

THE TWITTER VERSION

Collaboration is tricky, so communicate carefully, develop good relationships, and listen to people – even when they disagree with you.

THE SUMMARY VERSION

Communication is the process of getting ideas from one mind to another. When it goes well, we can share knowledge and skills and get more done. In fact, good collaboration is the building block for everything we're trying to achieve.

Good communication relies on shared concepts, so check that other people have the same understanding as you do of the words you're saying. Watch your body language and tone of voice too: they give away how you feel about what you're saying. Email is particularly tricky so compensate for the lack of non-verbal cues by expressing your emotions in messages.

Conflict is an inevitable flipside of collaboration. When you face conflict, start by getting a shared understanding, and then be clear about your needs as well as supportive of other people's: it is often possible to find win-win solutions.

There are particular things to bear in mind about groups too. Not all groups are wise: many ignore key information and prioritise getting along over getting things right. Seek out new information and dissenting voices to avoid groupthink and make teams more than the sum of their parts.

NOTES

1 **'Hell is other people.'** This line – in the original French, *'Enfer – c'est les autres'* – comes from Jean-Paul Sartre's 1944 play *Huis Clos*, although he later said the line had been misinterpreted.

2 **'without co-operation there is no construction'** Martin Nowak, quoted in Nowak, M. & Highfield, R. (2011). 'Supercooperators: The mathematics of evolution, altruism and human behaviour'. RSA Events, 2011. http://mindap.pl/1rTrOok.

3 **political scientist Robert Axelrod held tournaments..** Axelrod, R. (1984). *The Evolution of Cooperation*. Basic Books.

4 **'red in tooth and claw'** The line comes from Alfred, Lord Tennyson's 1849 poem 'In Memoriam A.H.H.', itself partly influenced by theories of natural selection, and it has been widely quoted in connection with Darwin and evolution ever since.

5 **we compensate for this by being 'generous, hopeful and forgiving'...** Martin Nowak, quoted in Nowak, M. & Highfield, R. (2011). 'Supercooperators: The mathematics of evolution, altruism and human behaviour'. RSA Events, 2011. http://mindap.pl/1rTrOok.

6 **some nine months premature...** See Chapter 1 for more on how our brains evolve and the implications of this for our natural development.

7 **We won the evolutionary game by learning to work together...** Further evidence of the 'evolution of cooperation' can be found in studies of instinctive fairness and cooperation in monkeys, such as Brosnan, S.F. & de Waal, F.B.M. (2003). 'Monkeys reject unequal pay'. *Nature*, 425: 297–299.

8 **efficiency depends on the goodwill of employees...** See for example the Japanese 'Human Relations' management school of the 1930s, cited for example in Chang, H-J. (2011). *23 Things They Don't Tell You About Capitalism*. Penguin, p. 47.

9 **even some types of fungus communicate...** Babikova, Z. et al (2013). 'Underground signals carried through common mycelial networks warn neighbouring plants of aphid attack'. *Ecology Letters*, 16(7): 835–843.

10 **we 'encode' it as a message and transmit it...** There are many theories of communication. Variants of this model also include noise, feedback and two-way communication, so things can get complicated pretty quickly. There is a nice discussion of this and other theories of communication in Krauss, R.M. & Fussell, S.R. (1996). 'Social psychological models of interpersonal communication'. In Higgins, E.T. & Kruglanski, A. (Ed.), *Social Psychology: Handbook of Basic Principles*. New York: Guilford Press , pp. 655–701.

11 **how people understand it may be very different...** These images come from exercises in Mindapples corporate training sessions, in which participants were asked to describe a picture to a colleague, who then redrew it – a representational model of the encoding-decoding process.

12 **a scene in the film *Brassed Off*...** *Brassed* Off (1996).

http://mindap.pl/1rp8qLV Quoted in Žižek, S. (2011). 'Great minds: Slavoj Žižek'. Intelligence Squared, Cadogan Hall, 1 July 2011 (c. 8 minutes). http://mindap.pl/ZizekIQ2.

13 **our minds are excellent at filling in the blanks...** This idea once circulated as a popular internet meme, but for a more detailed discussion of when and how it works see Rayner, K., White, S.J., Johnson, R.L. & Liversedge, S.P. (2006). 'Raeding wrods with jumbled lettres: There is a cost'. *Psychological Science*, 17: 192–193.

14 **'The world makes more sense than it should, because we force it to make sense.'** Quoted by the author from his 2014 lecture. Kahneman, D. (2014). *How To: Thinking, Fast and Slow*. Methodist Hall, 18 March 2014.

15 **We see the world as a series of symbols...** For a neuroscientific take on this, see Schapiro, A.C, Rogers, T.T., Cordova, N.I., Turk-Browne, N.B. & Botvinick, M.M. (2013). 'Neural representations of events arise from temporal community structure'. *Nature Neuroscience* 16(4): 486. Or for a more philosophical interpretation of language as symbols, see Wittgenstein, L. (1953). *Philosophical Investigations*. Blackwell.

16 **we find it easier to understand each other...** For one perspective on how communication becomes easier if we understand each other's world view, see for example Davidson, D. (1984). *Inquiries into Truth and interpretation*. Clarendon, New York.

17 **The language we speak can even affect how we think...** Fausey, C.M. & Boroditsky, L. (2011). 'Who dunnit? Cross-linguistic differences in eye-witness memory'. *Psychonomic Bulletin and Review* 18:150–157.

18 **The Pormpuraaw people in Australia...** Boroditsky, L. (2010). 'Lost in translation'. *Wall Street Journal*, 23 July 2010. http://mindap.pl/1hRvEla See this helpful piece on the TED blog too. http://mindap.pl/1kLSt5x.

19 **The structure of our language shapes our reality...** For a nice summary of the long-running debate about how, and how far, language limits our thoughts, see this *New York Times* article Deutscher, G. (2010). 'Does your language shape how you think?' *New York Times Magazine*, 26 August 2010. http://mindap.pl/1qK0nZJ.

20 **'The more similar our brain patterns during a conversation, the better we understand each other'** Quoted in Coghlan, A. (2010). 'We humans can mind-meld too'. *New Scientist*, 26 July 2010. http://mindap.pl/1tbOKh5. The original study is Stephens, G.J., Silbert, L.J. & Hasson, U. (2010). 'Speaker-listener neural coupling underlies successful communication'. *PNAS*, 107(32). See also Hasson, U., Ghazanfar, A.A., Galantucci, B., Garrod, S. & Keysers, C. (2012). 'Brain-to-brain coupling: A mechanism for creating and sharing a social world'. *Trends in Cognitive Sciences*, 16(2): 114–121. This is also related to mirror neurons, described in more detail in Chapter 8.

21 **There are many communication models around...** See for instance 'non-violent communication', 'active listening', 'clean language', the work of

Carl Rogers and Thomas Gordon amongst others, and many other conflict-resolution and therapeutic approaches.

22 **a classic study by Albert Mehrabian which proposed the '7–38–55 rule'...** This 'rule' actually comes from two studies: Mehrabian, A. & Wiener, M. (1967). 'Decoding of inconsistent communications'. *Journal of Personality and Social Psychology*, 6(1): 109–114. And Mehrabian, A. & Ferris, S.R. (1967). 'Inference of attitudes from nonverbal communication in two channels'. *Journal of Consulting Psychology*, 31 (3): 248–252.

23 **Mehrabian has often tried to correct the misinterpretation of his work...** In fact the study authors never actually claimed theirs was a generalised theory of communication. See for example the disclaimer on Mehrabian's own website: http://mindap.pl/1uF1Eov.

24 **The trouble with email...** This is obviously not a unique problem with email: phone calls, letters and other tools miss out aspects of non-verbal communication. The trouble with email and other digital messaging tools is that they miss out all of these cues whilst also speeding up our communications.

25 **a wireless brain-to-brain interface...** The pilot research was conducted by Rajesh Rao, Andrea Stocco and Chantel Prat in August 2013 and covered extensively by the media, including in Thomas, B. (2013). 'Welcome to the mind-meld: Our future of brain-to-brain communication' *Discover Magazine* blog, 25 October 2013. http://mindap.pl/1cat4fo.

26 **We learn things in small 'chunks'...** For more on the benefits of 'chunking' for how we take on information, see Chapter 6.

27 **the best strategy in an argument is not to argue back...** Fernbach, P.M., Rogers, T., Fox, C.R. & Sloman, S.A. (2013). 'Political extremism is supported by an illusion of understanding'. *Psychological Science*, 24(6): 939–946.

28 **the Thomas-Kilmann Conflict Mode Instrument...** Kilmann, R.H. & Thomas, K.W. (1977). Modified and reproduced by special permission of the Publisher, CPP, Inc., Mountain View, CA 94043 from the Thomas-Kilmann Conflict Mode Instrument by Kenneth W. Thomas and Ralph H. Kilmann. Copyright 1974, 2002 by CPP, Inc. All rights reserved. Further reproduction is prohibited without the Publisher's consent.

29 **'[teamwork] has to offer its members the best means for achieving their own ambitions.'** Tu, K. (2012). 'The secrets of superteams'. RSA Events, 1 November 2012. http://mindap.pl/RSAsuperteams.

30 **In his book *The Wisdom of Crowds*...** Surowiecki, J. (2004). *The Wisdom of Crowds*. Little, Brown. See also a classic overview of the benefits of groups in Barnlund, D.C. (1959). 'A comparative study of individual, majority, and group judgment'. *The Journal of Abnormal and Social Psychology*, 58(1): 55–60.

31 **a diverse group outperforms experts...** Page, S.E. (2007). *The Difference: How The Power of Diversity Creates Better Groups, Firms, Schools, and Societies*. New Jersey: Princeton University Press.

32 **can reinforce members' prejudices...** Isenberg, D.J. (1986). 'Group polarization: A critical review and meta-analysis'. *Journal of Personality and Social Psychology*, 50(6): 1141–1151. And see also the exploration in Sunstein, C. R. (2002). 'The law of group polarization'. *Journal of Political Philosophy*, 10: 175–195.

33 **give more weight to their own positions...** Yaniv, I.I. & Kleinberger E. (2000). 'Advice taking in decision making: Egocentric discounting and reputation formation'. *Organisational Behaviour and Human Decision Processes*, 83(2): 260–281.

34 **Groups are prone to all the same biases...** Kerr, N.L. & Tindale, R.S. (2004). 'Group performance and decision making'. *Annual Review of Psychology*, 55: 623–55.

35 **Groupthink has been blamed for some of the worst mistakes in human collaboration...** For a round-up of the impact of groupthink, try Merchant, K.A. & Pick, K. (2010). *Blind Spots, Biases and Other Pathologies in the Boardroom*. Business Expert Press, Chapter 5. See also the classic work on the subject, Janis, I. L. (1982). *Groupthink: Psychological Studies of Policy Decisions and Fiascoes*. Cengage Learning.

36 **Our instinct to follow the group consensus is often helpful...** For more on the positive benefits of social norms, see Basu, K. (1983). 'On why we do not try to walk off without paying after a taxi ride'. *Economic and Political Weekly*, 18(48).

37 **anyone who is seen as an outsider...** Mackie, D.M., Devos, T. & Smith, E.R. (2000). 'Intergroup emotions: Explaining offensive action tendencies in an intergroup context'. *Journal of Personality and Social Psychology* 79(4): 602. See also Brewer, M.B. (1999), 'The psychology of prejudice: Ingroup love and outgroup hate?' *Journal of Social Issues*, 55: 429–444.

38 **if groups are completely random...** Billig, M. & Tajfel, H. (2006). 'Social categorization and similarity in intergroup behaviour'. *European Journal of Social Psychology*, 3(1): 27–52.

39 **Groups are more prone to groupthink...** This helpful summary of the factors that contribute to groupthink comes from Freeman, D. & Freeman, J. (2010). *Use Your Head: The Inside Track on the Way We Think*. John Murray, chapter 13.

40 **Diversity is the enemy of groupthink...** Horwitz, S.K. & Horwitz, I.B. (2007). 'The effects of team diversity on team outcomes: A meta-analytic review of team demography'. *Journal of Management*, 33(6): 987–1015.

41 **keep crucial information to themselves...** Stewart, D. D. & Stasser, G. (1998). 'The sampling of critical, unshared information in decision-making groups: The role of an informed minority'. *European Journal of Social Psychology*, 28: 95–113.

42 **Good leaders need to consider every perspective...** Homan, A.C. & Greer, L.L. (2013). 'Considering diversity: The positive effects of considerate leadership in diverse teams'. *Group Processes & Intergroup Relations*, 16: 105–125.

43 **an unfortunate tendency to discuss things that everyone already knows...** Greitemeyer, T. & Schulz-Hardt, S. (2003). 'Preference-consistent evaluation of information in the hidden profile paradigm: Beyond group-level explanations for the dominance of shared information in group decisions'. *Journal of Personality and Social Psychology*, 84: 322–339.

44 **everyone's different too...** See Chapter 5 for more on how our personality traits affect our behaviour.

45 **more than 16 people...** Turquet, P.M. (1974). 'Leadership: The individual and the group'. In Gibbard, G.S., Hartman, J.J. & Mann, R.D. (1974). *Analysis of Groups.* Jossey-Bass.

46 **people's ideas get wasted...** Stroebe, W. & Diehl, M. (1994). 'Why groups are less effective than their members: On productivity losses in idea-generating groups'. *European Review of Social Psychology*, 5(1): 271–303.

47 **people are tired or distracted at the important moment...** Remember the experiment on hungry, tired judges? See Chapter 7 for more on how our mental resources affect our decisions.

48 **In his excellent book on creativity, Zig Zag...** Sawyer, K. (2013). *Zig Zag: The Surprising Path to Greater Creativity.* Jossey-Bass, p. 191.

49 **Sharing new information well can make groups wiser and more productive...** Reiter-Palmon, R., de Vreede, T. & de Vreede, G-J. (2013). 'Leading interdisciplinary creative teams. Challenges and solutions'. In Hemlin, S., Allwood, C.M, Martin, B. & Mumford, M.D. (2013). *Creativity and Leadership in Science, Technology and Innovation.* New York: Routledge.

50 **Groups that are specifically asked to pool information...** Stewart, D.D. & Stasser, G. (1995). 'Expert role assignment and information sampling during collective recall and decision making'. *Journal of Personality and Social Psychology*, 69(4): 619–28.

51 **The central importance of relationships...** Gere, J. & MacDonald, G. (2010). 'An update of the empirical case for the Need to Belong'. *Journal of Individual Psychology*, 66: 93–115.

52 **'There are three sides to every story: your side, my side, and the truth. And no-one is lying.'** Evans, R., (2004) *The Kid Stays in the Picture: A Hollywood Life.* Faber & Faber.

CHAPTER 10
THINK CREATIVELY

Invention. Imagination. Innovation. Ingenuity. Creativity is a subject overrun with clichés, conjuring up images of 'blue sky' thinking, beanbags and brainstorming meetings.

Yet creativity is a pretty serious business. The ability to come up with new ideas and solutions to problems drives progress and has given us the tools and technologies that we rely on today. Businesses recruit for it, schools are asked to nurture it, and most of us like to think we have it.

Creativity is unusual for being an area of psychology that investors care about. The economist Clayton Christensen once said that *'innovation is the target of investment, and investment is the fuel that keeps the economy going'.*[1]

The right innovations can empower customers, making products simpler and more affordable, improving people's quality of life, generating new revenue streams and creating more jobs. In Christensen's view, creativity is the key to business growth and the growth of the economy.[2]

TYPES OF CREATIVITY

Creativity is a very broad topic in psychology and most researchers distinguish between two types of creativity:[3]

- **'Large C' creativity**
  Arts, music, creative pursuits
- **'Small c' creativity**
  Creative thinking and innovation

Creative thinking is about pattern recognition, divergent thinking and non-linear problem-solving, coming up with fresh perspectives and seeing unexpected possibilities.

There is more to creativity than mere novelty. If every new idea were creative then a random number generator would be creative. Not all new ideas are creative, and not all creative ideas are new. Psychologist J. C. Flanagan defined creative thinking as doing things in *'an unusually neat, clever, or surprising way'*.[4] The quality of a creative idea is to make us wish we'd thought of it.

Creativity is more than an intellectual exercise too; it is very practical. In fact philosopher Robert Nozick defined creativity as a combination of novelty and utility: *'How creative something is depends both upon how novel it is and upon how valuable it is; and each of these has degrees.'*[5]

Although it is often argued that 'large C' creativity involves some degree of innate talent, 'small c' creative thinking is generally seen as a process. It is possible to practise creative thinking, and to support people to think in more creative ways, including through business practices. This type of creativity can be learned.

THE CREATIVE MIND

When we are faced with a problem, our instinct is often to focus on it and try to 'think it through'. This can be particularly true at work, when we have limited time and resources and our creativity is confined to short bursts.

Creative thinking works differently though: consciously 'working on it' can actually make it harder to find the solution. As the researcher Jonathan Schooler puts it: *'[we] assume that you get more done when you're consciously paying attention to a problem...but this is often a mistake'*.[6]

We can find a more fruitful approach to creative thinking by returning to the 'two systems thinking' model popularised by Daniel Kahneman.[7] We like to use our controlled 'System 2' for solving problems – seeking rational arguments and analysing things systematically. It feels like putting more conscious attention on the problem makes our minds more likely to give us the answer.

The trouble is that too much controlled thinking can make us narrow and linear, and less able to spot connections and find unexpected solutions. The more we focus on the problem, the more we lose sight of unexpected connections.

Kaufman and Singer proposed that creativity is not found in the controlled, rational System 2, but in our more intuitive, emotional System 1. The interaction between these two systems allows us to apply intuitive thinking to rational problems:[8]

> 'One of the wonders of system 1 is its ability to feed creative insights to system 2. This often happens precisely when system 2 is taking a rest.'

FLEXING YOUR MIND

The trick, then, is to give your unconscious, associative thought processes the freedom to roam. Letting our minds wander can increase our ability to find creative solutions. When we leave our conscious minds clear to think freely, we make space for our unconscious minds to make creative associations for us – the classic 'moment of inspiration'.[9]

Creativity research then points in the opposite direction to most studies on attention, memory and productivity. Concentration might actually be bad for creativity. Taking short breaks, daydreaming and 'switching off' between creative tasks can aid creative thinking.[10] There is even one experiment that suggests the relaxing effect of two pints of beer can make men 40 per cent better at lateral thinking.[11]

Our conscious minds still play an important role in creative thinking though: creativity comes not from unconscious intuition alone, but from the interplay between our experiential and rational thinking styles. Perhaps this might explain our reliance on alcohol for inspiration and coffee to get things done.

Kaufman and Singer neatly summed it up like this:[12]

'The key to both intelligence and creativity is the ability to flexibly switch between different modes of thought depending on the task demands.'

If there is a skill to practise with creativity, it is that of switching fluently between different ways of thinking, moving seamlessly from intuition to analysis and keeping your mind in a state of playful productivity.

INCREASING YOUR CREATIVITY

There are many things we can do to help our minds to work in this more flexible, creative way. Particular contexts can make it easier for us to think creatively, and we can also learn various techniques for breaking out of a fixed analytic style into a more flexible, creative mindset.

Since creativity relies on your unconscious mind, keeping yourself physically and emotionally healthy can affect your creative performance. Take regular breathers and restorers and find time to recharge. **Give your mind energy** to make creative associations for you, and watch it work.

A little light distraction can be stimulating, except when it disturbs our peace of mind. Distracting **noises** can be problematic, and so too can silence. We're all different, but the average noise level that seems to be most conducive to creative thought is around seventy decibels – about the level of a coffee shop.[13]

Nature is also good for creativity: walking in nature for as little as twenty minutes can aid problem solving, and even looking at pictures of natural scenes can help our minds switch out of fixed modes and think more freely.[14] In fact, **walking** can be helpful for creativity generally.[15]

Anything that lets you 'switch off' tends to be helpful. One study even suggested the benefits of **mindless work** interspersed between more challenging tasks to give our minds space to think.[16]

Generally speaking, most things that help us **stay healthy and rested** will also aid our creativity. The more mental energy we have, the more successful we get at making those all-important unconscious connections.

A CREATIVE MOOD?

There is some evidence that we are more creative when we are in a positive mood. Positive emotions can make us more open to new ideas and possibilities and can help us spot things we might otherwise have missed.[17]

Stress is particularly bad for creativity: when we are stressed, our focus narrows and our minds become closed – a survival mechanism to make sure we give our attention to immediate threats. This means we tend to miss creative possibilities. Creativity involves playfulness. It is very difficult to be playful when you feel afraid.

We also need to feel motivated to be creative. Decades of research have now shown that external incentives such as money or power are less effective for promoting creativity than more intrinsic, inner drivers like deeply held beliefs and valued social relationships. If we don't feel motivated to do a task, we might be able to force ourselves to do it on a conscious level – but it is very difficult to force our unconscious mind to engage fully.

Negative emotions can be helpful in focussing our minds on the problem though, and making us more determined to solve it, so the old cliché of the 'tortured artist' may hold true to some extent. Being aware of your emotional state and understanding the impact it has on your ability to focus, make connections and see possibilities can help you maintain your creativity in the face of challenges and adversity.[18]

PROBLEM CONSTRUCTION

Alongside these contextual and emotional factors, some cognitive tricks can help us think more creatively. The first is to examine how we are defining a problem.

When we consider any new situation, our minds make immediate assumptions about it. Some of these assumptions can be useful, helping us to focus our minds and select ideas. Ask someone to 'come up with an idea' and they may not know where to start; we naturally create constraints and conditions for our thinking to help us focus our minds better.

However, these assumptions can also trap us into closed thinking and cause us to edit out legitimate possibilities without even realising it. Paying closer attention to how we are unconsciously constructing a problem can help us spot creative solutions we may otherwise disregard.

Try this one for example. Join all nine dots with just four straight lines, without taking your pen from the paper:

Here is the solution: the puzzle can only be solved by taking the lines outside the 'box' of dots.

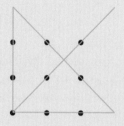

Most of us unconsciously assume that the puzzle must be solved within the box, even though that was not included in the puzzle instructions. In fact this puzzle is thought to be the origin of the phrase 'thinking outside the box'.[19]

The point behind this well-worn phrase is that our minds impose additional constraints on our thinking and make the problem impossible to solve. Learning how to frame problems more flexibly can lead to more original solutions.

The next time you are stuck on a problem, try restating it in different words, and write down your assumptions about it. The more you play with the precise parameters of the problem, the more you may notice any false assumptions you have made.

This process can aid creativity and divergent thinking, and practising problem definition seems to help train your mind to make more accurate assumptions about problems – helping you notice what is really possible.

FUNCTIONAL FIXEDNESS

We can also get distracted by the conventions about how things can be used – a bias known as 'functional fixedness'.

One good way to practise this is the 'alternative uses' exercise proposed by J P Guilford.

You can try this exercise yourself now: all you need to do is spend a minute now thinking of as many uses as you can for a coat hanger.[20]

Challenging assumptions and seeing objects for their basic properties can help us spot new possibilities. Some studies even suggest that exercises like this can increase our capacity to produce ideas by 67 per cent.[21] Creativity guru Edward de Bono also advises playing with stupid ideas and 'intermediate impossibilities' to expand your thinking.[22] Your final ideas need to be practical, but the steps you take to get there don't have to be.

Consider your assumptions about the coat hanger. Was it made of wire or something else? How big was it? Did you keep it in the same form or disassemble it? Did you assume, perhaps, that the coat hanger in question was the one pictured above, and not just any coat hanger as the problem says?

The more familiar things are, the harder it can be to see new possibilities in them. Creativity involves unpicking your experiences of the world, unlearning what you have learnt. The more aware you can be of your assumptions, the more possibilities you begin to see.

MENTAL DISTANCE

Questioning assumptions and redefining problems is easier when we have perspective on the situation.

Most of us find it easier to solve other people's problems than our own. The reason for this may be that we tend to be more creative about problems that feel a long way from our own experiences.

Anything that gives us distance from a problem seems to help us spot possibilities.[23] People who imagine themselves in the distant future[24] or a faraway land[25] tend to solve more insight problems. Telling people the situation is unlikely to happen can also enhance their creativity.[26]

We are also more creative when we engage in unrelated thoughts and tune out from the current demands of our surroundings. This is a form of 'mind wandering' and can be achieved by disengaging attention from what you are doing and getting perspective on your current thoughts. Whilst other tasks require focus, creativity requires distraction.[27]

One of the best ways to get distance from a problem is to go to sleep. One study showed that when participants in a pattern-recognition puzzle were allowed to sleep on it, the proportion solving it rose from 20 per cent to 60 per cent.[28]

So when you feel stuck in closed ways of thinking and need a fresh perspective, sleeping on it really can help.

WORKING ON IT

Perhaps the most important thing to remember in creative thinking is simply not to give up.

We are so used to solving problems in controlled, analytic ways that the unpredictable processes of creative thinking can feel frustrating – causing us to give up just as our minds start to make connections.

It may be that the most creative people just spend more time on problems. They are willing to tolerate the discomfort of not having a solution for longer before closing off the alternatives. Try to enjoy the process of exploration and defer the solution until the last possible moment whilst you try out potential solutions, to give your mind time to think about it.

There are still many things you can do to increase the chances of coming up with new ideas. Try this checklist for approaching problems and thinking more creatively:

• Find a relaxed and stimulating environment
• Keep yourself healthy and well-rested
• Manage your moods and emotional states
• Keep a healthy distance and perspective
• Redefine and rewrite the problem itself
• Write down and challenge your assumptions
• Play with stupid, impractical ideas
• Let your mind wander and even sleep on it
• Stay with it. Inspiration will come...

FROM CREATIVITY TO INNOVATION

Creativity is only useful if we can put it to use to solve problems, create new things and improve our lives. To do this, we need to look beyond just creating ideas, and explore how to refine them and apply them.

Unlike the pure process of creative thinking, practical creativity is a more collective endeavour. We tend to be better at solving problems when we work together, so putting ideas into practice usually involves working with other people and harnessing the creativity of teams.

In fact, most of the really difficult problems facing us today require a range of skills and perspectives to solve. As one study on creative teams puts it: *'the problems that organizations face today are generally too complex for one individual or a team from one discipline to solve'.*[29]

If we want to put our creativity to use, we need to learn how to share our skills, test our ideas and become more creative together. Collaboration is an important ingredient of creativity.[30]

In a business context, this means getting people in your organisation to think creatively together, and also putting the resulting ideas to good use to deliver commercial value. Both of these require us to work together in teams.

BRAINSTORMING

Brainstorming was first popularised in the 1950s by the advertising executive Alex Osborn as a technique for generating ideas in groups. The rules he proposed were fairly simple: say every idea that comes into your mind, the more the better, and don't criticise any of them, and then improve the ideas and combine them together.[31]

Brainstorming is an incredibly popular technique for group creativity yet, surprisingly, it can be less effective than working separately. The brainstorming process can prevent productive trains of thought from flowing: people have to wait a long time to speak and good ideas can get lost.[32]

However, other studies have shown that the efficacy of brainstorming varies a lot by how it is conducted.[33] Here are a few things to consider for successful brainstorming:

- **Facilitation matters**
  Brainstorming works best with a trained facilitator, one who can ensure everyone's ideas are heard.[34]
- **Size matters**
  Waiting time increases with group size, so keep brainstorming groups to fewer than ten people.[35]
- **Criticism is useful**
  Make it safe for people to say what they really think, including if they disagree.[36]
- **Digital tools can help**
  For large groups, try using technology so participants can share ideas anonymously and asynchronously.[37]

CREATIVE TEAMS

Four things in particular can make a team more creative.

The first is **proper resourcing**. Although a lack of resources can sometimes inspire ingenuity, more often it gets in the way, particularly when it stops people from doing useful things to progress their thinking like spending time on the problem, creating prototypes or holding meetings.[38]

The second is **motivation**. External incentives alone are inadequate for inspiring us to be creative: we can force ourselves to go to work, but we find it much harder to use our willpower to make our subconscious more creative. For creativity, we need inner drive for the task.[39] Lack of resources can also have an impact on motivation and harm a group's creativity in that way.[40]

The third is **diversity**. More diverse teams tend to come up with more creative solutions to problems, particularly groups with very different skills or experience. Diverse perspectives are only valuable if team members are open-minded enough to listen to them though, so diversity must be accompanied by a tolerant, open team culture.[41]

The fourth is **psychological safety**. Encouraging safe reflection and discussion of ideas is important. This doesn't just mean being positive about everything: criticism is actually good for creativity, enabling us to refine and improve ideas and make solutions that work in practice. Highly creative teams tend to be comfortable with critiquing each other's ideas without fear of causing offence.[42]

The principles of individual creativity apply here too. Just like individuals, creative teams also need to get comfortable questioning their assumptions, redefining problems together, and taking time to think and reflect.

GETTING BACK INTO DOING MODE

Most studies on brainstorming and creativity focus on the number and variety of ideas produced. Yet creativity does not stop at idea generation. Once you have a promising idea, there is still a long way to go before you know if it works in practice.

This is where 'innovation' comes in: not simply coming up with nice ideas, but applying these ideas successfully to business practices and commercial models. As Jamie Young puts it in his RSA paper *How to be ingenious*, *'if creativity is the process that conceives of new ideas, then innovation is the process that executes them'.*[43]

Sooner or later then, we need to get back into 'doing mode' and turn our ideas into action. The danger, though, is that teams often become less creative once a decision has been made and implementation begins.

In fact though, prototyping, piloting, evaluating and reviewing ideas are all part of the creative process too, and all require the same principles of creative thought. Staying creative when testing and implementing ideas is an important ingredient of successful innovation.

Innovation is not a separate department, but a daily habit, something encoded into the culture of your business. Creativity is about how we work, and any business, and any team, can approach its work in a creative way.

Innovation researcher Richard Florida has argued that we need to find ways to make all our work creative, and bring creativity into every part of our economy.[44] After all, it is a skill that anyone can learn, and you never know where good ideas might come from.

A CREATIVE BUSINESS

The key to fostering a creative culture in your business is flexibility. As with individual creativity, innovation does not come from a single process or method, but from a mental agility to switch between different styles of working.

To return to Kaufman and Singer, creativity is 'the ability to flexibly switch between different modes of thought'.[45]

The most important thing is not to get stuck in a particular way of working. Creativity is found not in focus, or in distraction, but in the gap in between.

Creative businesses excel at switching modes. The more fluent we can become collectively at switching between focussed productivity and playful exploration, the more creative our businesses will become. Traditional business practice is to create procedures for everything, to do things the same way every time. Creative businesses are able to switch from process thinking to playful thinking, questioning their assumptions and trying new approaches all the time.

This may present more challenges for managing and scaling operations, but these businesses are more likely to thrive in a changing market. Approach your business in a playful manner, even under pressure, and you may find you get some surprisingly serious results.

Creativity is the closest thing we have to a scalable asset, and we need to nurture it. As Maya Angelou once put it:[46]

> You can't use up creativity.
> The more you use, the more
> you have.

HABIT 10
SWITCH FLEXIBLY BETWEEN DIFFERENT MODES OF THOUGHT TO KEEP YOUR MIND CREATIVE

THINK CREATIVELY
IN A NUTSHELL

THE TWITTER VERSION

Creativity is essential in business, so make your mind flexible by questioning assumptions, playing with ideas and sticking with problems.

THE SUMMARY VERSION

Businesses need creativity because creativity drives business growth. New products and new markets depend on staff being creative, and businesses that are better at innovation also tend to do better in a changing market.

Creativity can be learnt – at least in terms of creative problem solving. It comes from flexibly switching your mind between analytic thinking and playful exploration. The more fluent you are at switching modes of thought, the more creative you can become.

Some things enhance creativity: positive moods, high wellbeing, inner drive for the task and freedom from stress and worry can all help us be more creative. There are other techniques too, such as unpicking problems and questioning your assumptions. And if in doubt, sleep on it.

Creativity isn't just an individual pursuit though: put ideas to the test by trying them out early on, and use small groups to brainstorm ideas. Critique ideas too though: editing is part of the creative process. Switch back into doing mode as soon as you can – but remember to stay flexible.

NOTES

1   'innovation is the target of investment, and investment is the fuel
    that keeps the economy going.' Christensen, C. (2013). 'The capitalist's
    dilemma' at the Royal Society for the Encouragement of Arts, Manufactures &
    Commerce, London, 9 September 2013. http://mindap.pl/1hRuX1D.

2   creativity is the key to business growth... More detail on Christensen's
    theories can be found in Christensen, C. (2013). *The Innovator's Dilemma:
    When New Technologies Cause Great Firms to Fail*. Harvard Business School
    Publishing.

3   researchers distinguish between two types of creativity... There are
    naturally many debates about how to define creativity, but see for example
    Plucker, J.A., Beghetto, R.A. & Dow, G.T. (2004). 'Why isn't creativity more
    important to educational psychologists? Potentials, pitfalls, and future
    directions in creativity research'. *Educational Psychologist*, 39(2): 83–96. A
    more complex model is proposed in Kaufman, J.C. & Beghetto, R.A. (2009).
    'Beyond big and little: The four c model of creativity'. *Review of General
    Psychology*, 13(1): 1–12.

4   'an unusually neat, clever, or surprising way' Flanagan, J.C. (1963).
    'The definition and measurement of ingenuity'. In Taylor, C.W. & Barron, F.
    (1963). *Scientific Creativity. Its Recognition and Development*. John Wiley.

5   'How creative something is depends both upon how novel it is and
    upon how valuable it is' Nozick, R. (1989). *The Examined Life: Philosophical
    Meditations*. Simon & Schuster.

6   '[we] assume that you get more done when you're consciously
    paying attention...' Jonathan Schooler, quoted in Lehrer, J.
    (2012). 'The virtues of daydreaming'. *The New Yorker*, 5 June 2012.
    http://mindap.pl/1uadnvV.

7   The 'two systems thinking' model... Kahneman, D. (2012). *Thinking, Fast
    and Slow*. Penguin. See also Stanovich, K.E. & West, R.F. (2000). 'Individual
    differences in reasoning: Implications for the rationality debate?' *Behavioral
    and Brain Sciences*, 23: 645–726.

8   'One of the wonders of system 1 is its ability to feed creative
    insights to system 2...' Kaufman, S.B. & Singer, J.L. (2012). 'The creativity
    of dual process "System 1" thinking'. *Scientific American* blog, 17 January
    2012. http://mindap.pl/1u9WUIh.

9   Letting our minds wander... See for example Takeuchi, H., Taki, Y.,
    Hashizume, H., Sassa, Y., Nagase, T., Nouchi, R. & Kawashima, R. (2011).
    'Failing to deactivate: the association between brain activity during a working
    memory task and creativity'. *NeuroImage*, 55(2): 681–7.

10 Taking short breaks... Baird, B., Smallwood, J., Mrazek, M.D., Kam,
    J.W., Franklin, M.S. & Schooler, J.W. (2012). 'Inspired by distraction mind
    wandering facilitates creative incubation'. *Psychological Science,* 23(10):
    1117–1122.

11 the relaxing effect of two pints of beer... Jarosz, A.F., Colflesh, G.J. &

Wiley, J. (2012). 'Uncorking the muse: Alcohol intoxication facilitates creative problem solving'. *Consciousness and Cognition*, 21: 487–493.

12 **'The key to both intelligence and creativity is the ability to flexibly switch between different modes of thought...'** Kaufman, S.B. & Singer, J.L. (2012). 'The creativity of dual process "System 1" thinking'. *Scientific American*, blog, 17 January 2012. http://mindap.pl/1u9WUIh.

13 **about the level of a coffee shop...** Mehta, R., Zhu, R. & Cheema, A. (2012). 'Is noise always bad? Exploring the effects of ambient noise on creative cognition'. *Journal of Consumer Research*, 39: 784–99.

14 **Nature is also good for creativity...** Atchley, R.A., Strayer, D.L. & Atchley, P. (2012). 'Creativity in the wild: Improving creative reasoning through immersion in natural settings'. *PLoS ONE* 7(12): e51474.

15 **walking can be helpful for creativity...** Oppezzo, M. & Schwartz, D.L. (2014). 'Give your ideas some legs: The positive effect of walking on creative thinking'. *Journal of Experimental Psychology: Learning, Memory, and Cognition*, 40(4): 1142–1152.

16 **the benefits of mindless work...** Elsbach, K.D. & Hargadon, A.B. (2006). 'Enhancing creativity through "mindless" work: A framework of workday design'. *Organization Science*, 17(4): 470–483.

17 **we are more creative when we are in a positive mood...** For a review of the effects of emotions on creativity, see Baas, M., De Dreu, C.K. & Nijstad, B.A. 2008. 'A meta-analysis of 25 years of mood-creativity research: Hedonic tone, activation, or regulatory focus?' *Psychological Bulletin*, 134: 779–806.

18 **Negative emotions can be helpful...** Bledow, R., Rosing, K. & Frese, M. (2013). 'A dynamic perspective on affect and creativity'. *Academy of Management Journal*, 56(2): 432–450.

19 **Join all nine dots with just four straight lines...** This puzzle is found in many management books and was apparently first recorded in the early twentieth century. It is thought to be the origin of the infamous phrase 'thinking outside the box'. There is a nice exploration of it and other variants – and a solution with just three lines – in Sawyer, K. (2013). *Zig Zag: The Surprising Path to Greater Creativity*. Jossey-Bass.

20 **the 'alternative uses' exercise proposed by J P Guilford...** Guilford, J.P. (1967). *The Nature of Human Intelligence*. McGraw-Hill.

21 **seeing objects for their basic properties...** McCaffrey, T. (2012). 'Innovation relies on the obscure: A key to overcoming the classic problem of functional fixedness'. *Psychological Science* 23: 215.

22 **Edward de Bono also advises playing with 'intermediate impossibilities'...** de Bono, E. (1973). *Po: Beyond Yes and No*. Penguin.

23 **Anything that gives us 'mental distance'...** For a review of this see Trope, Y., Liberman, N. & Wakslak, C. (2007). 'Construal levels and psychological distance: Effects on representation, prediction, evaluation, and behavior'. *Journal of Consumer Psychology*, 17(2): 83–95.

24 **People who imagine themselves in the distant future...** Förster, J.,

Friedman, R.S. & Liberman, N. (2004). 'Temporal construal effects on abstract and concrete thinking: Consequences for insight and creative cognition'. *Journal of Personality and Social Psychology*, 87: 177–189.

25 **or a faraway land...** Jia, L., Hirt, E.R. & Karpen, S.C. (2009). 'Lessons from a faraway land: The effect of spatial distance on creative cognition'. *Journal of Experimental Social Psychology*, 45(5): 1127–1131.

26 **Telling people the situation is unlikely to happen...** Schooler, J.W., Smallwood, J., Christoff, K, Handy, T.C., Reichle, E.D. & Sayette, M.A. (2011). 'Meta-awareness, perceptual decoupling and the wandering mind'. *Trends in Cognitive Science,* 15: 319–326.

27 **This is a form of 'mind wandering'...** Baird, B., Smallwood, J., Mrazek, M.D., Kam, J.W., Franklin, M.S. & Schooler, J.W. (2012). 'Inspired by distraction: Mind wandering facilitates creative incubation'. *Psychological Science*, 23(10): 1117–1122.

28 **go to sleep...** Wagner, U., Gais, S., Haider, H., Verleger, R. & Born, J. (2004). 'Sleep inspires insight'. *Nature*, 427(6972): 352–5.

29 **'the problems that organizations face today are generally too complex for one individual...'** Reiter-Palmon, R., de Vreede, T. & de Vreede, G-J. (2013). 'Leading interdisciplinary creative teams: Challenges and solutions'. In Hemlin, S., Allwood, C.M, Martin, B. & Mumford, M.D. (2013). *Creativity and Leadership in Science, Technology and Innovation.* New York: Routledge.

30 **we need to learn how to share our skills...** See more on collaboration and groups in Chapter 9.

31 **Brainstorming was first popularised in the 1950s by the advertising executive Alex Osborn...** Osborn, A.F. (1953). *Applied Imagination.* Scribner.

32 **it can be less effective than working separately...** Stroebe, W. & Diehl, M. (2011). 'Why groups are less effective than their members: On productivity losses in idea-generating groups'. *European Review of Social Psychology*, 5(1): 271–303.

33 **the efficacy of brainstorming varies a lot...** Isaksen, S.G. & Gaulin, J.P. (2005). 'A reexamination of brainstorming research: Implications for research and practice'. *Gifted Child Quarterly*, 49: 315.

34 **Facilitation matters...** Kramer, T.J., Fleming, G.P. & Mannis, S.M. (2001). 'Improving face-to-face brainstorming through modeling and facilitation'. *Small Group Research*, 32(5): 533–557.

35 **Size matters...** The best group size can depend on the task though, as discussed in De Vreede, G.-J., Briggs, R.O. & Reiter-Palmon, R. (2010). 'Exploring asynchronous brainstorming in large groups: A field comparison of serial and parallel subgroups'. *Human Factors*, 52(2): 189–202.

36 **Criticism is useful...** There is a useful discussion of this in Reiter-Palmon, R., de Vreede, T. & de Vreede, G-J. (2013). 'Leading interdisciplinary creative teams. Challenges and solutions'. In Hemlin, S., Allwood, C.M, Martin, B. &

Mumford, M.D. (2013). *Creativity and Leadership in Science, Technology and Innovation.* New York: Routledge.

37 **Digital tools can help...** Dennis, A.R. & Valacich, J.S. (1993). 'Computer brainstorms: More heads are better than one'. *Journal of Applied Psychology,* 78(4): 531–537.

38 **The first is proper resourcing...** Hoegl, M., Gibbert, M. & Mazursky, D. (2008). 'Financial constraints in innovation projects: When is less more?' *Research Policy,* 37: 1382–1391.

39 **For creativity, we need inner drive...** See Glucksberg, S. (1962). 'The influence of strength of drive on functional fixedness and perceptual recognition'. *Journal of Experimental Psychology,* 63: 36–41. The need for intrinsic motivation for creativity and innovation has also been well documented in Pink, D.H. (2011) *Drive: The Surprising Truth About What Motivates Us.* Canongate Books Ltd.

40 **Lack of resources can also have an impact on motivation...** See Chapter 3 for the effect of resources and perceived ability to complete a task on motivation levels.

41 **The third is diversity...** Horwitz, S.K. & Horwitz, I.B. (2007). 'The effects of team diversity on team outcomes: A meta-analytic review of team demography'. *Journal of Management,* 33(6): 987–1015. And see also Hoever, I.J., van Knippenberg, D., van Ginkel, W.P. & Barkema, H.G. (2012). 'Fostering team creativity: Perspective taking as key to unlocking diversity's potential'. *Journal of Applied Psychology,* 97(5): 982–996.

42 **The fourth is psychological safety...** Carmeli, A., Reiter-Palmon, R., & Ziv, E. (2010). 'Inclusive leadership and employee involvement in creative tasks in the workplace: The mediating role of psychological safety'. *Creativity Research Journal,* 22: 250–260.

43 **'if creativity is the process that conceives of new ideas, then innovation is the process that executes them'** Young, J. (2011). *How to be Ingenious: Comedians, Engineers and Survivalists.* RSA. http://mindap.pl/1mPyMYg.

44 **we need to find ways to make all our work creative...** See for instance his 2012 RSA lecture, Florida, R. (2012). 'Why creativity is the new economy'. RSA President's Lecture, 10 September 2012. http://mindap.pl/RSAflorida.

45 **To return to Kaufman and Singer...** Kaufman, S.B. & Singer, J.L. (2012). 'The creativity of dual process "System 1" thinking'. *Scientific American,* 17 January 2012. http://mindap.pl/1u9WUIh.

46 **'You can't use up creativity. The more you use, the more you have.'** Maya Angelou, quoted in Elliot, J.M. (1989). *Conversations with Maya Angelou.* http://mindap.pl/1ztBJRM.

THE 10 HABITS OF
A MIND FOR BUSINESS

1 Look after your health and find breathers and restorers to get the 5-a-day for your mind
2 Track the actions you take to raise energy and reduce tension and build them into your day
3 Connect your work to your skills and values to motivate yourself and others
4 Build your resources and supporting relationships to turn pressures into challenges
5 Work within your natural personality to stay comfortable and conserve your energy
6 Learn things in small chunks and design your daily routine to train your mind
7 Conserve your mental resources and avoid multi-tasking to make smarter decisions
8 Notice the moods of people around you and take charge of your emotional impact
9 Invest time in relationships and seek out diverse opinions to avoid groupthink
10 Switch flexibly between different modes of thought to keep your mind creative

CONCLUSION
A BUSINESS FOR MINDS

The former Archbishop of Canterbury, Rowan Williams, once began a lecture with a question that anyone writing a book like this really should consider.[1]

'And what follows if everyone agrees with you?'

So if you want to give your business a lift, or improve the performance of your team, how can you put the ideas in this book into practice? How do our businesses need to change to incorporate these principles into their work?

Good organisations often do a lot of these things already. What has changed though is that this is now a strategic issue, not just a question of delivery. If your business isn't mentally fit, you are risking poor decisions, inefficient working and lost creativity. This isn't just about how our businesses work: it is about whether they work.

So ask yourself: is your organisation fit for business?

For many leaders, the answer is an uncomfortable no. In a survey of over ten thousand workers worldwide by The Energy Project,[2] two-thirds said they weren't able to focus on one thing at a time, around half felt no connection to their company's mission, and half felt they weren't doing what they did best at work.

When it comes to making the most of our minds, there is plenty of room for improvement.

Knowing what's going on is the first step to putting things right. In the knowledge economy, the most important question is 'how are the minds of my staff performing right now?' If your measurements can't tell you that, you need better measurements.

Follow through on this and many gaps start to appear in the traditional models of management. As one study put it: *'Companies are running 21st-century businesses with 20th-century workplace practices and programs.'*[3]

How many leaders know the stress levels of their staff, or how this is affecting their judgment? How many managers really understand what motivates people and how they vary in their resources and personalities? How many staff have permission to manage their minds and work sustainably?

The time has come to transform our organisations to be better for our minds. This is not an exact science of course. You will need to use your judgement about how people are performing and what you can do to improve things.

Yet there are a number of conclusions that we can draw from research about the factors that are most likely to help businesses perform well. From staff engagement to recruiting the right people, modern science has much to offer us about building successful businesses.

SUSTAINABLE ENGAGEMENT

Staff engagement is a key driver of business performance. Engaged employees perform better in their jobs and are less likely to leave, and businesses with high engagement levels tend to outperform the stock market index, post higher shareholder returns[4] and show higher profit margins.[5]

Modern businesses are getting better at engaging their staff. Fair incentives, achievable goals, good relationships, choice and autonomy, and an inspiring purpose – get these things right, and discretionary effort goes up, productivity increases, and staff enjoy their work more too.

However, it is possible for staff to be **too engaged**. The more we care about our work and colleagues, the more likely we are to get stressed. Businesses that work hard to boost staff engagement can find themselves with a stress problem.

The goal is not simply high engagement, but **sustainable engagement** – high engagement with low stress. As one study put it: '*Engagement, as traditionally defined, is not sufficient to give employers the sustained performance lift they need*'.[6]

Employee engagement and psychological wellbeing actually interact with each other to predict performance.[7]

- **High engagement and high wellbeing**
  These are the most productive and happiest employees.
- **High engagement but low wellbeing**
  These employees will often 'burn out' or end up leaving their jobs.
- **Low engagement but high wellbeing**
  These people are more likely to stay but be less committed to their work.
- **Low engagement and low wellbeing**
  These employees tend to contribute the least, and also be the most reluctant to leave.

To manage employee engagement successfully, we need to measure the quality of work, not just the quantity – in short, we need to work smarter, not just harder.

DEVELOPING MENTAL RESOURCES

We know that wellbeing is good for business. It is associated with lower stress levels, better decisions, more creativity and good relationships,[8] as well as a healthier workforce.[9] It also correlates with many aspects of business performance, including customer satisfaction, brand reputation, staff productivity, talent retention and reduced sickness absence.[10]

The term 'wellbeing' rather undersells all these benefits though. It can be perceived as a luxury, something to be tackled once the work is finished. Perhaps this is why so few employers see wellbeing as core to their business.[11]

Rather than talking about wellbeing, talk about developing the **mental resources** of staff – the individual and collective brainpower in the organisation. If people are tired, worried or distracted, they make worse decisions, have less willpower and can't use their minds effectively. Promoting wellbeing means promoting productive, sustainable working.[12]

Framed in these broader terms, most businesses do many things for the minds of their staff without realising it.

Wellbeing promotion is about **joining up existing initiatives** as much as it is about new work. From bonus schemes to team away days, health insurance to flexible working, most policies and benefits are actually about developing the mental resources of staff. Do all this in a strategic way and it becomes much easier to quantify the impact of this investment.

Balancing pressure with resources is important: if people are overwhelmed they will not be able to work well. Since stress comes from a lack of skills and resources, learning and development are rather important, and so too is recruiting well and supporting people to do their jobs.

Relationships matter, both between colleagues and with leaders and managers. A good relationship with your manager can make a huge difference to how you feel about your work, whilst honest and effective communication can help people share resources and manage stress better.

Give people a clear purpose. Good strategy can give everyone a common goal and a sense that they can contribute successfully to it, whilst businesses with unclear missions or shifting priorities can leave people uncertain or overwhelmed.

Tolerance and fair treatment make a big difference. If people feel heard and are able to work in the way that suits them, they will work better. Bullying makes people unwell,[13] so anti-bullying and discrimination policies, and fair incentive structures, are essential for a high-performing workforce.

The other lesson, though, is that **we're all different**, and good wellbeing promotion isn't about one-size-fits-all solutions or telling people what to do. Gym memberships and healthy canteen food may work for physical health, but looking after people's minds is a little more complex. As one study put it, promoting wellbeing is about *'helping employees do what is naturally right for them by freeing them up to do so'*.[14]

So start by **asking people what works for them**, and develop your strategy from there. The more control and responsibility employees can take for improving wellbeing levels in the business, the more successful and sustainable your wellbeing strategy will be.

MENTAL HEALTH MATTERS

Healthy businesses rely on healthy people, and this means mentally as well as physically. Just like physical illness, mental illness is fairly common. Some studies suggest three in ten employees will experience some form of mental health problem in a year, and on any given day one worker in five will be experiencing a mental health issue of some kind.[15]

There is now a profound financial as well as ethical case for taking action on mental illness. In the UK alone, mental ill-health costs employers around £8.4 billion in sickness absence annually, and a further £15 billion in lost productivity. Staff members who become mentally unwell also often leave their jobs, robbing businesses of talent and costing some £2.4 billion in recruitment.[16]

Wellbeing alone is not enough to promote good mental health. In fact, the UK's Chief Medical Officer has argued that *'well-being in mental health is one poorly evidenced strand of a much bigger picture, and I recommend the bigger picture'*. We need to encourage people to look after their minds, minimise the factors that can make people ill, get people help early, and help people recover quickly. As the Chief Medical Officer concluded: *'This is "low-hanging fruit"; we must not ignore it, or focus instead on "well-being"'.*[17]

This can be a difficult topic for employers though. Managers often feel unequipped for the conversations, and staff may be reluctant to come forward. Research from Time to Change[18] and the Priory Group[19] suggests between half and two-thirds of UK employees would feel uncomfortable talking to their employer about their mental health. Talking about the positive side can be difficult too. As Dame Carol Black once observed, *'employees do not welcome health interference.'*[20]

Perhaps this is why so many businesses spend more on maintaining their photocopiers than they do maintaining the minds of their staff.

There is a great deal, though, that employers can do to support the mental health of their staff.

The first step is to **stop making people ill** in the first place. One in seven cases of absence due to mental ill-health is directly caused by work or working conditions,[21] and staff could have recourse to the law if work makes them ill.[22] Workload, resources, autonomy, relationships, bullying and discrimination, job security and safe working conditions can all affect our mental health. Just as we now accept the responsibility of employers to protect the physical safety of staff, it's time to consider their **psychological safety** too.

The second is to **offer prompt support** to people when they become unwell. This might include employee assistance, occupational health, HR support, mental health first aid and access to health services. Don't wait until people go off sick to help them: the quicker they get help the better for everyone.

The third is to **educate staff and managers** about their minds. Staff must feel able to identify problems before they become severe, and this is impossible if they lack basic knowledge. Teach people about their minds, and give them clear, easy ways to seek help when they need it.

The fourth is to **promote open dialogue** about mental health and illness. Again, just imagine how much harder it would be to look after your teeth if you were too scared to admit you had toothache. Help people feel safe to come forward and discuss their problems, confidentially if possible. It is much easier to address problems if they can be identified early.

Don't just talk about mental health problems though. The best thing any organisation can do to reduce mental ill-health is **promote a positive culture** of looking after our minds. We all have mental health, and talking about it can help people seek help when they need it, and keep themselves well in the first place.

If you want people to talk about problems with their minds, first you need to get them talking about their minds.

RECRUITING STAFF

All of this gets easier if you have the right minds in place to begin with. Hire people with the resources and drive to do a role, and they will be more motivated and less likely to get stressed if things go wrong. Hire someone who is uninterested or out of their depth, and all the incentives and resilience programmes in the world won't help you.

The application of psychology to recruitment is nothing new. Most major businesses use it in some form, and even smaller businesses apply some of the principles.

You can certainly learn a lot from a **standard intelligence test** and a **Big Five personality assessment**. Don't overcomplicate things though: if you stray into less rigorous models to select candidates you are both ethically and legally out on a limb. These tests also tell you very little about someone's skills, life experiences, cultural values, motivations or creativity, so you still need to find out what they have done well in the past, where their interests lie, and how they like to be challenged.

It can also be tempting to take refuge in the supposed objectivity of competency frameworks and psychometric testing, but unless you are careful about what you measure and why, the tests can end up **confirming your prejudices**. Very few jobs actually require specific personality traits to be accomplished successfully. You might think your Head of Sales needs to be an extravert, but that may just be your opinion, and people can surprise you.

The decisions you make about candidates are usually intuitive, and your intuition can be fooled. Biases and implicit associations creep in at every stage of the hiring process, from the way you write the job description, to where you advertise the post. Take time to **consider your assumptions**, write down what you want from a candidate before you advertise the role, beware of the familiar choices and keep asking whether you are recruiting with the role in mind, or a stereotype.

PROMOTING DIVERSITY

Diversity is a particularly important consideration. Diversity in all its forms is extremely good at helping businesses work smarter, but we often find it easier to hire people who are like us, and we need to correct for this.

Gender balance matters. When a team is under stress, a good gender balance can help negate some of the effects on judgement and perceptions of risk. The days of all-male boardrooms talking about 'rolling the dice' and 'punching our way out of the crisis' really should be a thing of the past.

Functional diversity is as important as cultural diversity: a wide spread of **knowledge, skills and experience** in an organisation can help spot innovation, make better decisions and avoid groupthink.

Try to get **a good mix of personalities**. 'Cultural fit' is important, but it can become an excuse to hire the same type of person. The result can be that you will reinforce your collective prejudices, become too cautious, or too risky in your decisions, and miss obvious factors affecting the business. Variety, properly managed, is almost always better.

Once people are in, try not to force them to be the person you hoped they were. The best way to help people work well is to **listen to their views** and give them the space to manage things their way. Sometimes new people can spot potential issues that others in the organisation can't, and you ignore these fresh perspectives at your peril.

Diversity is both an ethical and a commercial necessity, so put it at the heart of your strategy. A diverse, tolerant working culture can lead to better ideas and more innovative ways of working – and it may even avoid the occasional corporate disaster along the way.

DEVELOPING TALENT

Learning and development help us get more value from the minds in an organisation. If people have the knowledge and skills they need to do their jobs, they will work, and feel, better; if they don't, they will get stressed and demoralised.

Knowledge and experience have a huge impact on our work, shaping our decisions, building understanding and helping us communicate better. A strategic approach to learning requires developing both the **knowledge** and the **skills** of staff. Skills are acquired through repetition, whilst embedding knowledge takes more conscious reflection – so create opportunities to practise skills, but also for staff to share what they know and build a shared understanding.

Think about the **habits and assumptions** people learn from their peers too. We pick up a sense of how things are done from the people around us, and this can quickly become ingrained. A good learning strategy must look not just at the formal skills and knowledge being acquired, but what else people are learning on the job, and make sure these habits are making the organisation smarter and more inventive.

Teach people **how their minds work** too. It is much easier to run a successful business if decision-makers have been taught how the minds of their staff work and what they need to thrive.

If every leader and manager in the organisation is equipped with a working knowledge of their key assets – the minds of their staff – they will find it much easier to get the best from them. Without this knowledge, they may find themselves groping around in the dark.

MINDFUL MANAGEMENT

Many aspects of improving the mental performance of an organisation fall on managers, so managers often need more support to put these principles into practice, and they also need to understand these issues more than anyone.

The good news is that there are a number of things managers can do to help people perform to their potential.

- **Support staff to make time for their minds**
  This means giving staff permission to manage their daily routines, and take 'breathers' and 'restorers' to maintain their wellbeing, concentration and mental performance.
- **Conserve mental resources**
  Identify the drains on people's mental energy and get rid of them. Take big decisions early in the day, remove unnecessary distractions and help people prioritise effectively.
- **Set realistic goals**
  Map people's skills and resources when assigning tasks and manage them in the broadest sense – in appraisals, team meetings and planning.

- **Promote choice and autonomy**
  Micromanaging people might make you feel better, but you're just passing the stress on to everyone else.
- **Build a strength-based culture**
  Play to the strengths of your team by assigning tasks that suit people's skills and personality traits to reduce cognitive fatigue. Combining teams with diverse skills and personalities, and listening to people's opinions, can make teams more effective.
- **Focus on relationships**
  Good relationships with and between staff can improve motivation, reduce stress, help people communicate, and promote autonomy too. So make time for people, and treat them fairly.

Finally, remember to set a good example through your own behaviour. Teams pick up the moods and habits of their managers, so you can improve your team by improving your own performance, and by being a positive influence at work.[23]

THE CHALLENGE FOR LEADERS

If you lead an organisation, you are responsible not only for your own mind, but for the minds of all the people in your charge too – and you neglect them at your peril.

Here are a few things you can do as a leader to build a mentally healthy and high-performing workplace:

- Give people a **supportive work environment**, with minimal distractions and freedom from bullying.
- Give staff **permission** to manage their minds and their work, and remember that **everyone is different**.
- Manage **your moods** and express your emotions appropriately to set a **positive emotional tone**.

- Talk **openly** about how you maintain your own mind, and make it **easier for others** to talk about this too.
- Listen to **dissenting voices** and make space for people who think and feel **differently** from you.
- Set a **clear strategy** that plays to the **strengths** of the business and shows people how they can **succeed**.
- Speak about your **passion** for the business and help people see the **value** of their contributions to it.

Leaders set the tone for the whole organisation too, so you condition the culture by your own behaviour. These ideas don't just apply to other people; they apply to you too.

By managing your mind well, taking responsibility for your moods and your impact on others, and building and maintaining your own mental resources, you make it easier for everyone else to do the same.

A MIND FOR BUSINESS

In his book *The Power of Habit*, Charles Duhigg proposes the idea of a 'keystone habit' – *'a habit that, if embraced, changes everything'*.[24]

Managing our minds is just such a habit.

If you make time for your mind and maintain your mental resources every day, and embed this as a habit in every aspect of your work, it will have a systemic effect across the business – boosting motivation, inspiring innovation, improving decision-making and driving productivity.

The benefits of doing this will be felt at every level, from investors getting a better return on their assets, to CEOs managing risks and returns more reliably, managers running more motivated and innovative teams, staff enjoying greater health and job satisfaction, and customers getting a better service. Look after the minds, as the saying might go, and the pounds will take care of themselves.

All this starts with you though. It is very difficult to apply these principles to an organisation without first applying them to yourself. If you don't manage your mind it will end up managing you, and this will have an effect on your colleagues whether you mean it to or not.

Maintain your wellbeing, manage your moods, model the behaviours you want to see and consider the impact you have on the people around you. As they say on aeroplanes, always fit your own oxygen mask before helping others with theirs.

Change begins with each of us choosing to think differently. If you want to change the world, change your mind.

So what do you think? Does *your* mind mean business?

CHANGING MINDS, REVISITED

If we are to put our minds at the heart of our organisations, many things may need to change, in how we select and develop staff, take decisions, set objectives and reward success.

Some organisations may require a shift of mindset to take account of these new considerations, such as changes in management practices, new corporate attitudes, and the development of new ways of promoting and measuring performance. Leaders need to set an example; managers need to put ideas into practice.

Staff must play their part too. Individually we need to improve our awareness of what our minds need to thrive, notice when we are working well and when we aren't, and do our best to have a positive impact on ourselves and the people around us. This is in all our interests: no one really wants to be unimaginative, demotivated, stressed or miserable at work. Good business is good for everyone.

Responsibility also lies with board members and investors to put these issues on the corporate agenda, and to hold the executive to account for delivering on them. The mental state of a business should be a matter for debate at the highest level, not just once, but regularly, reviewing figures, assessing risks and monitoring the mental performance of their workforce. If the board don't know the mental state of staff, they don't really know what's going on in the business, and they won't see bad decisions coming until it is too late.

Investors have a lot to gain here as well. Businesses that invest in the minds of their people will attract more talent, manage risks better, get more from their staff and outperform their competitors. Many investors talk about the importance of a strong management team, so a natural extension of this is to assess the mental condition of staff too. Businesses that make the most of their mental resources deliver more value for investors. A mentally fit business is usually an investable business.

We have an ethical imperative to do this too, not just a commercial one: we spend nearly a third of our lives working, and if work is bad for our minds we will all pay for that, both individually and collectively, sooner or later.

This is an evolution rather than a revolution though: there have been many positive steps in recent decades towards creating safer, healthier and more successful workplaces. Many of the principles in this book seem obvious when we think about them. As George Orwell once observed, though, there are times when restating the obvious is the primary duty of intelligent people.[25] We may know what works, but it is all too easy to forget these principles in the heat of a deadline, and we need the evidence to remind us what matters.

The evidence will continue to improve of course. Neuroscience in particular is still only scratching the surface of what can be learnt about the human mind. New models are emerging all the time, from the work of Dennis Stevenson's MQ project in the UK[26] to Barack Obama's flagship 'BRAIN' initiative.[27]

As far as changing the way we work though, the future is already here. We don't need more theoretical studies: it's time to put what we know into practice and start sharing what works.

The time to start transforming our businesses is right now.

NOTES

1 **'And what follows if everyone agrees with you?'** Lord Williams of Oystermouth, 'No last words: Language as unfinished business'. Gifford Lectures, University of Edinburgh, 7 November 2013. http://mindap.pl/1p7dXoF. As he says in the lecture though, the question is actually a quote from David Lodge's novel, *Small World*. Thanks to my good friend Dougald Hine for pointing me at this particular gem.

2 **a survey of over ten thousand workers worldwide...** The research was conducted with 12,115 workers in the US, mainly knowledge workers. Schwartz, T. & Porath, C. (2014). 'Why you hate work'. *The New York Times Sunday Review*, 30 May 2014. http://mindap.pl/1lckraA.

3 **As one study put it...** Towers Watson (2012). *Global Workforce Study. Engagement at Risk: Driving Strong Performance in a Volatile Global Environment.* July 2012.

4 **post higher shareholder returns...** AON Hewitt (2011). *Trends in global employee engagement.*

5 **show higher profit margins...** Towers Watson (2012) *Global Workforce Study. Engagement at Risk: Driving Strong Performance in a Volatile Global Environment.* July 2012.

6 **sustainable engagement...** Towers Watson (2012) *Global Workforce Study. Engagement at Risk: Driving Strong Performance in a Volatile Global Environment.* July 2012.

7 **Employee engagement and psychological wellbeing...** Robertson, I.T. & Cooper, C.L. (2010). 'Full engagement: The integration of employee engagement and psychological well-being'. *Leadership and Organization Development Journal.* 31(4): 324–36. See also Fairhurst, D. & O'Connor, J. (2010). *Employee Well-being: Taking Engagement and Performance to the Next Level.* Towers Watson, February 2010.

8 **wellbeing is associated with...** Ryff, C.D., & Keyes, C.L.M (1995). 'The structure of psychological well-being revisited'. *Journal of Personality and Social Psychology* 69, 719–727.

9 **as well as a healthier workforce...** Ryff, C.D. Singer, B.H. & Love, G.D. (2004). 'Positive health: Connecting well-being with biology'. *Philosophical Transactions of Royal Society of London Biological Sciences.* 359(1449): 1383–1394.

10 **correlates with many aspects of business performance...** Harter, J.K., Schmidt, F.L. & Keyes, C.L. (2003). 'Well-being in the workplace and its relationship to business outcomes: A review of the Gallup studies'. In Keyes, C.L. and Haidt, J. (Eds). *Flourishing: Positive Psychology and the Life Well-lived* 2: 205–224. Washington, DC: American Psychological Association.

11 **few employers see wellbeing as core to their business...** In a survey of employers by *HR Magazine*, only 19 per cent felt that staff wellbeing was core to their business, and only 17 per cent had a comprehensive wellbeing

strategy linked to the success of their business. Jacobs, K. (2014). 'The health bomb'. *HR Magazine*, June 2014.

12 **developing the mental resources of staff...** Wellbeing and 'mental resources' in this sense are aligned to 'mental capital' which the UK Government has defined as *'a person's cognitive and emotional resources, including cognitive ability, how flexible and efficient they are at learning... "emotional intelligence" such as social skills and resilience in the face of stress'.* Government Office for Science (2008). *'Mental capital and wellbeing: Making the most of ourselves in the 21st century.*

13 **bullying makes people unwell...** Friedli, L. (2009). *Mental Health, Resilience and Inequalities – A Report for WHO Europe and the Mental Health Foundation.* London/Copenhagen: Mental Health Foundation and WHO Europe.

14 **'helping employees do what is naturally right for them...'** Harter, J.K., Schmidt, F.L. & Keyes, C.L. (2003). 'Well-being in the workplace and its relationship to business outcomes: A review of the Gallup studies'. In Keyes, C.L. and Haidt, J. (Eds). *Flourishing: Positive Psychology and the Life Well-lived* 2: 205–224. Washington, DC: American Psychological Association.

15 **three in ten employees will experience some form of mental health problem in a year...** Sainsbury Centre for Mental Health (2007). 'Mental health at work: Developing the business case'. London: SCMH, Policy Paper 8.

16 **costing some £2.4 billion in recruitment...** Sainsbury Centre for Mental Health (2007). 'Mental health at work: Developing the business case'. London: SCMH, Policy Paper 8.

17 **the UK's Chief Medical Officer concluded...** Davies, S. et al (2014). *Annual Report of the Chief Medical Officer 2013. Public Mental Health Priorities: Investing in the Evidence.* Disclosure: I am listed in the acknowledgements.

18 **Research from Time to Change...** Time to Change/HSCIC (2011). *Attitudes to Mental Illness – 2011.* http://mindap.pl/1mov2Qy.

19 **and the Priory Group...** Priory Group (2014). 'Mental health stigma silences employees'. *Priory* blog, 8 August 2014. http://mindap.pl/1sT7Iak.

20 **'employees do not welcome health interference.'** Dame Carol Black quoted by the author from *The BITC Workwell Summit*, King's Fund, 10 May 2011, citing Black, C. (2011). *Health and Wellbeing at Work.* Department of Work and Pensions.

21 **One in seven cases of absence...** CIPD/OPP (2006). 'Fight, flight or face it'. Oxford.

22 **staff could have recourse to the law...** Bevan, S. (2010). *The Business Case for Employee Health and Wellbeing.* The Work Foundation.

23 **remember to set a good example...** For more on good management, see CIPD (2012). *Managing for Sustainable Employee Engagement: Developing a Behavioural Framework.*

24 **'a habit that, if embraced, changes everything.'** The example Duhigg gives is of the CEO of Alcoa, who *'turned out to have an uncanny appreciation*

of how to pick what is termed a "keystone habit" – a habit that, if embraced, changes everything. In this case, the habit of workplace safety aligned the interests of employees (who didn't want to get injured), management (who hated to have to deal with missing staff and the paperwork around injury claims), and investors (who paid for injury claims and downtime)'. Duhigg, C. (2012). *The Power of Habit*. Random House.

25 **'restating the obvious is the primary duty of intelligent people.'** Orwell, G. (1939). 'Review of power: A new social analysis by Bertrand Russell'. *The Adelphi*, January 1939. OK, so he actually said 'intelligent men' but I think this is probably what he meant.

26 **Dennis Stevenson's MQ project...** Read more about this initiative to promote neuroscientific research into mental health at www.joinmq.org.

27 **Barack Obama's flagship 'BRAIN' initiative...** Obama, B. (2013). Remarks by the President on the BRAIN Initiative and American Innovation. The White House, 2 April 2013. http://mindap.pl/1ubYnQL.

What did you think of this book?

We're really keen to hear from you about this book, so that we can make our publishing even better.

Please log on to the following website and leave us your feedback.

It will only take a few minutes and your thoughts are invaluable to us.

www.pearsoned.co.uk/bookfeedback

FURTHER READING

So many books have been written about the mind, and about business, but here are a few popular psychology books that combine practical application with academic excellence.

The Happiness Hypothesis (2006, Heinemann) by Jonathan Haidt explains the 'elephant and the rider' concept and many other fascinating insights into health and happiness.

Use Your Head (2011, John Murray) by Daniel and Jason Freeman gives an excellent introduction to your mind and how to use it.

Psychobabble (2012, Pearson UK) by Stephen Briers is a refreshing antidote to all those dodgy self-help books out there.

Stumbling on Happiness (2006, HarperPress) by Daniel Gilbert is one of the really good books on happiness in a crowded field.

Robert Thayer's theories of mood regulation are outlined in more detail in his later book *Calm Energy: How People Regulate Mood with Food and Exercise* (2001, Oxford University Press).

For the 'conservation of resources' model of stress and pressure, see Stevan Hobfoll, *The Ecology of Stress* (1988, Taylor & Francis).

The best introduction to motivation is *Drive: The Surprising Truth About What Motivates Us* (2011, Canongate Books) by Daniel H. Pink.

For more on the Big Five personality traits, see *Personality: What Makes You the Way You Are* (2009, Oxford University Press) by Daniel Nettle.

Susan Cain's *Quiet* (2013, Penguin) is an excellent read for both introverts and extraverts alike.

One accessible introduction to neuroplasticity is *The Brain that Changes Itself: Stories of Personal Triumph from the Frontiers of Brain Science* (2008, Penguin) by Norman Doidge.

For a snappy approach to training your brain, try *Sort Your Brain Out* (2014, Capstone) by Jack Lewis and Adrian Webster.

The Power of Habit (2012, Random House) by Charles Duhigg is a masterful introduction to our habits and how to change them.

Thinking, Fast and Slow (2012, Penguin) by Daniel Kahneman is now the definitive introduction to decision-making and cognition.

Predictably Irrational: The Hidden Forces that Shape our Decisions (2009, HarperCollins) by Daniel Ariely explores many of our peculiar unconscious biases.

For how to think like a genius, see *Mastermind: How to think like Sherlock Holmes* (2013, Canongate Books) by Maria Konnikova.

Harvard's *Project Implicit* investigates the assumptions that shape our automatic reactions: www.projectimplicit.org

For an inspiring introduction to the power of fast thinking and intuition, try Malcolm Gladwell's classic *Blink: The Power of Thinking Without Thinking* (2006, Penguin).

For more on influence and persuasion see Robert Cialdini's classic *Influence: The Psychology of Persuasion* (2007, HarperBusiness).

Zig Zag: The Surprising Path to Greater Creativity (2013, Jossey Bass) by Keith Sawyer offers a refreshing and highly practical guide to the many aspects of creativity and innovation.

For an accessible introduction to positive psychology in the workplace, try *The Happiness Advantage* (2011, Virgin Books) by Shawn Achor.

And you can share the '5-a-day for your mind' and find out what people say works for them at www.mindapples.org.

INDEX